International Review of Strategic Management

VOLUME 1   1990

International Review of Strategic Management

VOLUME 1   1990

Edited by

D. E. Hussey

Harbridge Consulting Group Ltd.

JOHN WILEY & SONS

CHICHESTER · NEW YORK · BRISBANE · TORONTO · SINGAPORE

Copyright © 1990 by John Wiley & Sons Ltd.
          Baffins Lane, Chichester
          West Sussex PO19 1UD, England

International Review of Strategic Management ISSN 1047-7918

Published annually by John Wiley & Sons

Volume 1 — 1990 £50/$90 (Institutions)

Personal subscription at reduced rate
available for prepayment direct to the publisher.
For details telephone 0243 770 397 or write to
The Journals Subscriptions Department,
John Wiley and Sons Ltd,
Baffins Lane, Chichester, West Sussex, PO19 1UD, England.

Future volumes will be invoiced to subscribers prior to
publication, and subscriptions may be cancelled at any time.

British Library Cataloguing in Publication Data
International review of strategic management—vol 1 (1990)—
    658

ISBN 0 471 92608 6

Typeset by Photo·graphics, Honiton, Devon
Printed and bound in Great Britain by Courier International Ltd, Tiptree, Essex

CONTENTS

ABOUT THE CONTRIBUTORS

KATE ASCHER is manager of business development with the Port Authority of New York and New Jersey in New York City. Prior to joining the Port Authority, she worked as a management consultant with Harbridge Consulting Group in London, where she specialised in market strategy and analysis. Dr Ascher is the author of *The Politics of Privatisation* (Macmillan, 1985) and has published articles in *Local Government Studies, Financial Decisions, Personnel Management and Business Education*. She holds a Ph.D. and a M.Sc. in government from the London School of Economics and a B.A. from Brown University.

HELEN BUTCHER was appointed Information Manager and Consultant with BDO Binder Hamlyn Chartered Accountants and Consultants after spending two years as an information officer with a firm of solicitors. She is responsible for information services and libraries within the firm and for the promotion and use of online systems, as well as the management of firm wide information. She has a wide consultancy experience and lectures regularly on her subject. She has published several articles and books on online business information and information management.

ANDREW CAMPBELL is a founding director and fellow of the Ashridge Strategic Management Centre, and was previously a fellow in the Centre of Business Strategy at the London Business School, where he managed research into the strategic decision making processes of large UK companies, directed in-company management development programmes, and taught on the MBA programme. Previously he was a consultant with Mckinsey and Company. He is co-author with Michael Goold of the book *Strategies and Styles* (Blackwell, 1987).

MAGDOLNA CSATH is currently a visiting Professor at Virginia Polytechnic Institute and State University at Blacksburg, United States of America. She has held a number of senior academic, and consulting positions with leading organisations in Hungary. Her Ph.D. from the Hungarian Academy of Sciences was based on a study of strategic planning in Hungarian industry. Her book, written with L. Horvarth, on strategic management and published by the Economic and Law Publishing House, Budapest, won the 'Best Management Book of the Year Award'. She writes widely on strategic and educational subjects.

ADA DEMB is a faculty member in organisational systems with the International Institute for Management Development, Lausanne, Switzerland. She is Director of the International Programme for Board Members, and is involved in research on the role of boards and organisational issues in technology management. Previously she was Assistant Director of Research at the University of Hawaii College of Tropical Agriculture and Human Resources, which she joined from the International Institute of Applied Systems Analysis (Austria). She holds a doctorate in education from Harvard University. In addition to consultancy assignments with government and private industry, she has published a number of articles, and two books: *Computer Systems for Human Systems* (Pergamon Press, 1979), and *Organisation for Programme Management*, with C. Davies and R. Espejo (John Wiley, 1979).

MICHAEL GOOLD is a founding director and fellow of the Ashridge Strategic Management Centre. He runs the Centre's programme on strategic decisions. He was previously a senior fellow in the Centre for Business Strategy at the London Business School, which he joined after twelve years' consultancy experience with the Boston Consulting Group. With Andrew Campbell he wrote the book *Strategies and Styles* (Blackwell 1987), which was based on research he undertook into the role of the corporate centre in managing diversified companies.

JOHN HENRY is Senior Vice President of SRI's International Business Consulting Group, with responsibility for managing the group's four divisions and SRI's overseas offices. He has spent more than 20 years in consulting to clients whose businesses are influenced by major technological developments. He specialises in corporate strategy and management. AT SRI he established the Energy Centre and directed that business for more than 10 years. His papers on international business management and energy issues have appeared in the *Harvard Business Review*, the *Oil and Gas Journal*, the *Journal of Petroleum Technology* and other technical publications. He has been widely quoted in major national media. He holds B.S., M.S., and Ph.D. degrees in chemical engineering, and was recently awarded the Distinguished Alumnus from the Ohio State University.

DAVID HUSSEY has had many years of experience in corporate planning, as a practitioner in industry from 1964 to 1975, and as a consultant since

1976. Prior to moving into corporate planning, he was engaged in industrial development work in a developing country. He is managing director of Harbridge Consulting Group, the European operation of a well-known US consultancy, and is the author of several books on the subject of strategic management, including *Corporate Planning: Theory and Practice* (Pergamon 1974), which won the John Player management author of the year award. He was one of the founders of the Society for Strategic Planning, and has been associated with the official journal of the society, *Long Range Planning*, since its foundation. He is a member of the editorial board of *Strategic Directions*, and is a director of the Eastern Regional Board of the British Institute of Management.

MARIE McHUGH works for the Centre for Research in Management at the University of Ulster, Northern Ireland. Her major current research interests are focused on the issue of competitiveness in a regional context. She has been involved in writing articles based on these and other research projects, and has also undertaken consultancy work in the public sector.

PATRIC McNAMEE is a reader in the Centre for Research in Management at the University of Ulster. He has written widely on strategic management, including *Tools and Techniques for Strategic Management* (Pergamon 1985). His most recent book is a standard text for the Chartered Institute of Management Accountants. He has taught in the United States and Scandinavia in addition to the United Kingdom, where he also undertakes consultancy.

MICHAEL MAINELLI is Director of Strategic Planning and Information Technology at BDO Binder Hamlyn Management Consultants. His career includes several years' consulting to organisations in finance, energy, utilities, manufacturing and retailing. He has worked in strategic planning, strategic information planning and applying advanced, integrated technology in large-scale databases, office automation, cartography, and CAD/CAM in a variety of commercial and scientific applications. He has developed BDO's approach to strategic planning, and directs a variety of consulting work for several industries.

GEN-ICHI NAKAMURA has 20 years of business experience and 15 years of academic experience. He has been developing an extensive consultancy practice in Asia, Europe and the United States. He is Chairman and Principal Researcher/Consultant of SMI 2I Co. Ltd, Principal of Gen-Ichi-Nakamura Associates, Managing Partner of Ansoff, Buchner, Nakamura and Partners in West Germany, and co-founder of the Japan Strategic Management Society. He is also the author of a number of books, primarily on strategic management and related subjects. His recent works are *The Practice of Divestment Strategy* and *Corporate Identity Development within the Context of Strategic Management*. Both are in the Japanese language.

BLAIR NARE is the Director of Fiscal Policy Analysis for the New York State Division of the Budget. Prior to assuming this position she was manager of Business Analysis for the Port Authority of New York and New Jersey and, before that, Product Manager for the International Group of Data Resources (DRI). She earned her MBA from the Columbia University Graduate School of Business in 1984 after several years' experience in both the public sector and consulting organisations. Her publications include *Writing Skills* (a college text published by McGraw-Hill in 1970) and a variety of articles in DRI's economic journals.

FRED NEUBAUER is Faculty Member—multinational corporate strategy and planning at IMD, and Adjunct Professor of Business at the Pennsylvania State University at Harrisburg, USA. He holds a doctorate from the University of Würtzburg and an MBA (Dipl Kfm) from the University of Frankfurt. He has extensive management consulting experience with multinational companies in the area of strategic management, and is author of three books and numerous articles on business policy and strategic planning. With Dr Ada Demb, he is currently involved in a multinational study on the governance of corporations.

JOHN PENDLEBURY is Managing Director of Coopers & Lybrand Associates Europe. He is an engineer by education and training with industrial experience in the electrical, electronics, computer, consumer goods and process industries prior to joining Coopers & Lybrand. Dr Pendlebury is also qualified as a cost accountant. Since joining Coopers & Lybrand he has added 15 years' experience in a variety of industrial environmental projects, and has been a member of the consulting practices in a number of countries, including the United States, France, Italy and Benelux. In his present capacity he works widely in Europe and is a frequent visitor to manufacturing companies in the United States and the Far East. He was responsible for the development of the manufacturing and distribution practice of Coopers and Lybrand in the United Kingdom.

MICHAEL PORTER is a professor at Harvard Business School. His books on competitive analysis and strategy have made him one of the most significant influences on strategic management, and probably one of the most widely read authors on this subject. In addition to his teaching, researches and writing, he is a consultant to leading companies throughout the world. *Competitive Strategy* (Free Press 1980) remains the standard work on its subject.

ED TOZER is a director of Planning and Strategy Ltd, and specialises in strategic Information Systems (IS) and Information Technology (IT) consultancy. He has 25 years' experience in the IT industry, and his career has included extended spells working with Arthur Andersen & Co and James Martin. He is a Fellow of the British Computer Society and a Fellow of the Institute of Management Consultants. He has led IS strategy assignments for clients in a wide variety of industries, including manufacturing, distribution and retail, banking, securities, oil and chemicals. He was editor of the Pergamon Infotech state of the art report *Application Development Tools* and is the author of *Planning for Effective Information Systems* (Pergamon 1988). He teaches courses in the subject.

TOM WURSTER is a vice president and director of the Boston Consulting Group, Inc. in the Los Angeles office. Dr Wurster has 11 years of experience in management consulting, and specialises in strategy and organisational change. He is a graduate of Cornell University, where he earned his AB. He received his MBA degree with honours from the University of Chicago, and his Ph.D. in economics from Yale. He has worked with clients in most major industries, with a focus over recent years on financial services and aerospace industries. In addition to his work with BCG, Dr Wurster teaches a course on strategy development and organisational change at the John E. Anderson Graduate School of Business at UCLA. Prior to joining BCG, he worked for the Federal Reserve Board, the Congressional Budget Office and the Bank of America.

INTRODUCTION

This is the first volume of what will become an annual critical review of developments and best practice in strategic management. It is intended that each book will consist of a number of chapters linked to a theme, amounting to 50% to 60% of the content. The remaining chapters will be chosen for topical importance or to provide (over successive volumes) a comprehensive picture of the whole field of strategic management. In every volume there will be one contribution giving a state of the art survey of the subject. Since different authors may take differing views of trends and priorities, and as new developments are constantly emerging, this annual chapter should become a rich source of ideas for those concerned with the subject.

The scope of strategic management is wide, and over time all facets will be considered. We can look at strategic management from several viewpoints. Figure A shows one way in which we might begin to conceptualise the subject.

The main value of the diagram is to emphasise the interdependence of the four headings. *Process* covers topics such as the way strategy is formulated, the climate of the organisation, and the integration of the different elements of planning. Closely allied to process is *System*, which covers topics such as how planning is organised, how information flows

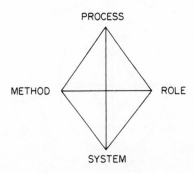

Figure A Concepts of strategic management

are designed to assist planning, and how the control system is established. *Role* covers the part played by various people within the process, such as the corporate planner, line managers, functional managers, and of course the chief executive himself and the board to which he reports. Role is closely allied to process, since what managers do in the context of planning is to a large degree affected by the culture of the organisation. *Method* covers all the techniques that may be used in the process of strategy formulation, and the principles of strategic decision making on which they are based.

Figure A is bounded by an interface with the world at large, and aspects of this business environment may become important enough to cover in this series.

This model covers many of the topics that will be included in this review series as it evolves, but the model is not quite complete. Figure B adds three further areas of complexity.

A first addition is *national differences*. We may from time to time wish to explore how planning is practised in particular countries, and how differences of politics and culture may affect the way strategic management is applied.

Organisational differences provide us with a second fertile field for exploration. In this context the word organisation is used to mean entity,

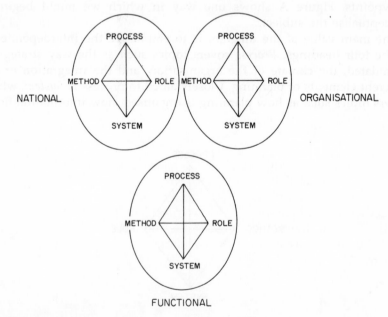

Figure B   Additional issues

and we would expect to find that a global, large business had to approach strategic management in a different way to a medium sized, local firm. Firms which operate in only one industry face a less complex planning situation than those which are in many industries. A further difference is between businesses, government organisations and non-profit-making activities, such as a charity or church.

Our final area of difference is *functional*. The role that different functions play in the process of planning has been identified in the first model. Here we are concerned with the detail of planning which will be different for, say, a human resource department than it would be for a manufacturing unit. Functional level planning is only a part of the strategic management process, but the requirements of functional plans are seen as within the scope of this review series.

In this first volume the chapters can be grouped according to this scheme, although it has not been the intention to cover every element of the scheme in the first volume. The main theme of this first book is building competitive advantage, but even within this theme the scheme still works.

	Competitive Advantage	Other
ROLE		Neubauer/Demb
SYSTEM	Butcher/Mainelli	
PROCESS	Wurster	Goold and Campbell
METHOD	Porter	
	McNamee	
	Henry	
	Tozer	
NATIONAL	Nakamura	Csath
ORGANISATIONAL		Ascher
FUNCTIONAL	Pendlebury	

The state of the art review spans all these classifications. In a subject like this, it is essential that authors go beyond the narrow brief suggested by this model, and the reader will find insights into other aspects of the subject within each chapter. The reason is that strategic management is a subject which draws many threads together, and we have to be aware of all the strands as well as the few selected to weave the tapestry in front of us.

Part 1

STATE OF THE ART REVIEW

1

DEVELOPMENTS IN STRATEGIC MANAGEMENT

D. E. Hussey

Harbridge Consulting Group Ltd

Planning has been in a continual state of evolution since it began to be seen as an important management tool in the mid-1960s. As with all management advances, early planning built on practice and the development of the subject was aided by a few key publications. It is reasonable to put 1965 as the start of modern planning. That year saw the publication of the first book on strategy (Ansoff, 1965), and also what was probably the first survey of planning in practice (Scott, 1965). Both books had considerable impact at the time, although it is Igor Ansoff's work that has become a classic of management literature. Also around 1965 and for several years afterwards, the Long Range Planning Service of the Stanford Research Institute produced numerous survey-based monographs on planning for its subscribers.

As the subject developed, new terms were constantly being coined to show the different emphases that new generations of experts brought to the 'art'. Around 1965, the in-term was *long range planning*, the emphasis being on the need to plan beyond the *annual budget*. Before the end of the decade, the common term was *corporate planning* used as the realisation dawned that effective planning had to cover all aspects of the entity, in both the short and long term. By the early 1970s those at the forefront were beginning to use the term *strategic management*, as the view developed that strategy was more important than forecasting.

In the middle of the 1970s the term strategic management appeared in a book (Ansoff, Declerk and Hayes, 1976). Here the emphasis changed to a broader management task of managing strategy in its totality. (This term will be returned to later, and will be supported by

International Review of Strategic Management.
Edited by D. E. Hussey. © 1990 John Wiley & Sons Ltd

reference to some research which shows the evolution of planning in a more precise way.) The publication of this book marked what might be termed the modern age of planning, and it is the point at which I have selected to begin my state of the art review. There have probably been more useful developments in planning theory and practice since 1976 than in the previous years, although many of these build on methods and concepts already in use by the more advanced organis- ations. There have been no revolutionary developments in strategy, and it is fair to claim that even the most useful of the new concepts is an evolutionary step, owing much to the practice of advanced organisations, and to the work of the experts who have gone before. Those who have stayed with planning since the mid-1960s will have grown easily into each new concept. Anyone who returned to strategy after a break of several years might well find that evolution has left his or her knowledge of the subject well behind.

Given the change of emphasis implied by the term strategic management it is not surprising that many of the major advances of the past few years should be in the area of strategic analysis and decision making. Competitor analysis, globalisation, empirical evidence from the PIMS database and from acquisition studies, developments in information technology and ways of considering manufacturing are among the new and important contributions of the recent past. The behavioural stream shows equally important strands of new thinking, including work on innovation, studies of the different styles of planning, the role that management training can play in the implementation and formulation of strategy, re-evaluations of the way in which strategic decisions are actually made, and at the head of this stream of work the lessons from *In Search of Excellence* (Peters and Waterman, 1982), and the many subsequent appraisals that this spawned.

Both the behavioural and analytical branches will be covered in this chapter and an attempt made to identify the most significant contributions of the numerous people who have taken the development of planning forward. Identifying who is first with a theory is incredibly difficult, and is not the objective. Instead I hope to leave an overall impression of modern planning thinking, with references to some of the most helpful books and articles. But let us start with the term *strategic management*, and some of the research which demonstrates how different concepts of planning have evolved.

STRATEGIC MANAGEMENT

Ansoff, Declerk and Hayes (1976) edited the book that established the new way of thinking about strategy. It derived from an earlier conference at Vanderbilt University and was a response to the increasing complexity of modern business. The differences of emphasis between strategic planning and strategic management are as shown below:

Strategic planning	Strategic management
External linkages (e.g. products, markets, environment)	Adds internal elements (e.g. organisation, style, climate)
Strategy formulation to solve problems	Adds implementation and control
Focuses on the 'hard' aspects of the external environment	Also concerned with social and political aspects

Thus strategic management may be seen as a more complete way of managing a business, concerned not only with markets and decision making, but also with social developments, implementation and the 'fit' of strategy with organisational structure and climate.

Gluck, Kaufman and Walleck (1980) published a study of developments in planning systems over time, and concluded that there had been four phases in the evolution of formal strategic planning. The stages are shown in Figure 1.1. The dates are my own observations and do not appear in the study, but relate to empirical observations of my own and related observations on the evolution of planning approaches (Hussey,

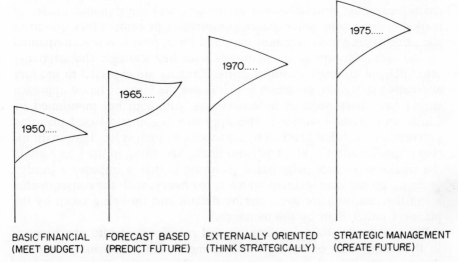

BASIC FINANCIAL   FORECAST BASED   EXTERNALLY ORIENTED   STRATEGIC MANAGEMENT
(MEET BUDGET)   (PREDICT FUTURE) (THINK STRATEGICALLY) (CREATE FUTURE)

Figure 1.1 Phases in the evolution of strategic planning (Derived from Gluck, Kaufman and Walleck, *Harvard Business Review*, July/August, 1980)

1979). Approaches to planning tend to coexist, which means that it is possible to find all forms. Gluck and his co-authors noted that at the time of their work only a few companies were managing strategically, and that all of these were multinational and diversified companies.

Phase 1 could also be described as extended budgeting, and the approach is largely based on taking the figures in the budget out for a few more years. This tends to emphasise the existing aspects of the business, and allows little room for major changes in strategy. In these companies any new strategic thinking occurs outside of the planning system.

In phase 2 the approach tries to match the company's strategies to the perversities of the real world. The feeling is that more accurate forecasting would lead to better planning, and the emphasis in this approach is on forecasting techniques and models. Operational research techniques were high on the list of the planner's tools when this approach was at its most popular, and you would be invited to attend seminars with titles such as 'Corporate planning, the control of company destiny.' The Gluck study observes that one benefit of this approach was greater attention to resource allocation, and the growing use of portfolio analysis techniques to aid this.

Repeated frustration from the discontinuity of the events in the world in which we operate created a realisation that accurate forecasting was not possible. The figure suggests 1970 as the time when phase 3, externally based planning, began to appear, but for the majority of companies the trigger was the 1973 oil crisis, which overnight put the world into a situation of unexpected turbulence. Externally based planning is characterised by more attention to markets, and the dynamic causes of market change, and much closer examination of competitors. Resource allocation takes a more dynamic part, and the approach was accompanied by the formal grouping of businesses with like strategic characteristics into SBUs, or strategic business units. Planners are expected to produce alternative strategies, an action which under the forecast-based approach would have been seen as indecisiveness. Although not mentioned by Gluck, an extreme example of this approach is scenario-based planning practice in very different forms by organisations such as Reed International (see Chandler and Cockle, 1982) and Shell. According to the Gluck study the weakness of externally based planning is that it imposes a burden of choice on top management which is too heavy, with the consequential result that many major decisions by default end up being taken by the planners rather than by the managers.

Phase 4 melds strategic planning and management into one process. In their definition of strategic management, Gluck and his co-authors differ a little from the Ansoff definition. They define it as a *system of corporate values, planning responsibilities, or organisational responsibilities that couple strategic thinking with operational decision making at all levels and across all functional lines of authority in a corporation.* The main difference between phases 3 and 4 is of management philosophy rather than technique, and as the Ansoff view described earlier suggests, more emphasis is placed on the 'soft' internal aspects of management such as values and culture. Some of these themes will be picked up later when we look at the main behavioural advances in planning.

STYLES OF STRATEGIC MANAGEMENT

Goold and Campbell (1987) published an important research-based study of styles of strategic management (Chapter 10 of this book is based on this work). They saw the styles as arising from the attempt by top managers to determine the appropriate role for the corporate office vis-à-vis the business units, during which process trade-offs have to be made. The desire to give strong leadership from the centre conflicts with the desire to encourage entrepreneurial activity at the business unit level. Styles arise as a result of the way in which the group chief executive determines where the trade-offs have to be made.

A number of possible styles were identified on a matrix of planning influence from the corporate level (high, medium and low), and corporate control influence (flexible, tight strategic and tight financial). Of the nine possible positions on that matrix (which appears in diagram form on page 222), three were found in the sample of companies studied. These were labelled *strategic planning*, with a high planning influence accompanied by flexible control; *strategic control*, which has medium level planning influence and tight strategic control; and *financial control*, with low planning influence and tight financial control.

Figure 1.2 summarises the main differences between the styles.

There are strengths and weaknesses to each style, and the head office can both add and subtract value under each style. The authors conclude that the appropriate style is one that fits the situation of the business, and that appropriate matching is an important determinant of business success. In this way it is something like leadership where the right style is relevant to the situation in which the leader operates. Business factors fall under two headings: those related to the business nature, and those related to the resources in the organisation. Among the former are issues such as the ferocity of the competitive environment, size and length of payback of investments, and the shape of the corporate portfolio. Among the latter are the financial health of the company, the personality of the chief executive and the skills of senior management.

	STRATEGIC PLANNING	STRATEGIC CONTROL	FINANCIAL CONTROL
STRATEGY RESPONSIBILITY	BUSINESS LEVEL BUT MULTIPLE PERSPECTIVES	DIVISIONAL & BUSINESS UNIT	UNIT AND EVEN PROFIT CENTRE
REVIEW	EXTENSIVE TO INFLUENCE PROPOSALS AND RAISE QUALITY	EXTENSIVE - RAISE QUALITY	BUDGET KEY PLANNING PROCESS
CORPORATE SUPPORT	FOR STRATEGIC THEMES	AVOIDANCE OF CENTRAL STRATEGIES	MAJOR USE OF ACQUISITION (CENTRE OR UNIT)
INTER DIVISIONAL COORDINATION	CENTRAL COORDINATION	LITTLE STRONG DIV. LEVEL COORDINATION	GROUP LEVEL MGRS FLOW INFO CENTRE/UNITS
SOURCE OF NEW IDEAS	CENTRE OR UNIT	FROM UNITS (DIVESTMENT CORPORATE)	SUGGESTIONS FROM CENTRE
SOURCE OF GOALS	FROM PLANS	OBJECTIVES SET	SHORT TERM PAYBACK CRITERIA
REPORTING	DETAILED TO CENTRE	DETAILED	FREQUENT MONITORING
CONTROL	FLEXIBLE STRATEGY KEY	TIGHT-INCENTIVES AND SANCTIONS	BUDGET AS CONTRACT STRONG PRESSURE ON PROBLEM UNITS - MANAGEMENT CHANGE
RESOURCE ALLOCATION	CENTRE ALLOCATES, SETS PRIORITIES	CENTRE ALLOCATES SETS PRIORITIES	CENTRE FUNDS ALL GOOD PROJECTS

Figure 1.2 Styles of strategic management (Derived from Goold and Campbell, *Strategies and Styles*)

The Goold and Campbell contribution is important, but raises two issues in my mind. The first is whether the research on the evolution of planning, and that on styles of planning are in fact intertwined in some way. Is the evolutionary argument as straightforward as it seems, or are some of the successive steps reflections of differences in style? There is an interesting area for further thought here.

My second issue is about the chief executive, and a query about whether it is the individual in this slot who is in fact the most significant factor affecting style, and that this will override all but extreme situations among the other factors. The research covers 16 companies and by chance I have a professional consulting relationship with two of them. One, a strategic control company, was an assignment where I helped formulate corporate level strategy and design a planning process. The only reason the process is more strategic control than strategic planning is because of the deepseated beliefs of the chief executive in delegation of autonomy to the people closest to the 'coal face'. The other company is a strategic planning firm. My association with that company began in 1978 and has been continuous and involved many planning assignments, although none to do with the process. Over this period I have observed three changes in planning style, which in my opinion have again been the result of chief executive influence rather than a change in business circumstances. My surmises do not make the Goold and Campbell contribution any less valuable, and I believe that they have opened up a seam of understanding from which planning will extract even more valuable nuggets in the future. There is also a clear connection between their findings and some of the behaviourally oriented contributions that are described later in this chapter.

ANALYTICAL ADVANCES

Analytical Evolution

Analytical concepts play a key role in strategic management. Without analysis it may be difficult to see the new patterns, or even to understand the opportunities and threats within the present and expected situation. Without analysis it is difficult to determine whether a particular course of action is likely to be beneficial or harmful to the organisation. Yet, as Ohmae (1982) neatly indicates, analysis does not make strategy. It is the creative and innovative skills of people which make strategy. He coined the phrase strategic thinking, and his book would have been worth referencing for this alone. In fact it also contains some refreshingly new slants on analytical concepts, enhanced by examples which are largely from Japanese businesses.

Recent years have shown significant advances in analytical approaches. Forecasting techniques are not much in favour in strategic management, and have given way to techniques which improve understanding of the dynamics which affect business results, and which allow the human mind to grasp very complex situations.

Hussey (1984) sees one of the main purposes of the analytical approaches as shifting what he calls the 'perceptual boundaries' of a business. The point is that all managers are prisoners within the boundaries of their own perception, and although corporate planning is supposed to remove those boundaries it does not always do so. This perception can never match reality completely, because all the facts can never be known. Often the perception is very wrong, in that deeply held beliefs about how an industry works, or what a particular company is good at just do not match reality. The British motor cycle industry disappeared because its managers did not understand that the new Japanese competitors were working to different strategic concepts than had been the norm hitherto. Perceptual boundaries are often shared across a whole company, passed on from one manager to another, and are seen as if they are an immutable reality. Where the match with reality is close, this is not a problem. Where it is far from the truth, as for example with a company which sees all competition in a domestic context, although the rest of the industry operates globally, the consequences can be severe. Good analytical approaches put information into new patterns, and in so doing challenge the perceptions. Hussey recommends the use of several approaches, rather than reliance on one method, because different facets of reality are illuminated by different methods of analysis.

Competitor Analysis

One of the biggest changes of emphasis that has taken place over the past decade has been in a new awareness of competitor analysis, and in the industry forces that affect a company's power to make profits. The credit for starting this movement must go to Porter (1980) whose approach to industry analysis has been one of the strongest influences on the development of strategic management. The basic concept of industry analysis is a model and set of general principles which looks at the dynamic tensions between industry firms, those that buy from them, and those that supply them. The power of the various players is also affected by the availability of substitutes, and the ease of entry into or exit from the industry.

The Porter contribution included an awareness that the structure of the industry should affect the formulation of strategies, and that these are likely to be different in an emerging industry, for example, than in a highly fragmented mature industry. His work predates the publication of his first book and his initial model appeared in Porter (1975). Not all of his conclusions are original, in that elements of his approach had been in use for decades. What his contribution has been is the addition of some original elements, and the pulling of the old and new into a sound model with well-codified rules. The result is a concept which has probably been one of the most important single influences on strategic management throughout the entire history of the subject. It is this work which contributed to a challenge to some of the concepts behind some of the then popular techniques of portfolio analysis, about which more will be said later.

Porter (1980) also put the spotlight on competitor analysis, including the systematic collection of information and ways of interpreting this within the framework of the industry structure. It is fair to attribute to Porter's influence the immense interest in competitor analysis that has occurred since 1980, and although others have made a significant contribution to the further development of competitor analysis, none has had as dramatic an influence. A further concept was added, Porter (1985), in value chains which might best be described as an analytical approach to the identification of areas of differentiation throughout all the activities of a company, which he divides into primary activities such as marketing and support activities such as human resources. The complexity of the approach and the need for detailed information makes it something which does not suit all organisations.

The PIMS Contribution

One of the difficulties facing strategists is that so many principles of good strategic thinking have been drawn from experience, common sense, or from case study observation. There are few areas where principles have been derived from statistically relevant researches or formal analysis. One exception is in the area of acquisition success and failure, on which more will be said later. Another is the contribution made to our knowledge of strategy by the PIMS organisation. The initials stand for the Profit Impact of Market Strategy, and the organisation has collected quantified information to explore the relationship between strategy and performance since 1972. The database in 1987 consisted of 3000 strategic business units run by 450 companies, covering a wide spectrum of industries. The majority of participants are in North America, but there are members from other countries, particularly countries in Europe.

Buzzell and Gale (1987) reported the PIMS findings in a detailed book which marks another landmark in the development of strategic management. The validation of the principles is in the book, and this reference is important for the serious planner. In summary, the main findings are:

- The most important linkage between strategy and performance is quality. Those in the top third on relative quality gained on average 5%–6% higher profitability than those in the bottom third. Quality is a concept that relates to the product in its market segment. It is not an argument that a small family saloon should be produced to the same engineering standards as a Rolls Royce car, but that it should have the appropriate quality standards for what it is. The argument is developed that in the end quality is free, in that better market performance brings volume increases, and that the reduction in unit costs exceeds the costs of quality.
- Market share and profitability are strongly related: 3.5 points of ROI are achieved for 10 points of market share. This is not a mandate to chase market share at any cost, since in some situations such an action could be uneconomic or even impossible. It does endorse the view that market share is critical, and should be sought when this is sensible. Porter's work, discussed above, provides a means of

analysing whether increased market share is realistic in a given situation.

- Higher ROI occurs when capital intensity is low.
- Much conventional wisdom about 'dogs' and 'cash cows' is erroneous. In reality many cows are dry and many dogs yield milk! The PIMS information does not provide insight on how businesses are managed and it may be that there are factors which affect the conclusion and which are outside the scope of the data.
- Vertical integration is not a universal good or bad strategy. Its success depends on the situation of the company. Many of the conclusions that can be drawn from PIMS on this issue are tentative and should perhaps be interpreted as the first words on a new line of thinking, rather than the ultimate conclusion.

Acquisition

The main conclusion from all the studies of acquisition strategy is that the failure rate is high. These facts were established by Kitching (1967, 1973, 1974), all outside the date chosen for the start of this review. More recent work such as Porter (1987) merely confirms the earlier findings, which are basically that all mergers have a high chance of failing, and that this is increased if the acquired company is in an unrelated business. The modern argument is that acquisition can and should be used to increase value added by the company. This is really little different from the argument of the 1960s and 1970s about synergy: the theory that two plus two should equal five. All the research shows that the result usually obtained is less than four!

Decline of Portfolio Analysis

Perhaps one of the most significant changes of emphasis in analytical approaches since 1976 has been the decline of portfolio analysis. In the early 1970s there were many variants of this technique in common use, of varying degrees of sophistication. All provided a matrix on which one axis measured market prospects and the other competitive performance. Businesses within the group were plotted on this matrix, and strategic principles in common use were based on a perception of the cash flow and profit implications of the sector of the matrix in which each business was plotted. It was argued that a high growth business would consume cash in order to finance growth. To balance it a company needed some businesses which had a strong position in low growth markets, as these, the so-called cash cows, would produce a cash surplus which could support growth in other areas. Nasty businesses with poor shares and low growth were held to make losses and consume cash. In all the methods there was a high growth, low market share area where the company had to decide to press for market share or get out.

The Boston Consulting Group was the organisation most associated with this technique, and as the pioneer its original technique was the least sophisticated, and relied on some very broad assumptions. The attack started in the late 1970s as the logic of industry analysis and of the PIMS findings began to cast doubts on the validity of some of the assumptions made in some of the methods. Of course there must have been some companies who tried to manage totally by the portfolio matrix, and the criticism of Porter (1987) was valid in these cases. He argued that the search for growth through acquisition candidates foundered on the fact that the spread of personal computers and databases had created a state of perfect knowledge so that there were no bargains to be had. Unless a business could be bought cheaply, the result of portfolio management could be a lower rather than a greater ROI.

There is validity to the arguments in Porter (1987) and Buzzell and Gale (1987) that a major direction of strategy should be the creation of added value through the various activities in a group, in terms of shared knowledge and skills, and shared resources. Some of the ideas suggested for this seem to argue for a greater degree of centralisation, at a time when the behavioural findings are for more autonomy at the sharp end, and fewer and smaller head office functions.

In all areas of management there is a tendency to over-react. Just as some companies used portfolio analysis as if it were the total salvation, so other companies have now rejected a technique which if well applied can help a company to make judgements about the relative strategic value of its various components. In addition, the approach can help the exploration of added value in the interfaces between businesses within a group, and in developing scenarios about the future shape of the total organisation.

Hussey (1982) made a comparison between the factors considered in industry analysis and in the concept of portfolio analysis he used. There is a very close fit. The issue in my mind is that any technique should be used wisely and not as a magic black box which produces the one true answer, that it should be used in combination with other methods of analysis, and that if portfolio analysis is used it should follow industry analysis, so that every business plotted is thoroughly understood. There is still considerable value in sensible use of portfolio analysis, despite the views that some now hold to the contrary.

Manufacturing Strategy

It is probably fair to say that manufacturing was the forgotten area of strategy in the 1960s, and remains in this position. A major contribution to thinking about manufacturing strategy was made by Skinner (1978), although many of the chapters in this had been published before, some in the mid-1960s. The argument is that manufacturing tends to be managed from the bottom up. It is rarely considered in the formulation of strategy, and is expected to produce the results of that strategy. One effect of this is that it is often forced to try to perform to conflicting objectives, such as maximum flexibility and lowest cost, and because of this fails on both counts. If manufacturing decisions were considered during the strategy process, and if manufacturing executives were expected to be proactive rather than reactive, better strategies would result.

Japan offers an example where the marketing and manufacturing strategies are considered jointly and it is this approach, which in the end is what brings competitive advantage, that has contributed to her success in world markets. There are other examples. *Swatch*, for example, was a marketing initiative conceived to recover market share in the watch business which had been lost to the Far Eastern countries. However, it was recognised that these fun watches had to be produced to a price that was conditioned by the market and unrelated to current watch production costs. A new total manufacturing strategy was thought out and new plants built dedicated to the *Swatch* concept.

Skinner argues that one of the important concepts is to see the problem as 'How can we compete?' rather than as the more usual 'How can we increase productivity?' One of his concepts is the focused factory, the argument that a plant should be set up with a limited number of objectives, and not be expected to perform a number of opposing tasks. For example, to make components that require two different standards of quality using the same machines and with the same people may be technically possible, but is probably undesirable (for example aircraft spares and normal industrial components). The reason is that the quality objectives may be in conflict. Similarly, a factory that mass produces a machine, and tries also to produce spares on the same equipment is likely to run into difficulties because here too there are conflicting objectives. The Skinner concept of the focused factory is a major contribution to our thinking about manufacturing strategy.

As firms become global there is increasing need to consider manufacturing strategy in a careful manner. The firm that is global needs to consider the location and number of plants that are required: the firm that is under competitive attack by a global firm needs to consider how to organise its production so that it remains able to compete.

Globalisation

One trend in business today is for more and more industries to go global. Writers on strategic management have noted and kept pace with the trend, but have not succeeded in getting far enough ahead of established practice to lead it. I find it difficult to single out any landmark writing on this subject, although there have been many helpful books and articles. The few that I list here add a little to our overall understanding of globalisation, and because I found them useful I include them.

Stopford and Turner (1985) provided a model showing the factors that influence global positioning. Each force can drive a firm either towards or away from global operations. The model is reproduced in Figure 1.3.

Cvar (1986) made a study of patterns of success and failure in global competition. The success factors are shown in Figure 1.4, which was derived from her work.

The analysis suggests that there are certain characteristics in industries that become global, in that there has to be the opportunity for high levels of demand for standardised products which also give rise to economies of scale. Globalisation is not a naturally occurring state but is man made, and the triggers are the identification of common segments in different countries that enable a product to be defined globally. In turn, this enables supply sources to be consolidated, so that the competitive cost advantages can be gained.

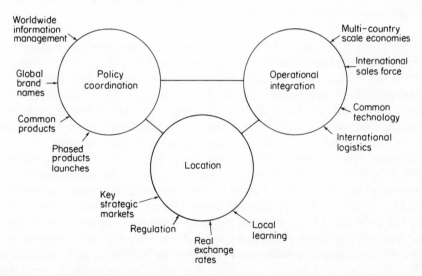

Figure 1.3 Factors influencing global positioning (From Stopford, J. M., and Turner, L., *Britain and the Multinationals*. Wiley, 1985. Reproduced with permission)

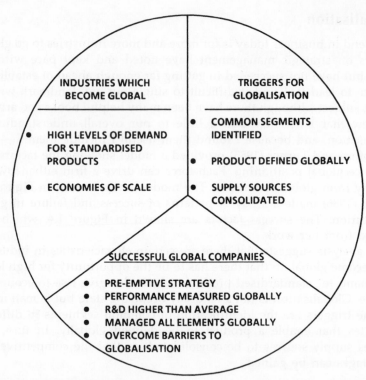

Figure 1.4 Global competition. (From research findings by Cvar, M. R. (1986) Case studies in global competition: Patterns of success and failure. In Porter, M. E. *Competition in Global Industries,* Harvard Business School, Boston)

The study also showed that the successful global companies had five factors in common. They had all developed a pre-emptive strategy, effectively becoming the agency that created the global market. All managed their companies on a global concept and measured their performance on this basis. It was also observed that all had higher than average R&D compared to their industry. All had demonstrated a measure of single mindedness in overcoming obstacles to globalisation.

Ohmae (1985) offers a conceptual argument to the need to become global. He argues that industries that have the right characteristics to become global will succeed only if they operate in the three geographic centres of the world: the United States, Japan and Europe. Those that stay in only one or two of these areas are unlikely to succeed in the long run because the volumes of production which will fall to those competitors that do penetrate the total triad will give an immense cost advantage. The argument is based on the fact that these areas contain some 600 million people in the largest and most sophisticated markets of the world.

ADVANCES IN BEHAVIOURAL THINKING

Behavioural Evolution

The behavioural aspect has always been important in strategic management. Even the earliest books would usually stress the need to ensure involvement of line managers in the planning process, in order to increase the chance that the plans would in fact be implemented. At the same time as the planning literature was piling up, so too was the output of the behaviouralists.

For almost two decades the planners did little more than give a nod to the behaviouralists. Hussey and Langham (1979) addressed this in a work that brought together the two streams of thinking, but this book did not succeed in changing thinking. My belief is that the planners thought it something that would be good for the personnel and OD people, while these specialists thought it good for the planners. So few bought it!

A more influential stream of thinking, although somewhat narrower in scope, came out of the Harvard Business School programme which explored the relationship of strategy and structure. The progress of this programme and its results are summarised in Galbraith and Nathanson (1978) and described in a series of publications between 1970 and 1977. Most studies were published in the early part of the decade, and examined the linkages through a study of statistical and empirical evidence in various countries. The programme was inspired by Chandler (1962) and added much to our knowledge about the intertwined nature of strategy and structure.

It was not until the 1980s that behavioural issues became part of the regular agenda of strategic management, and this change in thinking owes much to the publication of one book, *In Search of Excellence*, and is one of the most significant developments in the state of the art.

In Search of Excellence

Peters and Waterman (1982) spawned an 'excellence' industry after the runaway success of their study of the common factors in successful US companies. The fact that after the study some of the companies fell off their pedestals does not in my opinion reduce the value of the findings: it perhaps does emphasise that there are other factors that were not uncovered in the study. Strategy was not seen as a critical factor. It is perhaps of interest that at about the time of the publication, the 3Ms company, which probably featured more than any other in the book, was itself aware of the weakness in its approach to strategy, and began to go through the sort of analysis described in this chapter. What does emerge from the Peters and Waterman study, which is of fundamental importance, is an emphasis on the 'soft' aspects of management.

The basics are easy to list, but ⁻¹uch more difficult to do. The following summary is adapted from Hussey (1988):

(1) *Getting things done.* All the successful companies had a 'bias for action'. This did not mean that they did not think, but they certainly got down to implementing the results of those thoughts.

(2) *Staying close to the customer.* The customer is paramount, is served well, and is the source of many of the best new product ideas. This may be what we have all learned to call the marketing concept, but knowing the buzzword is not the same as applying the philosophy.

(3) *Leaders and innovators.* Innovation is encouraged, and there is adequate autonomy for the growth of entrepreneurial leaders.

(4) *People and productivity.* People, at whatever level, are seen as the source for productivity. 'We and they' attitudes are not fostered. The individual is important.

(5) *Staying close to the business.* The best companies have managers who regularly, using the words favoured by the Industrial Society, 'walk the job'. Managers understand what goes on at the basic level.

(6) *Staying with what you know.* The authors used the phrase 'stick to the knitting', which implies staying in your rut. I prefer to interpret this finding as to ensure that the company knows how it is going to manage any new area it decides to move into. Never to move from the business base is perhaps too conservative a view. Never to assume that you are immediately capable of managing *every* business is a very sensible concept.

(7) *Simple structure and small staffs.* All the best companies had simple organisational structures (no complex matrix organisations). Corporate staffs are very small, reducing the barriers between those at the top of the organisation and those at the coal face.

(8) *Mixed centralisation and decentralisation.* Autonomy is pushed down about as far as it will go. At the same time, the core values that the companies consider to be important are centralised.

Echoes of these findings are heard in many different places. For me the contribution of Peters and Waterman goes above the actual findings of their study. They have put the behavioural aspects of strategic management firmly on the map.

Implementation

I should like to be able to document considerable advances in the thinking on the implementation of strategy. In fact I have found only two streams of thought, which I include because I believe them to be important, although I would not claim that the ideas are as yet widely accepted.

The first is a research study (Alexander, 1985), which identified the ten most common strategy implementation problems. What is interesting is the number of causes that relate in some way to people issues. In the list that follows the problems are summarised from Alexander's research, but the comments are my own interpretation.

(1) *It took longer than expected.* This could be due to several causes, varying from failure to identify all the key actions to failure to build commitment.

(2) *There were major unidentified problems during implementation.* On the surface this appears an analytical issue, or possibly in some cases a realisation that we are not always able to anticipate everything. It may also be an involvement issue, in that wide involvement can often identify problems and actions that would otherwise be missed.

(3) *Implementation activities were not coordinated effectively enough.* This is most likely to be a failure in management.

(4) *Management was distracted by other activities and crises and did not implement.* This may have been appropriate if priorities changed. Just as likely is the possibility that management was not committed to the plan: a behavioural issue.

(5) *The capabilities of managers involved in implementation actions were inadequate.* This may be a recruitment or training issue. Those who make plans should not assume that everyone is competent to fulfil all necessary actions or to work in a different way.

(6) *Inadequate training and instruction were given to lower level employees.* It is easy to assume that the factory workers can operate new plant without help, that clerks will easily change to a new procedure, or that sales people will change priorities. Such assumptions may be damaging.

(7) *Events in the outside world impacted on the plan.* This could be poor planning, or the fact that there will always be some unpredictable changes.

(8) *Departmental managers did not provide enough leadership.* This again is a behavioural problem, which could have been caused by ignorance or poor management.

(9) *Key implementation tasks and activities were not adequately defined.*

(10) *The information systems were inadequate to monitor performance.* Clearly if you do not know whether or not an action has been implemented it is difficult to manage the process.

The second stream of thought has echoes in many of Alexander's findings, but also has added dimensions. It is the use of training and education, particularly of management, tied to the corporate strategy.

Management Training and Corporate Strategy

It would be wrong to claim that the authors quoted have created the sort of swing in opinion that has followed a Porter or a Peters. What is important is that there is a movement to use training strategically, particularly in the United States, and that the authors from empirical observation have provided what should be an influential building block in the development of strategic management.

Lusterman (1985), in a survey of management training in the United States, found a significant increase in training which was caused by changes in the business circumstances or strategy. Further, it was noted that there were many situations where training had a bottom line objective or was directly tied to the implementation of new strategies. Nilsson (1987) stresses the need to formulate the executive development programme in the context of corporate strategy. He stresses how training can contribute to the company's philosophy and shared values. The book is based on the author's experience with Hewlett-Packard.

Hussey (1988) bases his conclusions on research into management training in the United Kingdom and experience in designing initiatives that are intended to achieve a strategic objective.

Figure 1.5 illustrates the main essentials of the argument. Most organisations ignore the top box of the model, and base their management development plans on an assessment of the needs of individuals. This is an important component of the new approach, but it is argued that the strategies and objectives of the organisation are even more important, and will change, supplement or over-ride what may be identified from a study of the individuals.

There may also be forms of training that are necessary for legal reasons. This additional category of requirements is included for completeness. These three groups of input when considered together will often cause a reconsideration of the training initiatives currently being applied by the company, and these should be considered as a fourth component of the model. The result is likely to be a different policy, strategy and initiatives for management training.

Hussey identifies six situations where a training programme can be used to make a major contribution to strategic management.

(1) *Strategy formulation.* The right programmes can be used to challenge the assumptions on which current plans are based, or to examine strategic options.
(2) *Strategy implementation.* An appropriate initiative can be used to enable an understanding of the strategy to be gained in broad terms, and in its impact on an individual and his or her job. Commitment

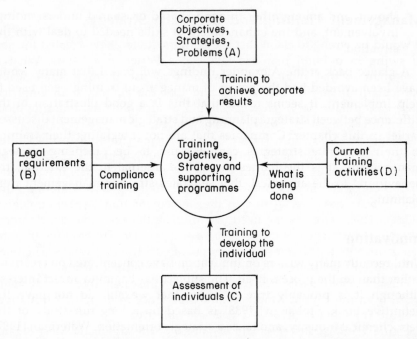

Figure 1.5 Training strategy (Copyright Harbridge Consulting Group Ltd. 1988)

can be built as people discover the reason for the strategy, and decide for themselves that it makes sense. Implications of the strategy can be explored and converted into personal action plans. Appropriate training can be given to correct deficiencies in those who are involved in implementing the change.

(3) *Policy implementation.* A change in policy, such as a decision to put more effort behind competitor analysis, can often be effectively implemented with the aid of training programmes, which can build commitment to the policy and ensure that people are both able and willing to implement it.

(4) *Corporate culture.* Training may be a major tool in creating a culture or changing a culture. In turn this will help ensure that strategies and culture are compatible.

(5) *Environmental change.* Significant changes in the business environment may provide threats or opportunities. Appropriate training initiatives can help the organisation to identify and deal with major changes.

(6) *Solving problems.* Training programmes may also be designed to solve particular problems, such as how to increase market share, or improve profitability. The mechanism is similar to the other categories

shown, and among other things is based on shared understanding, involvement, and the enhancement of skills needed to deal with the situation.

A glance back at the Alexander findings will reveal that many would have been avoided had the power of management training been used to help implement. It seems to me that this is a good illustration of the difference between strategic planning and strategic management discussed earlier in this chapter. Companies that are not integrating their training to their corporate strategies cannot claim to be practising strategic management. It is the harnessing of the internal to the external, the behavioural to the analytical, that separates strategic management from planning.

Innovation

Until recently many writers on innovation have concentrated on creativity rather than on the process itself. The subject has begun to attract interest, although it is probably true to argue that we still do not have the definitive book. Stobaugh (1988) is based on a long-run study of the petrochemical industry, and takes a strategic orientation. Waterman (1987) concentrates on renewal, and advocates a way of linking planning and organisation via the 7C and 7S models. The 7C model has, as its name suggests, a number of linked factors built around the alliteration of the letter C. Culture, Control, Crisis points, Causes and commitment, Communication, Chance and information, and Capability. The 7S model is very similar to the well-known concept developed by McKinsey, and links Structure, Strategy, Symbolic behaviour, Staff, Shared values, Systems, and Skills. Waterman combines Culture with Shared values, and Skills with Capability to produce what he terms the renewal ring. His argument is about using this renewal ring to gain and keep a competitive edge.

A simpler but effective model has been published by Harbridge House, Inc. (1987) (Figure 1.6). This was derived from a study of the management practices of organisations that were successful innovators in the United States.

The definition of innovation by the inventors of this model is:

A better thing to do or a better way to do it that contributes to an organisation's goals. It may be a method, structure, process or product.

The model accepts that creativity is important, but argues that there is much to do to change creativity to innovation. The middle circle represents the management tasks, the first is developing a vision of where the innovator wants to go. The second is building commitment to the

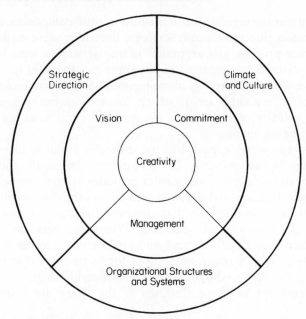

Figure 1.6 Harbridge House innovation model (Copyright © 1986, Harbridge House, Inc.)

vision through communication, involvement, reinforcement, support and influence. The third task is to manage the process by providing direction and control to the project.

The innovator operates in a broader context, that of the organisation. This is illustrated by the outer ring, and each segment directly relates to the segment of the middle ring which it touches. Thus the innovation has to be compatible with the strategic direction of the firm, the climate and culture must encourage innovation, and the structures and systems must support the innovation process.

The emphasis on innovation seems to me to be another of the important differences between strategic management today compared with that of a decade ago. Clearly there is room for many more contributions to a subject which is now receiving considerable attention. Whether the works referenced will retain their positions as important influencers of thought remains to be seen. Certainly they take us forward, and do a good service in opening up the subject to a wider audience.

Decision Making

In this review of developments, it seems right that a mention should be made of the concept developed by Quinn (1980) of *logical incrementalism*.

He studied the strategic decision making in nine companies, and reached the conclusion that most major strategic decisions were made outside of the planning process. His argument is that strategies tend to evolve, as internal decisions and external happenings run together to create a new shared consensus among top management. Major decisions are made in a series of incremental steps, which themselves build consensus and show the validity of the action. He sees the process as logical, and as capable of being managed.

The idea has some appeal, but the difficulty I find is in extrapolating the findings to the universe. The sample is very small, and the Goold and Campbell work referenced earlier provides at least one set of findings that strategic decision-making processes are not the same in all companies. There is always the dilemma that observed behaviour is not necessarily the most effective way of operating. Whereas Peters and Waterman's (1982) *In Search of Excellence* took successful companies as its criteria for the sample, Quinn's requirement was for companies that had recently undergone, or were undergoing, a major strategic shift.

My assessment of these findings is that they are interesting, but unproven.

CONCLUSION

The art and science of strategic management has made considerable progress over the past decade or so. Fortunately this progress continues, and there are no signs of a drying up of the flow of concepts of practical value.

If I were to rewrite this chapter in ten years' time, I would hope to be able to record many more developments in the areas of manufacturing, globalisation, information systems and technology. I would also hope that the behavioural side would have expanded to take a disproportionately large share of space, because I believe that many of our problems are caused by analysis without full consideration of people issues.

Overall I see grounds for optimism in the progress already achieved and in the directions in which we appear to be headed.

REFERENCES

Alexander, L. D. (1985) Successfully implementing strategic decisions. *Long Range Planning*, **18**(3), 91–97.

Ansoff, H. I. (1965) *Corporate Strategy*. McGraw-Hill, New York.

Ansoff, H. I., Declerk, R. P., and Hayes, R. L. (eds) (1976) *Strategic Planning to Strategic Management*. Wiley, Chichester.

Buzzell, R. D., and Gale, B. T. (1987) *The PIMS Principles*. Free Press, New York.
Chandler, A. D. (1962) *Strategy and Structure*. MIT Press, Cambridge, MA.
Chandler, J., and Cockle, P. (1982) *Techniques of Scenario Planning*. McGraw-Hill, New York.
Cvar, M. R. (1986) Case studies in global competition: patterns of success and failure. In Porter, M. E. (ed.) *Competition in Global Industries*. Harvard Business School, Boston.
Galbraith, J. R., and Nathanson, D. A. (1978) *Strategy Implementation: The Role of Strategy and Process*. West, St. Paul, MN, pp. 26–48.
Gluck, F. W., Kaufman, S. P., and Walleck, A. S. (1980) Strategic management for competitive advantage. *Harvard Business Review*, July/August, Harvard, Boston.
Goold, M., and Campbell, A. (1987) *Strategies and Styles*. Blackwell, Oxford.
Hussey, D. E. (1979) Evolution of planning approaches. *Professional Administration*, April.
Hussey, D. E. (1982) *Corporate Planning: Theory and Practice*, 2nd edn. Pergamon, Oxford, p. 137.
Hussey, D. E. (1984) Strategic management: Lessons from success and failure. *Long Range Planning*, **17**(1), pp. 43–53.
Hussey, D. E. (1988) *Management Training and Corporate Strategy*. Pergamon, Oxford.
Hussey, D. E., and Langham M. J. (1979) *Corporate Planning: The Human Factor*. Pergamon, Oxford.
Innovation: Creating the Future. Harbridge House, Inc., Boston, MA, 1987.
Kitching, J. (1967) Why do mergers miscarry? *Harvard Business Review*, November/December.
Kitching, J. (1973) *Acquisitions in Europe*. Business International, Geneva.
Kitching, J. (1974) Winning and losing with European acquisitions. *Harvard Business Review*, March/April.
Lusterman, S. (1985) *Trends in Corporate Education and Training*. Conference Board, USA.
Nilsson, W. P. (1987) *Achieving Strategic Goals Through Executive Development*. Addison-Wesley, Reading, MA.
Ohmae, K. (1983) *The Mind of the Strategist*. Penguin, London.
Ohmae, K. (1985) *Triad Power*. Free Press, New York.
Peters, T. J., and Waterman, R. H. (1982) *In Search of Excellence*. Harper & Row, New York.
Porter, M. E. (1975) *Note on the Structural Analysis of Industries*. Harvard Business School, Boston.
Porter, M. E. (1980) *Competitive Strategy*. Free Press, New York.
Porter, M. E. (1985) *Competitive Advantage*. Free Press, New York.
Porter, M. E. (1987) From competitive advantage to corporate strategy. *Harvard Business Review*, May–June.
Quinn, J. B. (1980) *Strategies for Change*. Irwin, Homewood.
Scott, B. W. (1965) *Long Range Planning in American Industry*. American Management Association.
Skinner, W. (1978) *Manufacturing in the Corporate Strategy*. Wiley, New York.
Stobaugh, R. (1988) *Innovation and Competition*. Harvard Business School, Boston.
Stopford, J. M., and Turner, L. (1985) *Britain and the Multinationals*. Wiley, Chichester, p. 41.
Waterman, R. H. (1987) *The Renewal Factor*. Bantam, New York.

Part 2

GAINING COMPETITIVE ADVANTAGE

2

FROM COMPETITIVE ADVANTAGE TO CORPORATE STRATEGY

Michael E. Porter

Professor of Business Administration, Harvard Business School

Corporate strategy, the overall plan for a diversified company, is both the darling and the stepchild of contemporary management practice— the darling because CEOs have been obsessed with diversification since the early 1960s, the stepchild because almost no consensus exists about what corporate strategy is, much less about how a company should formulate it.

The track record of corporate strategies has been dismal

A diversified company has two levels of strategy: business unit (or competitive) strategy and corporate (or companywide) strategy. Competitive strategy concerns how to create competitive advantage in each of the businesses in which a company competes. Corporate strategy concerns two different questions: what businesses the corporation should be in and how the corporate office should manage the array of business units.

Corporate strategy is what makes the corporate whole add up to more than the sum of its business unit parts.

The track record of corporate strategies has been dismal. I studied the diversification records of 33 large, prestigious US companies over the 1950–1986 period and found that most of them had divested many more acquisitions than they had kept. The corporate strategies of most companies have dissipated instead of created shareholder value.

International Review of Strategic Management. Edited by D. E. Hussey. Published 1990 by John Wiley & Sons Ltd. Reprinted by permission of *Harvard Business Review* 'From competitive advantage to corporate strategy', May/June 1987. © 1987 by the President and Fellows of Harvard College; all rights reserved.

The need to rethink corporate strategy could hardly be more urgent. By taking over companies and breaking them up, corporate raiders thrive on failed corporate strategy. Fueled by junk bond financing and growing acceptability, raiders can expose any company to takeover, no matter how large or blue chip.

Recognizing past diversification mistakes, some companies have initiated large-scale restructuring programs. Others have done nothing at all. Whatever the response, the strategic questions persist. Those who have restructured must decide what to do next to avoid repeating the past; those who have done nothing must awake to their vulnerability. To survive, companies must understand what good corporate strategy is.

A SOBER PICTURE

While there is disquiet about the success of corporate strategies, none of the available evidence satisfactorily indicates the success or failure of corporate strategy. Most studies have approached the question by measuring the stock market valuation of mergers, captured in the movement of the stock prices of acquiring companies immediately before and after mergers are announced.

These studies show that the market values mergers as neutral or slightly negative, hardly cause for serious concern.[1] Yet the short-term market reaction is a highly imperfect measure of the long-term success of diversification, and no self-respecting executive would judge a corporate strategy this way.

Studying the diversification programs of a company over a long period of time is a much more telling way to determine whether a corporate strategy has succeeded or failed. My study of 33 companies, many of which have reputations for good management, is a unique look at the track record of major corporations. (For an explanation of the research, see the insert 'Where the data come from'.) Each company entered an average of 80 new industries and 27 new fields. Just over 70% of the new entries were acquisitions, 22% were start-ups, and 8% were joint ventures. IBM, Exxon, Du Pont, and 3M, for example, focused on start-ups, while ALCO Standard, Beatrice, and Sara Lee diversified almost solely through acquisitions (Exhibit 2.1 has a complete rundown).

My data paint a sobering picture of the success ratio of these moves (see Exhibit 2.2). I found that on average corporations divested more than half their acquisitions in new industries and more than 60% of their acquisitions in entirely new fields. Fourteen companies left more than 70% of all the acquisitions they had made in new fields. The track record in unrelated acquisitions is even worse—the average divestment rate is a startling 74% (see Exhibit 2.3). Even a highly respected company like General Electric divested a very high percentage of its acquisitions, particularly those in new fields. Companies near the top of the list in Exhibit 2.2. achieved a remarkably low rate of divestment. Some bear witness to the success of well-thought-out corporate strategies. Others, however, enjoy a lower rate simply because they have not faced up to their problem units and divested them.

I calculated total shareholder returns (stock price appreciation plus dividends) over the period of the study for each company so that I could compare them with its divestment rate. While companies near the top of the list have above-average shareholder returns, returns are not a reliable measure of diversification success. Shareholder return often depends heavily on the inherent attractiveness of companies' base industries. Companies like CBS and General Mills had extremely profitable base businesses that subsidized poor diversification track records.

I would like to make one comment on the use of shareholder value to judge performance. Linking shareholder value quantitatively to diversification performance only works if you compare the shareholder value that is with the shareholder value that might have been without diversification. Because such a comparison is virtually impossible to make, my own measure of diversification success—the number of units retained by the company—seems to be as good an indicator as any of the contribution of diversification to corporate performance.

My data give a stark indication of the failure of corporate strategies.[2] Of the 33 companies, 6 had been taken over as my study was being completed (see the note on Exhibit 2.2). Only the lawyers, investment bankers, and original sellers have prospered in most of these acquisitions, not the shareholders.

PREMISES OF CORPORATE STRATEGY

Any successful corporate strategy builds on a number of premises. These are facts of life about diversification. They cannot be altered, and when ignored, they explain in part why so many corporate strategies fail.

Competition occurs at the business unit level. Diversified companies do not compete; only their business units do. Unless a corporate strategy places primary attention on nurturing the success of each unit, the strategy will fail, no matter how elegantly constructed. Successful corporate strategy must grow out of and reinforce competitive strategy.

Diversification inevitably adds costs and constraints to business units. Obvious costs such as the corporate overhead allocated to a unit may not be as important or subtle as the hidden costs and constraints. A business unit must explain its decisions to top management, spend time complying with planning and other corporate systems, live with parent

Exhibit 2.1 Diversification profiles of 33 leading US companies

Company	No. total entries	All entries into new industries	Percent acquisitions	Percent joint ventures	Percent start-ups	Entries into new industries that represented entirely new fields	Percent acquisitions	Percent joint ventures	Percent start-ups
ALCO Standard	221	165	99	0	1	56	100	0	0
Allied Corp.	77	49	67	10	22	17	65	6	29
Beatrice	382	204	97	1	2	61	97	0	3
Borden	170	96	77	4	19	32	75	3	22
CBS	148	81	67	16	17	28	65	21	14
Continental Group	75	47	77	6	17	19	79	11	11
Cummins Engine	30	24	54	17	29	13	46	23	31
Du Pont	80	39	33	16	51	19	37	0	63
Exxon	79	56	34	5	61	17	29	6	65
General Electric	160	108	47	20	33	29	48	14	38
General Foods	92	53	91	4	6	22	86	5	9
General Mills	110	102	84	7	9	27	74	7	19
W.R. Grace	275	202	83	7	10	66	74	5	21
Gulf & Western	178	140	91	4	6	48	88	2	10
IBM	46	38	18	18	63	16	19	0	81
IC Industries	67	41	85	3	12	17	88	6	6
ITT	246	178	89	2	9	50	92	0	8

33

Johnson & Johnson	88	77	77	0	23	18	56	0	44
Mobil	41	32	53	16	31	15	60	7	33
Proctor & Gamble	28	23	61	0	39	14	79	0	21
Raytheon	70	58	86	9	5	16	81	19	6
RCA	53	46	35	15	50	19	37	21	42
Rockwell	101	75	73	24	3	27	74	22	4
Sara Lee	197	141	96	1	4	41	95	2	2
Scovill	52	36	97	0	3	12	92	0	8
Signal	53	45	67	4	29	20	75	0	25
Tenneco	85	62	81	6	13	26	73	8	19
3M	144	125	54	2	45	34	71	3	56
TRW	119	82	77	10	13	28	64	11	25
United Technologies	62	49	57	18	24	17	23	17	39
Westinghouse	129	73	63	11	26	36	61	3	36
Wickes	71	47	83	0	17	22	68	0	32
Xerox	59	50	66	6	28	18	50	11	39
Total	3,788	2,644				906			
Average	114.8	80.1	70.3	7.9	21.8	27.4	67.9	7.0	25.9

Note: Beatrice, Continental Group, General Foods, RCA, Scovill, and Signal were taken over as the study was being completed. Their data cover the period up through takeover but not subsequent divestments.

Exhibit 2.2 Acquisition track records of leading US diversifiers ranked by percent divested

Company	All acquisitions in new industries	Percent made by 1980 and then divested	Percent made by 1975 and then divested	Acquisitions in new industries that represented entirely new fields	Percent made by 1980 and then divested	Percent made by 1975 and then divested
Johnson & Johnson	59	17	12	10	33	14
Proctor & Gamble	14	17	17	11	17	17
Raytheon	50	17	26	13	25	33
United Technologies	28	25	13	10	17	0
3M	67	26	27	24	42	45
TRW	63	27	31	18	40	38
IBM	7	33	0*	3	33	0*
Du Pont	13	38	43	7	60	75
Mobil	17	38	57	9	50	50
Borden	74	39	40	24	45	50
IC Industries	35	42	50	15	46	44
Tenneco	50	43	47	19	27	33
Beatrice	198	46	45	59	52	51
ITT	159	52	52	46	61	61
Rockwell	55	56	57	20	71	71
Allied Corp.	33	57	45	11	40	80
Exxon	19	62	20*	5	80	50*

Sara Lee	135	62	65	39	80	76
General Foods	48	63	62	19	93	93
Scovill	35	64	77	11	64	70
Signal	30	65	63	15	70	67
ALCO Standard	164	65	70	56	72	76
W.R. Grace	167	65	70	49	71	70
General Electric	51	65	78	14	100	100
Wickes	38	67	72	15	73	70
Westinghouse	46	68	69	22	61	59
Xerox	33	71	79	9	100	100
Continental Group	36	71	72	15	60	60
General Mills	86	75	73	20	65	60
Gulf & Western	127	79	78	42	75	72
Cummins Engine	13	80	80	6	83	83
RCA	16	80	92	7	86	100
CBS	54	87	89	18	88	88
Total	2,021			661		
Average per company†	61.2	53.4	56.5	20.0	60.0	61.5

*Companies with three or fewer acquisitions by the cutoff year.
†Companies with three or fewer acquisitions by the cutoff year are excluded from the average to minimize statistical distortions.
Note: Beatrice, Continental Group, General Foods, RCA, Scovill, and Signal were taken over as the study was being completed. Their data cover the period up through takeover but not subsequent divestments.

Exhibit 2.3 Diversification performance in joint ventures, start-ups, and unrelated acquisitions (companies in same order as in Exhibit 2.2)

Company	Joint ventures as a percent of new entries	Percent made by 1980 and then divested	Percent made by 1975 and then divested	Start-ups as a percent of new entries	Percent made by 1980 and then divested
Johnson & Johnson	0	†	†	23	14
Proctor & Gamble	0	†	†	39	0
Raytheon	9	60	60	5	50
United Technologies	18	50	50	24	11
3M	2	100*	100*	45	2
TRW	10	20	25	13	63
IBM	18	100*	†	63	20
Du Pont	16	100*	†	51	61
Mobil	16	33	33	31	50
Borden	4	33	33	19	17
IC Industries	3	100*	100*	13	80
Tenneco	6	67	67	13	67
Beatrice	1	†	†	2	0
ITT	2	0*	†	8	38
Rockwell	24	38	42	3	0
Allied Corp.	10	100	75	22	38
Exxon	5	0	0	61	27
Sara Lee	1	†	†	4	75
General Foods	4	†	†	6	67
Scovill	0	†	†	3	100
Signal	4	†	†	29	20
ALCO Standard	0	†	†	1	†
W.R. Grace	7	33	38	10	71
General Electric	20	20	33	33	33
Wickes	0	†	†	17	63
Westinghouse	11	0*	0*	26	44
Xerox	6	100*	100*	28	50
Continental Group	6	67	67	17	14
General Mills	7	71	71	9	89
Gulf & Western	4	75	50	6	100
Cummins Engine	17	50	50	29	0

Exhibit 2.3 Continued

Company	Joint ventures as a percent of new entries	Percent made by 1980 and then divested	Percent made by 1975 and then divested	Start-ups as a percent of new entries	Percent made by 1980 and then divested
RCA	15	67	67	50	99
CBS	16	71	71	17	86
Average per company‡	7.9	50.3	48.9	21.8	44.0

*Companies with two or fewer entries.
†No entries in this category.
‡Average excludes companies with two or fewer entries to minimize statistical distortions.
Note: Beatrice, Continental Group, General Foods, RCA, Scovill, and Signal were taken over as the study was being completed. Their data cover the period up through takeover but not subsequent divestments.

company guidelines and personnel policies, and forgo the opportunity to motivate employees with direct equity ownership. These costs and constraints can be reduced but not entirely eliminated.

Shareholders can readily diversify themselves. Shareholders can diversify their own portfolios of stocks by selecting those that best match their preferences and risk profiles.[3] Shareholders can often diversify more cheaply than a corporation because they can buy shares at the market price and avoid hefty acquisition premiums.

These premises mean that corporate strategy cannot succeed unless it truly adds value—to business units by providing tangible benefits that offset the inherent costs of lost independence and to shareholders by diversifying in a way they could not replicate.

PASSING THE ESSENTIAL TESTS

To understand how to formulate corporate strategy, it is necessary to specify the conditions under which diversification will truly create shareholder value. These conditions can be summarized in three essential tests:

(1) *The attractiveness test.* The industries chosen for diversification must be structurally attractive or capable of being made attractive.

(2) *The cost-of-entry test.* The cost of entry must not capitalize all the future profits.
(3) *The better-off test.* Either the new unit must gain competitive advantage from its link with the corporation or vice versa.

Of course, most companies will make certain that their proposed strategies pass some of these tests. But my study clearly shows that when companies ignored one or two of them, the strategic results were disastrous.

How Attractive is the Industry?

In the long run, the rate of return available from competing in an industry is a function of its underlying structure, which I have described in another HBR article.[4] An attractive industry with a high average return on investment will be difficult to enter because entry barriers are high, suppliers and buyers have only modest bargaining power, substitute products or services are few, and the rivalry among competitors is stable. An unattractive industry like steel will have structural flaws, including a plethora of substitute materials, powerful and price-sensitive buyers, and excessive rivalry caused by high fixed costs and a large group of competitors, many of whom are state supported.

Diversification cannot create shareholder value unless new industries have favorable structures that support returns exceeding the cost of capital. If the industry doesn't have such returns, the company must be able to restructure the industry or gain a sustainable competitive advantage that leads to returns well above the industry average. An industry need not be attractive before diversification. In fact, a company might benefit from entering before the industry shows its full potential. The diversification can then transform the industry's structure.

In my research, I often found companies had suspended the attractiveness test because they had a vague belief that the industry 'fit' very closely with their own businesses. In the hope that the corporate 'comfort' they felt would lead to a happy outcome, the companies ignored fundamentally poor industry structures. Unless the close fit allows substantial competitive advantage, however, such comfort will turn into pain when diversification results in poor returns. Royal Dutch Shell and other leading oil companies have had this unhappy experience in a number of chemicals businesses, where poor industry structures overcame the benefits of vertical integration and skills in process technology.

Another common reason for ignoring the attractiveness test is a low entry cost. Sometimes the buyer has an inside track or the owner is anxious to sell. Even if the price is actually low, however, a one-shot gain will not offset a perpetually poor business. Almost always, the company finds it must reinvest in the newly acquired unit, if only to replace fixed assets and fund working capital.

Diversifying companies are also prone to use rapid growth or other simple indicators as a proxy for a target industry's attractiveness. Many that rushed into fast-growing industries (personal computers, video games, and robotics, for example) were burned because they mistook early growth for long-term profit potential. Industries are profitable not because they are sexy or high tech; they are profitable only if their structures are attractive.

What is the Cost of Entry?

Diversification cannot build shareholder value if the cost of entry into a new business eats up its expected returns. Strong market forces, however, are working to do just that. A company can enter new industries by acquisition or start-up. Acquisitions expose it to an increasingly efficient merger market. An acquirer beats the market if it pays a price not fully reflecting the prospects of the new unit. Yet multiple bidders are commonplace, information flows rapidly, and investment bankers and other intermediaries work aggressively to make the market as efficient as possible. In recent years, new financial instruments such as junk bonds have brought new buyers into the market and made even large companies vulnerable to takeover. Acquisition premiums are high and reflect the acquired company's future prospects—sometimes too well. Philip Morris paid more than four times book value for Seven-Up Company, for example. Simple arithmetic meant that profits had to more than quadruple to sustain the preacquisition ROI. Since there proved to be little Philip Morris could add in marketing prowess to the sophisticated marketing wars in the soft-drink industry, the result was the unsatisfactory financial performance of Seven-Up and ultimately the decision to divest.

In a start-up, the company must overcome entry barriers. It's a real catch-22 situation, however, since attractive industries are attractive because their entry barriers are high. Bearing the full cost of the entry barriers might well dissipate any potential profits. Otherwise, other entrants to the industry would have already eroded its profitability.

In the excitement of finding an appealing new business, companies sometimes forget to apply the cost-of-entry test. The more attractive a new industry, the more expensive it is to get into.

Will the Business be Better Off?

A corporation must bring some significant competitive advantage to the new unit, or the new unit must offer potential for significant advantage to the corporation. Sometimes, the benefits to the new unit accrue only once, near the time of entry, when the parent instigates a major overhaul of its strategy or installs a first-rate management team. Other diversification yields ongoing competitive advantage if the new unit can market its product, through the well-developed distribution system of its sister units, for instance. This is one of the important underpinnings of the merger of Baxter Travenol and American Hospital Supply.

When the benefit to the new unit comes only once, the parent company has no rationale for holding the new unit in its portfolio over the long term. Once the results of the one-time improvement are clear, the diversified company no longer adds value to offset the inevitable costs imposed on the unit. It is best to sell the unit and free up corporate resources.

The better-off test does not imply that diversifying corporate risk creates shareholder value in and of itself. Doing something for shareholders that they can do themselves is not a basis for corporate strategy. (Only in the case of a privately held company, in which the company's and the shareholder's risk are the same, is diversification to reduce risk valuable for its own sake.) Diversification of risk should only be a by-product of corporate strategy, not a prime motivator.

Executives ignore the better-off test most of all or deal with it through arm waving or trumped-up logic rather than hard strategic analysis. One reason is that they confuse company size with shareholder value. In the drive to run a bigger company, they lose sight of their real job. They may justify the suspension of the better-off test by pointing to the way they manage diversity. By cutting corporate staff to the bone and giving business units nearly complete autonomy, they believe they avoid the pitfalls. Such thinking misses the whole point of diversification, which is to create shareholder value rather than to avoid destroying it.

CONCEPTS OF CORPORATE STRATEGY

The three tests for successful diversification set the standards that any corporate strategy must meet; meeting them is so difficult that most diversification fails. Many companies lack a clear concept of corporate strategy to guide their diversification or pursue a concept that does not address the tests. Others fail because they implement a strategy poorly.

My study has helped me identify four concepts of corporate strategy that have been put into practice—portfolio management, restructuring, transferring skills, and sharing activities. While the concepts are not always mutually exclusive, each rests on a different mechanism by which the corporation creates shareholder value and each requires the diversified company to manage and organize itself in a different way. The first two require no connections among business units; the second two depend on them (see Exhibit 2.4). While all four concepts of strategy have succeeded under the right circumstances, today some make more sense than others. Ignoring any of the concepts is perhaps the quickest road to failure.

Portfolio Management

The concept of corporate strategy most in use is portfolio management, which is based primarily on diversification through acquisition. The corporation acquires sound, attractive companies with competent managers who agree to stay on. While acquired units do not have to be in the same industries as existing units, the best portfolio managers generally limit their range of businesses in some way, in part to limit the specific expertise needed by top management.

The acquired units are autonomous, and the teams that run them are compensated according to unit results. The corporation supplies capital and works with each to infuse it with professional management techniques. At the same time, top management provides objective and dispassionate review of business unit results. Portfolio managers categorize units by potential and regularly transfer resources from units that generate cash to those with high potential and cash needs.

In a portfolio strategy, the corporation seeks to create shareholder value in a number of ways. It uses its expertise and analytical resources to spot attractive acquisition candidates that the individual shareholder could not. The company provides capital on favorable terms that reflect corporatewide fund-raising ability. It introduces professional management skills and discipline. Finally, it provides high-quality review and coaching, unencumbered by conventional wisdom or emotional attachments to the business.

The logic of the portfolio management concept rests on a number of vital assumptions. If a company's diversification plan is to meet the attractiveness and cost-of-entry tests, it must find good but undervalued companies. Acquired companies must be truly undervalued because the parent does little for the new unit once it is acquired. To meet the better-off test, the benefits the corporation provides must yield a significant competitive advantage to acquired units. The style of operating through

Exhibit 2.4 Concepts of corporate strategy

	Portfolio management	Restructuring	Transferring skills	Sharing activities
Strategic prerequisites	Superior insight into identifying and acquiring undervalued companies	Superior insight into identifying restructuring opportunities	Proprietary skills in activities important to competitive advantage in target industries	Activities in existing units that can be shared with new business units to gain competitive advantage
	Willingness to sell off losers quickly or to opportunistically divest good performers when buyers are willing to pay large premiums	Willingness and capability to intervene to transform acquired units	Ability to accomplish the transfer of skills among units on an ongoing basis	Benefits of sharing that outweigh the costs
	Broad guidelines for and constraints on the types of units in the portfolio so that senior management can play the review role effectively	Broad similarities among the units in the portfolio	Acquisitions of beachhead positions in new industries as a base	Both start-ups and acquisitions as entry vehicles
		Willingness to cut losses by selling off units where restructuring proves unfeasible		Ability to overcome organizational resistance to business unit collaboration
	A private company or undeveloped capital markets	Willingness to sell units when restructuring is complete, the results are clear, and market conditions are favorable		
	Ability to shift away from portfolio management as the capital markets get more efficient or the company gets			

Organizational prerequisites	Autonomous business units	Autonomous business units	Largely autonomous but collaborative business units	Strategic business units that are encouraged to share activities
	A very small, low-cost, corporate staff	A corporate organization with the talent and resources to oversee the turnarounds and strategic repositionings of acquired units	High-level corporate staff members who see their role primarily as integrators	An active strategic planning role at group, sector, and corporate levels
	Incentives based largely on business unit results	Incentives based largely on acquired units' results	Cross-business-unit committees, task forces, and other forums to serve as focal points for capturing and transferring skills	High-level corporate staff members who see their roles primarily as integrators
			Objectives of line managers that include skills transfer	Incentives based heavily on group and corporate results
			Incentives based in part on corporate results	

Continued

44

Exhibit 2.4 Continued

	Portfolio management	Restructuring	Transferring skills	Sharing activities
Common pitfalls	Pursuing portfolio management in countries with efficient capital marketing and a developed pool of professional management talent	Mistaking rapid growth or a 'hot' industry as sufficient evidence of a restructuring opportunity	Mistaking similarity or comfort with new businesses as sufficient basis for diversification	Sharing for its own sake rather than because it leads to competitive advantage
	Ignoring the fact that industry structure is not attractive	Lacking the resolve or resources to take on troubled situations and to intervene in management	Providing no practical ways for skills transfer to occur	Assuming sharing will occur naturally without senior management playing an active role
		Ignoring the fact that industry structure is not attractive	Ignoring the fact that industry structure is not attractive	Ignoring the fact that industry structure is not attractive
		Paying lip service to restructuring but actually practicing passive portfolio management		

highly autonomous business units must both develop sound business strategies and motivate managers.

In most countries, the days when portfolio management was a valid concept of corporate strategy are past. In the face of increasingly well-developed capital markets, attractive companies with good managements show up on everyone's computer screen and attract top dollar in terms of acquisition premium. Simply contributing capital isn't contributing much. A sound strategy can easily be funded; small to medium-size companies don't need a munificent parent.

Other benefits have also eroded. Large companies no longer corner the market for professional management skills; in fact, more and more observers believe managers cannot necessarily run anything in the absence of industry-specific knowledge and experience. Another supposed advantage of the portfolio management concept—dispassionate review—rests on similarly shaky ground since the added value of review alone is questionable in a portfolio of sound companies.

The benefit of giving business units complete autonomy is also questionable. Increasingly, a company's business units are interrelated, drawn together by new technology, broadening distribution channels, and changing regulations. Setting strategies of units independently may well undermine unit performance. The companies in my sample that have succeeded in diversification have recognized the value of inter-relationships and understood that a strong sense of corporate identity is as important as slavish adherence to parochial business unit financial results.

But it is the sheer complexity of the management task that has ultimately defeated even the best portfolio managers. As the size of the company grows, portfolio managers need to find more and more deals just to maintain growth. Supervising dozens or even hundreds of disparate units and under chain-letter pressures to add more, management begins to make mistakes. At the same time, the inevitable costs of being part of a diversified company take their toll and unit performance slides while the whole company's ROI turns downward. Eventually, a new management team is installed that initiates wholesale divestments and pares down the company to its core businesses. The experiences of Gulf & Western, Consolidated Foods (now Sara Lee), and ITT are just a few comparatively recent examples. Reflecting these realities, the US capital markets today reward companies that follow the portfolio management model with a 'conglomerate discount'; they value the whole less than the sum of the parts.

In developing countries, where large companies are few, capital markets are undeveloped, and professional management is scarce, portfolio management still works. But it is no longer a valid model for corporate strategy in advanced economies. Nevertheless, the technique is in the limelight today in the United Kingdom, where it is supported so far by a newly energized stock market eager for excitement. But this enthusiasm will wane—as well it should. Portfolio management is no way to conduct corporate strategy.

Restructuring

Unlike its passive role as a portfolio manager, when it serves as banker and reviewer, a company that bases its strategy on restructuring becomes an active restructurer of business units. The new businesses are not necessarily related to existing units. All that is necessary is unrealized potential.

The restructuring strategy seeks out undeveloped, sick, or threatened organizations or industries on the threshold of significant change. The parent intervenes, frequently changing the unit management team, shifting strategy, or infusing the company with new technology. Then it may make follow-up acquisitions to build a critical mass and sell off unneeded or unconnected parts and thereby reduce the effective acquisition cost. The result is a strengthened company or a transformed industry. As a coda, the parent sells off the stronger unit once results are clear because the parent is no longer adding value and top management decides that its attention should be directed elsewhere. (See 'An uncanny British restructurer' at the end of this chapter, for an example of restructuring.)

A strong sense of corporate identity is as important as slavish adherence to business unit financial results

When well implemented, the restructuring concept is sound, for it passes the three tests of successful diversification. The restructurer meets the cost-of-entry test through the types of company it acquires. It limits acquisition premiums by buying companies with problems and lackluster images or by buying into industries with as yet unforeseen potential. Intervention by the corporation clearly meets the better-off test. Provided that the target industries are structurally attractive, the restructuring model can create enormous shareholder value. Some restructuring companies are Loew's, BTR, and General Cinema. Ironically, many of today's restructurers are profiting from yesterday's portfolio management strategies.

To work, the restructuring strategy requires a corporate management team with the insight to spot undervalued companies or positions in industries ripe for transformation. The same insight is necessary to actually turn the units around even though they are in new and unfamiliar businesses.

These requirements expose the restructurer to considerable risk and usually limit the time in which the company can succeed at the strategy. The most skillful proponents understand this problem, recognize their mistakes, and move decisively to dispose of them. The best companies realize they are not just acquiring companies but restructuring an industry. Unless they can integrate the acquisitions to create a whole new strategic position, they are just portfolio managers in disguise. Another important difficulty surfaces if so many other companies join the action that they deplete the pool of suitable candidates and bid their prices up.

Perhaps the greatest pitfall, however, is that companies find it very hard to dispose of business units once they are restructured and performing well. Human nature fights economic rationale. Size supplants shareholder value as the corporate goal. The company does not sell a unit even though the company no longer adds value to the unit. While the transformed units would be better off in another company that had related businesses, the restructuring company instead retains them. Gradually, it becomes a portfolio manager. The parent company's ROI declines as the need for reinvestment in the units and normal business risks eventually offset restructuring's one-shot gain. The perceived need to keep growing intensifies the pace of acquisition; errors result and standards fall. The restructuring company turns into a conglomerate with returns that only equal the average of all industries at best.

Transferring Skills

The purpose of the first two concepts of corporate strategy is to create value through a company's relationship with each autonomous unit. The corporation's role is to be a selector, a banker, and an intervenor.

The last two concepts exploit the interrelationships between businesses. In articulating them, however, one comes face-to-face with the often ill-defined concept of synergy. If you believe the text of the countless corporate annual reports, just about anything is related to just about anything else! But imagined synergy is much more common than real synergy. GM's purchase of Hughes Aircraft simply because cars were going electronic and Hughes was an electronics concern demonstrates the folly of paper synergy. Such corporate relatedness is an ex post facto rationalization of a diversification undertaken for other reasons.

Portfolio management is no way to conduct corporate strategy

Even synergy that is clearly defined often fails to materialize. Instead of cooperating, business units often compete. A company that can define the synergies it is pursuing still faces significant organizational impediments in achieving them.

But the need to capture the benefits of relationships between businesses has never been more important. Technological and competitive developments already link many businesses and are creating new possibilities for competitive advantage. In such sectors as financial services, computing, office equipment, entertainment, and health care, interrelationships among previously distinct businesses are perhaps the central concern of strategy.

To understand the role of relatedness in corporate strategy, we must give new meaning to this often ill-defined idea. I have identified a good way to start—the value chain.[5] Every business unit is a collection of discrete activities ranging from sales to accounting that allow it to compete. I call them value activities. It is at this level, not in the company as a whole, that the unit achieves competitive advantage.

I group these activities in nine categories. *Primary* activities create the product or service, deliver and market it, and provide after-sale support. The categories of primary activities are inbound logistics, operations, outbound logistics, marketing and sales, and service. *Support* activities provide the input and infrastructure that allow the primary activities to take place. The categories are company infrastructure, human resource management, technology development, and procurement.

The value chain defines the two types of interrelationships that may create synergy. The first is a company's ability to transfer skills or expertise among similar value chains. The second is the ability to share activities. Two business units, for example, can share the same sales force or logistics network.

The value chain helps expose the last two (and most important) concepts of corporate strategy. The transfer of skills among business units in the diversified company is the basis for one concept. While each business unit has a separate value chain, knowledge about how to perform activities is transferred among the units. For example, a toiletries business unit, expert in the marketing of convenience products, transmits ideas on new positioning concepts, promotional techniques, and packaging possibilities to a newly acquired unit that sells cough syrup. Newly entered industries can benefit from the expertise of existing units and vice versa.

These opportunities arise when business units have similar buyers or channels, similar value activities like government relations or procurement, similarities in the broad configuration of the value chain (for example, managing a multisite service organization), or the same strategic concept (for example, low cost). Even though the units operate separately, such similarities allow the sharing of knowledge.

Of course, some similarities are common; one can imagine them at some level between almost any pair of businesses. Countless companies have fallen into the trap of diversifying too readily because of similarities; mere similarity is not enough.

Transferring skills leads to competitive advantage only if the similarities among businesses meet three conditions:

(1) The activities involved in the businesses are similar enough that sharing expertise is meaningful. Broad similarities (marketing intensiveness, for example, or a common core process technology such as bending metal) are not a sufficient basis for diversification. The resulting ability to transfer skills is likely to have little impact on competitive advantage.

(2) The transfer of skills involves activities important to competitive advantage. Transferring skills in peripheral activities such as government relations or real estate in consumer goods units may be beneficial but is not a basis for diversification.

(3) The skills transferred represent a significant source of competitive advantage for the receiving unit. The expertise or skills to be transferred are both advanced and proprietary enough to be beyond the capabilities of competitors.

The transfer of skills is an active process that significantly changes the strategy or operations of the receiving unit. The prospect for change must be specific and identifiable. Almost guaranteeing that no shareholder value will be created, too many companies are satisfied with vague prospects or faint hopes that skills will transfer. The transfer of skills does not happen by accident or by osmosis. The company will have to reassign critical personnel, even on a permanent basis, and the participation and support of high-level management in skills transfer is essential. Many companies have been defeated at skills transfer because they have not provided their business units with any incentives to participate.

Transferring skills meets the tests of diversification if the company truly mobilizes proprietary expertise across units. This makes certain the company can offset the acquisition premium or lower the cost of overcoming entry barriers.

The industries the company chooses for diversification must pass the attractiveness test. Even a close fit that reflects opportunities to transfer skills may not overcome poor industry structure. Opportunities to transfer skills, however, may help the company transform the structures of newly entered industries and send them in favorable directions.

The transfer of skills can be one-time or ongoing. If the company exhausts opportunities to infuse new expertise into a unit after the initial post-acquisition period, the unit should ultimately be sold. The corporation is no longer creating shareholder value. Few companies have grasped this point, however, and many gradually suffer mediocre returns. Yet a company diversified into well-chosen businesses can transfer skills eventually in many directions. If corporate management conceives of its role in this way and creates appropriate organizational mechanisms to facilitate cross-unit interchange, the opportunities to share expertise will be meaningful.

By using both acquisitions and internal development, companies can build a transfer-of-skills strategy. The presence of a strong base of skills sometimes creates the possibility for internal entry instead of the acquisition of a going concern. Successful diversifiers that employ the concept of skills transfer may, however, often acquire a company in the target industry as a beach-head and then build on it with their internal expertise. By doing so, they can reduce some of the risks of internal entry and speed up the process. Two companies that have diversified using the transfer-of-skills concept are 3M and Pepsico.

Sharing Activities

The fourth concept of corporate strategy is based on sharing activities in the value chains among business units. Procter & Gamble, for example, employs a common physical distribution system and sales force in both paper towels and disposable diapers. McKesson, a leading distribution company, will handle such diverse lines as pharmaceuticals and liquor through superwarehouses.

The ability to share activities is a potent basis for corporate strategy because sharing often enhances competitive advantage by lowering cost or raising differentiation. But not all sharing leads to competitive advantage, and companies can encounter deep organizational resistance to even beneficial sharing possibilities. These hard truths have led many companies to reject synergy prematurely and retreat to the false simplicity of portfolio management.

A cost–benefit analysis of prospective sharing opportunities can determine whether synergy is possible. Sharing can lower costs if it achieves economies of scale, boosts the efficiency of utilization, or helps a company move more rapidly down the learning curve. The costs of General Electric's advertising, sales, and after-sales service activities in major appliances are low because they are spread over a wide range of appliance products. Sharing can also enhance the potential for differentiation. A shared order-processing system, for instance, may allow new features and services that a buyer will value. Sharing can also reduce the cost of differentiation. A shared service network, for example, may make more advanced, remote servicing technology economically feasible. Often, sharing will allow an activity to be wholly reconfigured in ways that can dramatically raise competitive advantage.

Sharing must involve activities that are significant to competitive advantage, not just any activity. P&G's distribution system is such an instance in the diaper and paper towel business, where products are bulky and costly to ship. Conversely, diversification based on the opportunities to share only corporate overhead is rarely, if ever, appropriate.

Sharing activities inevitably involves costs that the benefits must outweigh. One cost is the greater coordination required to manage a shared activity. More important is the need to compromise the design or performance of an activity so that it can be shared. A salesperson handling the products of two business units, for example, must operate in a way that is usually not what either unit would choose were it independent. And if compromise greatly erodes the unit's effectiveness, then sharing may reduce rather than enhance competitive advantage.

Many companies have only superficially identified their potential for sharing. Companies also merge activities without consideration of whether they are sensitive to economies of scale. When they are not, the coordination costs kill the benefits. Companies compound such errors by not identifying costs of sharing in advance, when steps can be taken to minimize them. Costs of compromise can frequently be mitigated by redesigning the activity for sharing. The shared salesperson, for example, can be provided with a remote computer terminal to boost productivity and provide more customer information. Jamming business units together without such thinking exacerbates the costs of sharing.

Despite such pitfalls, opportunities to gain advantage from sharing activities have proliferated because of momentous developments in technology, deregulation, and competition. The infusion of electronics and information systems into many industries creates new opportunities to link businesses. The corporate strategy of sharing can involve both acquisition and internal development. Internal development is often possible because the corporation can bring to bear clear resources in launching a new unit. Start-ups are less difficult to integrate than acquisitions. Companies using the shared-activities concept can also make acquisitions as beach-head landings into a new industry and then integrate the units through sharing with other units. Prime examples of companies that have diversified via using shared activities include P&G,

Du Pont, and IBM. The fields into which each has diversified are a cluster of tightly related units. Marriott illustrates both successes and failures in sharing activities over time. (See 'Adding value with hospitality' at the end of this chapter.)

Following the shared-activities model requires an organizational context in which business unit collaboration is encouraged and reinforced. Highly autonomous business units are inimical to such collaboration. The company must put into place a variety of what I call horizontal mechanisms—a strong sense of corporate identity, a clear corporate mission statement that emphasizes the importance of integrating business unit strategies, an incentive system that rewards more than just business unit results, cross-business-unit task forces, and other methods of integrating.

A corporate strategy based on shared activities clearly meets the better-off test because business units gain ongoing tangible advantages from others within the corporation. It also meets the cost-of-entry test by reducing the expense of surmounting the barriers to internal entry. Other bids for acquisitions that do not share opportunities will have lower reservation prices. Even widespread opportunities for sharing activities do not allow a company to suspend the attractiveness test, however. Many diversifiers have made the critical mistake of equating the close fit of a target industry with attractive diversification. Target industries must pass the strict requirement test of having an attractive structure as well as a close fit in opportunities if diversification is to ultimately succeed.

CHOOSING A CORPORATE STRATEGY

Each concept of corporate strategy allows the diversified company to create shareholder value in a different way. Companies can succeed with any of the concepts if they clearly define the corporation's role and objectives, have the skills necessary for meeting the concept's prerequisites, organize themselves to manage diversity in a way that fits the strategy, and find themselves in an appropriate capital market environment. The caveat is that portfolio management is only sensible in limited circumstances.

A company's choice of corporate strategy is partly a legacy of its past. If its business units are in unattractive industries, the company must start from scratch. If the company has few truly proprietary skills or activities it can share in related diversification, then its initial diversification must rely on other concepts. Yet corporate strategy should not be a once-and-for-all choice but a vision that can evolve. A company should choose its long-term preferred concept and then proceed pragmatically toward it from its initial starting point.

Both the strategic logic and the experience of the companies I studied over the last decade suggest that a company will create shareholder value through diversification to a greater and greater extent as its strategy moves from portfolio management toward sharing activities. Because they do not rely on superior insight or other questionable assumptions about the company's capabilities, sharing activities and transferring skills offer the best avenues for value creation.

Sharing allows activities to change completely in ways that increase competitive advantage

Each concept of corporate strategy is not mutually exclusive of those that come before, a potent advantage of the third and fourth concepts. A company can employ a restructuring strategy at the same time it transfers skills or shares activities. A strategy based on shared activities becomes more powerful if business units can also exchange skills. As the Marriott case illustrates, a company can often pursue the two strategies together and even incorporate some of the principles of restructuring with them. When it chooses industries in which to transfer skills or share activities, the company can also investigate the possibility of transforming the industry structure. When a company bases its strategy on interrelationships, it has a broader basis on which to create shareholder value than if it rests its entire strategy on transforming companies in unfamiliar industries.

My study supports the soundness of basing a corporate strategy on the transfer of skills or shared activities. The data on the sample companies' diversification programs illustrate some important characteristics of successful diversifiers. They have made a disproportionately low percentage of unrelated acquisitions, *unrelated* being defined as having no clear opportunity to transfer skills or share important activities (see Exhibit 2.3). Even successful diversifiers such as 3M, IBM, and TRW have terrible records when they have strayed into unrelated acquisitions. Successful acquirers diversify into fields, each of which is related to many others. Procter & Gamble and IBM, for example, operate in 18 and 19 interrelated fields respectively and so enjoy numerous opportunities to transfer skills and share activities.

Companies with the best acquisition records tend to make heavier-than-average use of start-ups and joint ventures. Most companies shy away from modes of entry besides acquisition. My results cast doubt on the conventional wisdom regarding start-ups. Exhibit 2.3 demonstrates that while joint ventures are about as risky as acquisitions, start-ups are not. Moreover, successful companies often have very good records with start-up units, as 3M, P&G, Johnson & Johnson, IBM, and United Technologies illustrate. When a company has the internal strength to start up a unit, it can be safer and less costly to launch a company than to rely solely on an acquisition and then have to deal with the problem of integration. Japanese diversification histories support the soundness of start-up as an entry alternative.

My data also illustrate that none of the concepts of corporate strategy works when industry structure is poor or implementation is bad, no matter how related the industries are. Xerox acquired companies in related industries, but the businesses had poor structures and its skills were insufficient to provide enough competitive advantage to offset implementation problems.

An Action Program

To translate the principles of corporate strategy into successful diversification, a company must first take an objective look at its existing businesses and the value added by the corporation. Only through such an assessment can an understanding of good corporate strategy grow. That understanding should guide future diversification as well as the development of skills and activities with which to select further new businesses. The following action program provides a concrete approach to conducting such a review. A company can choose a corporate strategy by:

(1) *Identifying the interrelationships among already existing business units.* A company should begin to develop a corporate strategy by identifying all the opportunities it has to share activities or transfer skills in its existing portfolio of business units. The company will not only find ways to enhance the competitive advantage of existing units but also come upon several possible diversification avenues. The lack of meaningful interrelationships in the portfolio is an equally important finding, suggesting the need to justify the value added by the corporation or, alternatively, a fundamental restructuring.

(2) *Selecting the core businesses that will be the foundation of the corporate strategy.* Successful diversification starts with an understanding of the core businesses that will serve as the basis for corporate strategy. Core businesses are those that are in an attractive industry, have the potential to achieve sustainable competitive advantage, have important interrelationships with other business units, and provide skills or activities that represent a base from which to diversify.

The company must first make certain its core businesses are on sound footing by upgrading management, internationalizing strategy, or improving technology. My study shows that geographic extensions of existing units, whether by acquisition, joint venture, or start-up, had a substantially lower divestment rate than diversification.

The company must then patiently dispose of the units that are not core businesses. Selling them will free resources that could be better deployed elsewhere. In some cases disposal implies immediate liquidation, while in others the company should dress up the units and wait for a propitious market or a particularly eager buyer.

(3) *Creating horizontal organizational mechanisms to facilitate interrelationships among the core businesses and lay the groundwork for future related diversification.* Top management can facilitate interrelationships by emphasizing cross-unit collaboration, grouping units organizationally and modifying incentives, and taking steps to build a strong sense of corporate identity.

(4) *Pursuing diversification opportunities that allow shared activities.* This concept of corporate strategy is the most compelling, provided a company's strategy passes all three tests. A company should inventory activities in existing business units that represent the strongest foundation for sharing, such as strong distribution channels or world-class technical facilities. These will in turn lead to potential new business areas. A company can use acquisitions as a beach-head or employ start-ups to exploit internal capabilities and minimize integrating problems.

(5) *Pursuing diversification through the transfer of skills if opportunities for sharing activities are limited or exhausted.* Companies can pursue this strategy through acquisition, although they may be able to use start-ups if their existing units have important skills they can readily transfer.

Such diversification is often riskier because of the tough conditions necessary for it to work. Given the uncertainties, a company should avoid diversifying on the basis of skills transfer alone. Rather it should also be viewed as a stepping-stone to subsequent diversification using shared activities. New industries should be chosen that will lead naturally to other businesses. The goal is to build a cluster of related and mutually reinforcing business units. The strategy's logic implies that the company should not set the rate of return standards for the initial foray into a new sector too high.

(6) *Pursuing a strategy of restructuring if this fits the skills of management or no good opportunities exist for forging corporate interrelationships.* When a company uncovers undermanaged companies and can deploy adequate management talent and resources to the acquired units, then it can use a restructuring strategy. The more developed the

capital markets and the more active the market for companies, the more restructuring will require a patient search for that special opportunity rather than a headlong race to acquire as many bad apples as possible. Restructuring can be a permanent strategy, as it is with Loew's, or a way to build a group of businesses that supports a shift to another corporate strategy.

(7) *Paying dividends so that the shareholders can be the portfolio managers.* Paying dividends is better than destroying shareholder value through diversification based on shaky underpinnings. Tax considerations, which some companies cite to avoid dividends, are hardly legitimate reason to diversify if a company cannot demonstrate the capacity to do it profitably.

Creating a Corporate Theme

Defining a corporate theme is a good way to ensure that the corporation will create shareholder value. Having the right theme helps unite the efforts of business units and reinforces the ways they interrelate as well as guides the choice of new businesses to enter. NEC Corporation, with its 'C&C' theme, provides a good example. NEC integrates its computer, semiconductor, telecommunications, and consumer electronics businesses by merging computers and communication.

It is all too easy to create a shallow corporate theme. CBS wanted to be an 'entertainment company', for example, and built a group of businesses related to leisure time. It entered such industries as toys, crafts, musical instruments, sports teams, and hi-fi retailing. While this corporate theme sounded good, close listening revealed its hollow ring. None of these businesses had any significant opportunity to share activities or transfer skills among themselves or with CBS's traditional broadcasting and record businesses. They were all sold, often at significant losses, except for a few of CBS's publishing-related units. Saddled with the worst acquisition record in my study, CBS has eroded the shareholder value created through its strong performance in broadcasting and records.

Moving from competitive strategy to corporate strategy is the business equivalent of passing through the Bermuda Triangle. The failure of corporate strategy reflects the fact that most diversified companies have failed to think in terms of how they really add value. A corporate strategy that truly enhances the competitive advantage of each business unit is the best defense against the corporate raider. With a sharper focus on the tests of diversification and the explicit choice of a clear concept of corporate strategy, companies' diversification track records from now on can look a lot different.

AUTHOR'S NOTE

The research for this article was done with the able assistance of my research associate Cheng G. Ong. Malcolm S. Salter, Andrall E. Pearson, A. Michael Kechner, and the Monitor Company also provided helpful comments.

REFERENCES

1 The studies also show that sellers of companies capture a large fraction of the gains from merger. See Michael C. Jensen and Richard S. Ruback, 'The Market for Corporate Control: The Scientific Evidence,' *Journal of Financial Economics*, April 1983, p. 5, and Michael C. Jensen, 'Takeovers: Folklore and Science,' *HBR*, November–December 1984, p. 109.
2 Some recent evidence also supports the conclusion that acquired companies often suffer eroding performance after acquisition. See Frederick M. Scherer, 'Mergers, Sell-Offs and Managerial Behavior,' in *The Economics of Strategic Planning*, ed. Lacy Glenn Thomas (Lexington, Mass.: Lexington Books, 1986), p. 143, and David A. Ravenscraft and Frederick M. Scherer, 'Mergers and Managerial Performance,' paper presented at the Conference on Takeovers and Contests for Corporate Control, Columbia Law School, 1985.
3 This observation has been made by a number of authors. See, for example, Malcolm S. Salter and Wolf A. Weinhold, *Diversification Through Acquisition* (New York: Free Press, 1979).
4 See Michael E. Porter, 'How Competitive Forces Shape Strategy,' *HBR*, March–April 1979, p. 86.
5 Michael E. Porter, *Competitive Advantage* (New York: Free Press, 1985).

WHERE THE DATA COME FROM

We studied the 1950–1986 diversification histories of 33 large diversified US companies. They were chosen at random from many broad sectors of the economy.

To eliminate distortions caused by World War II, we chose 1950 as the base year and then identified each business the company was in. We tracked every acquisition, joint venture, and start-up made over this period—3788 in all. We classified each as an entry into an entirely new sector or field (financial services, for example), a new industry within a field the company was already in (insurance, for example), or a geographic extension of an existing product or service. We also classified each new field as related or unrelated to existing units. Then we tracked whether and when each entry was divested or shut down and the number of years each remained part of the corporation.

Our sources included annual reports, 10K forms, the F&S Index, and Moody's, supplemented by our judgment and general knowledge of the industries involved. In a few cases, we asked the companies specific questions.

It is difficult to determine the success of an entry without knowing the full purchase or start-up price, the profit history, the amount and timing of ongoing investments made in the unit, whether any write-offs or write-downs were taken, and the selling price and terms of sale. Instead, we employed a relatively simple way to gauge success: *whether the entry was divested or shut down*. The underlying assumption is that a company will generally not divest or close down a successful business except in a comparatively few special cases. Companies divested many of the entries in our sample within five years, a reflection of disappointment with performance. Of the comparatively few divestments where the company disclosed a loss or a gain, the divestment resulted in a reported loss in more than half the cases.

The data in Exhibit 2.1 cover the entire 1950–1986 period. However, the divestment ratios in Exhibit 2.2 and Exhibit 2.3 do not compare entries and divestments over the entire period because doing so would overstate the success of diversification. Companies usually do not shut down or divest new entries immediately but hold them for some time to give them an opportunity to succeed. Our data show that the average holding period is five to slightly more than ten years, though many divestments occur within five years. To gauge accurately the success of diversification, we calculated the percentage of entries made by 1975 and by 1980 that were divested or closed down as of January 1987. If we had included more recent entries, we would have biased upward our assessment of how successful these entries had been.

As compiled, these data probably understate the rate of failure. Companies tend to announce acquisitions and other forms of new entry with a flourish but divestments and shutdowns with a whimper, if at all. We have done our best to root out every such transaction, but we have undoubtedly missed some. There may also be new entries that we did not uncover, but our best impression is that the number is not large.

AN UNCANNY BRITISH RESTRUCTURER

Hanson Trust, on its way to becoming Britain's largest company, is one of several skillful followers of the restructuring concept. A conglomerate with units in many industries, Hanson might seem on the surface a portfolio manager. In fact, Hanson and one or two other conglomerates have a much more effective corporate strategy. Hanson has acquired companies such as London Brick, Ever Ready Batteries, and SCM, which the city of London rather disdainfully calls 'low tech'.

Although a mature company suffering from low growth, the typical Hanson target is not just in any industry; it has an attractive structure. Its customer and supplier power is low and rivalry with competitors moderate. The target is a market leader, rich in assets but formerly poor in management. Hanson pays little of the present value of future cash flow out in an acquisition premium and reduces purchase price even further by aggressively selling off businesses that it cannot improve. In this way, it recoups just over a third of the cost of a typical acquisition during the first six months of ownership. Imperial Group's plush properties in London lasted barely two months under Hanson ownership, while Hanson's recent sale of Courage Breweries to Elders recouped £1.4 billion of the original £2.1 billion acquisition price of Imperial Group.

Like the best restructurers, Hanson approaches each unit with a modus operandi that it has perfected through repetition.

Hanson emphasizes low costs and tight financial controls. It has cut an average of 25% of labor costs out of acquired companies, slashed fixed overheads, and tightened capital expenditures. To reinforce its strategy of keeping costs low, Hanson carves out detailed one-year financial budgets with divisional managers and (through generous use of performance-related bonuses and share option schemes) gives them incentive to deliver the goods.

It's too early to tell whether Hanson will adhere to the last tenet of restructuring—selling turned-around units once the results are clear. If it succumbs to the allure of bigness, Hanson may take the course of the failed US conglomerates.

ADDING VALUE WITH HOSPITALITY

Marriott began in the restaurant business in Washington, DC. Because its customers often ordered takeouts on the way to the national airport, Marriott eventually entered airline catering. From there, it jumped into food service management for institutions. Marriott then began broadening its base of family restaurants and entered the hotel industry. More recently, it has moved into restaurants, snack bars, and merchandise shops in airport terminals and into gourmet restaurants. In addition, Marriott has branched out from its hotel business into cruise ships, theme parks, wholesale travel agencies, budget motels, and retirement centers.

Marriott's diversification has exploited well-developed skills in food service and hospitality. Marriott's kitchens prepare food according to more than 6000 standardized recipe cards; hotel procedures are also standardized and painstakingly documented in elaborate manuals. Marriott shares a number of important activities across units. A shared procurement and distribution system for food serves all Marriott units through nine regional procurement centers. As a result, Marriott earns 50% higher margins on food service than any other hotel company. Marriott also has a fully integrated real estate unit that brings corporatewide power to bear on site acquisitions as well as on the designing and building of all Marriott locations.

Marriott's diversification strategy balances acquisitions and start-ups. Start-ups or small acquisitions are used for initial entry, depending on how close the opportunities for sharing are. To expand its geographic base, Marriott acquires companies and then disposes of the parts that do not fit.

Apart from this success, it is important to note that Marriott has divested 36% of both its acquisitions and its start-ups. While this is an above-average record, Marriott's mistakes are quite illuminating. Marriott has largely failed in diversifying into gourmet restaurants, theme parks, cruise ships, and wholesale travel agencies. In the first three businesses, Marriott discovered it could not transfer skills despite apparent similarities. Standardized menus did not work well in gourmet restaurants. Running cruise ships and theme parks was based more on entertainment and pizzazz than the carefully disciplined management of hotels and mid-price restaurants. The wholesale travel agencies were ill fated from the start because Marriott had to compete with an important customer for its hotels and had no proprietary skills or opportunities to share with which to add value.

3

EMERGING PERSPECTIVES ON CORPORATE STRATEGY

Thomas S. Wurster

The Boston Consulting Group, Inc.

BACKGROUND

During the 1960s and 1970s, corporate portfolio strategy was at the center of strategy development. Over the last decade, the focal point in many organizations shifted to business unit strategies. Today, corporate strategy is back again as a major focus for most corporations.

This renewed attention reflects the fact that growth is still an imperative for many large corporations and achieving it often requires reshaping the corporate portfolio. However, this focus also results from some major shortfalls in the quality of corporate strategy and strategic thinking in large corporations that have shown up during the last two decades (and from shortfalls in actual performance versus promised performance) and the associated need for improvement. The restructuring wave has been driven partially by this failure, as restructurers emerge as practitioners of corporate strategy and portfolio repositioning. They have done so by understanding, often better than their corporate counterparts, the linkages between shareholder value maximization and the corporate portfolio and by acting on this understanding. In the process, their actions have contributed to the continuing wave of acquisitions, divestitures, and LBOs throughout the global economy.

During the next decade, the challenge for the corporation is to reaffirm its role in corporate strategy development and to improve the quality of its effort and implementation. In this article, we explore the appropriate tasks of the corporation in corporate strategy and the necessary shape of the organization that addresses these tasks.

International Review of Strategic Management.
Edited by D. E. Hussey. © 1990 John Wiley & Sons Ltd

THE HISTORICAL PERSPECTIVE

The portfolio was one of the earliest formal approaches to modern corporate strategy and encompassed two analytical concepts:

(1) Financial flow of funds (funding, portfolio diversification, and portfolio balancing).
(2) Strategic attractiveness (synergies, linkages, and intangible relationships).

One element of the original portfolio approach was balancing the sources and uses of funds within the corporation in order to achieve cash neutrality. When the portfolio approach was first developed, capital market imperfections were perceived to create constraints on sources of economic funds; the portfolio was a useful tool in evaluating cash flow at a time when cash flow analysis was not a widespread corporate planning tool. However, capital markets are now widely accessible and deemed to be relatively 'efficient', so that internal cash balancing is not necessary for many large corporations in developed economies (except, interestingly enough, those companies undergoing restructuring or those that have restructured). Indeed, in some cases, the markets actively discourage internal portfolio financing, reflecting a market belief that the internal allocation decisions may be less efficient than the external market. In addition, portfolio rebalancing for financial diversification is not rewarded, since stockholders can do it directly at lower cost than the corporation.

Today then, most of the financial justifications for corporate strategy have diminished substantially in importance, particularly for companies operating in highly developed capital markets. As a result, for these companies, the primary role for (and contribution of) corporate strategy must be based on strategic logic, not financial policy. (For companies operating in markets with less well-developed capital markets, the relative role and importance of financial policy in corporate strategy increases.) In turn, this means focusing corporate strategy on creating sources of competitive advantage and growth, orienting towards strategic attractiveness, and maximizing value-enhancing linkages among business units. And, in this context, shareholder value methodologies are one way of linking strategic policy with financial policy and valuation.

Measuring and prioritizing strategic attractiveness, therefore, has been the major long-term contribution of the corporate portfolio approach, although the ways of defining and measuring attractiveness have changed markedly. The original portfolio approach recognized the need for and the value of comparing business units within the portfolio in terms of simple, single summary measures of their strategic attractiveness. Since then, the definition and measurement of strategic attractiveness have become much richer, taking into account multiple dimensions that capture inherent industry attractiveness and the value of competitive advantage, as well as competitive position within the industry.

The corporate portfolio approach, however, while useful in highlighting strategic focus, was not always very helpful in getting requisite action. Centralized strategy development, segmented from line managers, rarely produced effective implementation. Often it put the divisional managers in conflict with their corporate counterparts. In addition, the analytical work itself often suffered from the lack of bottom–up input and was confined to too few strategic portfolio frameworks. (A portfolio is just a way of describing a collection of businesses; there are frequently a number of different portfolio descriptions that need to be examined simultaneously in any particular situation.)

By separating line management from the change process, the corporate portfolio approach created execution difficulties. The 'rational economic man' model embedded in much portfolio work assumed a linear decision-making structure on the part of organizational participants—a linear model of strategy development, implementation and organizational change, best summed up by a view:

> Here is the data; here is the analysis; here is the conclusion. Now, let us implement. Take the resulting actions. Get the required results.

The implications of this approach for the change process and for the roles to be played by the various participants are profound. This linear approach presumes that the entire change process is divisible—that strategy formulation and organizational change are most effectively managed by dividing the process into a series of stages, each of which is best handled by specialists. The result was the creation during the 1970s of large specialized strategic planning departments at the corporate office engaged in strategy creation. The lesson of the linear approach is that virtually no amount of analysis, regardless of its level of sophistication, is likely to effect organizational change, until the beliefs of the managers themselves are changed. Effecting change requires first recognizing and defining beliefs, and then systematically challenging their reign over an organization.

Another weakness of the approach was the (often implicit) assumption of static market conditions: the very linearity encouraged long time frames for developing and implementing strategy. But, the environment often had changed by the time plans were ready to be implemented. In reality, strategies must be flexible; action plans must be adjustable. In a learning organization, it must be acceptable to be wrong, and quick changes in direction are one effective way to handle error. This tight loop of feedback and flexible response was made difficult by the linear structure to strategy development.

EMERGING ORGANIZATIONAL FORMS FOR CORPORATE STRATEGY

These experiences have led to better ways of effecting strategic and organizational change at the strategic business unit (s.b.u.) level: the process has shifted to line-centered strategy development, supported by high quality staff work, where implementation is integrated with the process of strategy development. (This is often referred to as 'strategic management'.) A profound and long-lasting consequence of this reorientation is the distribution of strategy development capability to the s.b.u.s and its integration with s.b.u. line management. This move reflects a recognition that the change agents (s.b.u. line managers) must play the pivotal role in the strategy development process—that without their full involvement and commitment the process is unlikely to succeed.

In turn, this has contributed to the integration of strategy development with the process of organizational change. In the field of strategy, there has long been a debate as to whether strategy drives structure or structure drives strategy. The distributed approach focuses on the integration of both strategy and structure: the process of belief formation (organizational change), the process of strategy development and the process of organizational reorientation are interactive and therefore mutually determinant. In this approach, successful implementation depends on congruence between beliefs, data, structure, and action—the organization must believe in the strategy and its ability to carry it out with success. Consequently, the degree to which the critical players share common strategic beliefs drives successful implementation. The process of distributed strategy development, integrated with the process of changing organizational beliefs, forms a critical pathway to achieving this set of common strategic convictions among the line management team.

Restructuring the Process of Strategy Development

The resulting distribution of strategy development to each strategic business unit has fostered increasing success in strategic implementation at the business unit level. However, in general, this has been at the expense of progress in developing the role of the center in shaping corporate strategy.

With the distribution of most of the analytical components of s.b.u. strategy development, corporate line (or staff) managers are finding it increasingly difficult to challenge business unit managers' plans effectively. This situation is, somewhat paradoxically, exacerbated by the very success of the integrated process of strategy development and organizational change: through this integrated process, the s.b.u. line managers typically have developed a new set of strong, shared beliefs about the direction of strategy, making successful challenge by external agents (e.g. corporate line managers or staff) even more difficult than before. Without satisfactory mechanisms or resources for confronting the business units' strategies, the process is contributing to some poor corporate decisions, often implemented in powerful ways as a result of the success of the consensus-building and buy-in created with distributed strategy development. The net result is ongoing misallocation of corporate resources among business units, creating lower levels of growth and profitability from the corporate portfolio than are theoretically (and practically) achievable, and creating incentives for the corporate raider, who is focusing on correcting these errors.

In addition, there is currently a shortage of corporate (as opposed to business unit) strategy development being undertaken in this environment: in many companies, the strategic business unit is the primary unit of strategy, and the corporation is largely the arithmetic sum of its units. This is creating a growth shortfall for many large corporations. This orientation is probably reinforced by the fact that corporate strategy departments are often very constrained in their ability to take action other than indirectly (primarily through persuasion), and have been further weakened by a period of staff cutbacks and budget reductions.

The challenge for corporate strategy development during the 1990s is to readdress these two shortcomings:

- providing effective strategic challenge to individual business unit plans; and
- developing corporate strategy.

Providing Effective Strategic Challenge to Business Unit Plans

A major challenge for corporate strategy is to regain a greater role for the center in business unit strategy development in order to add value by applying critical strategic thinking to the business units. This needs to be done in a way that leverages the power created by the shift to integrated line-centered strategy development and organizational change.

This requires new approaches, rather than a return to old organizational structures. Generically, this should include paying greater attention to:

- more effective uses of corporate-level management resources (people) in the strategy development project teams within the s.b.u.s; and
- a more structured process for making explicit the belief systems of the s.b.u.s, in order to make transparent to the corporation critical assumptions or premises in the plans.

While an effective project team must maintain its s.b.u. line management focus, fresh, new ways of staffing with a vertical slice of management resources from the center must be employed. In addition, most new strategic directions are based on some simplifying assumptions about the way the world works: paying greater attention to extracting and clarifying these beliefs or premises opens up the process for discussion with corporate line management and makes it more productive. The challenge in cataloging current and emerging beliefs is to create an 'open architecture' structure to emerging strategy direction, that lends itself to ready inspection and discussion, rather than the 'closed architecture' system that is so often reflected in s.b.u. plans. Appropriate senior corporate involvement on the strategy development teams of the s.b.u.s can facilitate this process, since those individuals who are somewhat outside the current organization have a greater likelihood of seeing clearly the major beliefs or premises on which a change in strategic direction is based. The challenge is to put in place a new system that creates closer integration of the center to the details of s.b.u. strategy development.

Developing Corporate Strategy

Additional changes must be put in place to improve the quality of corporate strategy (in contrast to s.b.u. strategy) work. This will require changes in the relative responsibility and authority of corporate planning and modifications in the skill set of corporate planners. During the 1980s, the proportion of the planning budget devoted to corporate planning has declined, consistent with the distribution of strategy development. However, greater corporate resources devoted to corporate strategy development and organizational change are now required, as well as greater attention to recruiting candidates who possess more than analytical skills. High quality corporate strategy requires two additional skills: an understanding of strategic thinking (in contrast to analytical techniques) and knowledge of how people and companies change. One consequence may be greater integration of the human resources, training and strategy development functions at the corporate level, given the integration of strategy development with the process of organizational change. Line management experience, project management skills, and execution capabilities are critical to effectively fulfilling the corporate planning function. Further increasing the stature of the corporate planning position by careful attention to the career track of the office holder is also warranted. And, in service organizations, the integration with the human resources and training functions is essential.

As a result, a selective reinforcement of the corporate staff in scope and power is likely, in order to ensure that the business unit strategies are sensible and in order to develop true corporate strategy.

The resulting shape of the corporate organization structure will undoubtedly vary greatly; a single model of structure is unlikely to emerge, since it will depend on the company's business mix and size. One approach that has been found effective is to create a corporate office consisting of a small number of senior line managers who have as their primary responsibility corporate strategy and corporate vision. While each may be assigned a group of divisions (clustered with as great a degree of commonality as possible), their role is as an advisor to the s.b.u.s (rather than as the individual with full responsibility for the s.b.u.s). Therefore, the corporate management team is almost entirely focused on its strategic role. One can accomplish this with very few corporate managers, since they are all devoting substantial portions of their time to issues of corporate strategy.

RESTRUCTURING THE ANALYTICS OF CORPORATE STRATEGY

Two major issues in the substance of corporate strategy must be addressed in the coming years:

- portfolio allocation and linkages; and
- corporate growth and strategic platforms.

Portfolio Allocation and Linkages

Even after three decades of corporate portfolio work, there is still a pronounced tendency in large corporations for capital allocation to be averaged (i.e. 'everybody gets some'), resulting in two forms of portfolio misallocation:

- overfunding businesses earning less than the cost of capital; and
- underfunding businesses earning more than the cost of capital.

The misallocation results from a variety of mechanisms that make internal investment allocation not as effective as 'arm's length' investment allocation. These include an inclination to be less disciplined with capital for low return businesses than the market, a willingness to tolerate longer time frames for turnaround of low return businesses than are consistent with the time frames of the market, and a tendency to overestimate strategic linkages. Whatever the mechanism, the net result is that the corporation chooses to invest in a way that is suboptimal when compared with the way the market would invest. As a result, attractive portions of the portfolio—where the focus should be to reinvest—are not scrutinized as aggressively as they should be for investment and growth opportunities, both defensive and offensive. For example, this often leads to the corporation 'satisficing' at lower levels of market share in high return businesses than may be possible and than are consistent with achieving the highest returns on capital in the portfolio. In addition, unattractive portions of the portfolio are not systematically examined for disinvestment.

In many cases, these portfolio misallocations have been unintentionally exacerbated by the trend toward focusing on strategic linkages within the portfolio. The creation of valid strategic linkages at the corporate portfolio level is one of the prime values that the corporate holding company can provide. Unfortunately, one of the shortfalls of corporate strategy has been identifying linkages among business units that did not create real corporate value, often meaning that more businesses earning less than the cost of capital on a stand-alone basis survived than should have, since businesses earning less than the cost of capital are often justified on the basis of apparent linkages to more successful businesses earning well in excess of the cost of capital. (This often happens with backward or forward integration strategies.) There are, in reality, fewer linkages in effect than have been claimed; paradoxically, corporate entities need to find more in order to create value.

As a result, many companies created negative value by stressing portfolio linkages and synergies that were of considerably smaller value than their internal estimates suggested, creating opportunities that were exploited by restructurers. For example, Beatrice Foods attempted to create (at significant cost) umbrella branding for the many individually strong brand positions within its portfolio; United Airlines, in the temporary guise of Allegis, focused on integrating (for the customer) its hotel, rental car, and airline businesses. These were linkages that were not economic vis-à-vis existing branding strategies, in the case of Beatrice Foods, and not attractive to customers, in the case of United. (Although United's strategy was never really given a chance to prove itself, it was flawed behaviorally in concept.)

The task for corporate strategy is to reinforce the valid linkages that do exist. One way to do this effectively is to start by evaluating all businesses initially as stand-alone entities. With their contribution or value to the portfolio as stand-alone entities well defined, the 'gap' that must be closed by synergistic linkages becomes measurable. Corporations need to pay careful attention to the size of the gap, and make realistic assessments as to whether it can be closed, based on quantifiable or intangible linkages. They should do so fully cognizant of the inherent tendency to protect poor performers in the portfolio. If the gap cannot be closed, then action should be taken.

For diversified companies that start with no linkages, it is imperative that they take two steps. First, they must decide which of their (many) areas of activity will be chosen for future focus. Second, they must aggressively concentrate on adding value to the corporation in these targeted areas. Given their starting point, this will often require strategic additions to the corporate architecture, as the corporation adds bridging acquisitions that enable the corporation to add value. Throughout, the corporation must always ask whether the company is adding as much value to these individual entities as alternative owners might or as the managers themselves might.

Corporate Growth and Strategic Platforms

It has become popular to urge companies to stay close to the core in pursuing growth through internal development, acquisition, and diversification. The orientation towards relatedness—either product, market or customer group—gains further credence when one examines the patterns of success of corporate acquisitions, particularly during the 1970s: related acquisitions have been more successful than unrelated acquisitions.

However, application of the principle of relatedness can be very constraining. It often restricts rather than enhances the contribution that can be made at the portfolio level to the corporation's growth and profitability. For companies without growth opportunities in closely related products, markets or customer groups, the focus effectively eliminates future sources of growth and vitality for the corporation. In addition, it often does not maximize shareholder value and may lead to inappropriate acquisition and diversification strategies.

In many companies, the orientation of corporate strategy is shifting from product–market–customer group relatedness to the broader concept of *strategic platform*. A strategic platform is defined as the ability of the corporation to handle businesses in similar strategic environments (with similar key success factors) or businesses with similar 'soft' skills. This reflects the fact that understanding and exploiting similar sources of competitive advantage is a leverageable, corporate strategic asset. In addition, it acknowledges the fact that in many industries, competitive advantage is shifting (or has shifted) from 'hard' advantages, such as economies of scale and factor costs, to 'soft' advantages, such as time-based responsiveness and customer service. These 'soft' advantages also can be exploited at the corporate level as well as within the individual strategic business units. Once defined, the strategic platform provides the vehicle for future growth, including acquisition and diversification strategy.

Similar strategic environments are defined on the basis of similar value-added structures and similar ways of gaining competitive advantage, rather than solely on the basis of related products, markets, or customer groups. For example, for some companies, this may redefine the strategic platform to be high marketing valued-added products, in which distribution and product positioning are the key sources of competitive advantage, rather than restrict the focus to specific markets or customer groups. The redefined strategic platform may, in turn, open up the opportunity space while simultaneously achieving a reinforced orientation to its basic sources of strategic advantage. This is an alternative unifying principle in building a corporate strategy: growing businesses in the portfolio that are manageable in similar ways and build on the management teams' skills in managing similar strategic environments.

To create an effective strategic platform, corporations must do a better job of distinguishing strategic relatedness from relatedness in product, market, or customer group sense. These two approaches are not always highly correlated, which is a primary cause of acquisition integration failures. For example, many of the major oil companies have moved towards broad-scale forward integration, often justified as a means for getting 'closer to the end user'. Unfortunately, many of these forward integration businesses have different business characteristics and management requirements than the core. Core businesses often are 'volume' businesses that require deployment of large blocks of project capital, where being larger creates economies of scale that translate to higher levels of profitability for the market leader; many of the downstream businesses are fragmented or specialization businesses that are marketing-intensive and often volatile. It has been difficult for a number of the major oil companies to manage these businesses effectively—they defined relatedness inappropriately (in terms of derived products for already served end markets and customer groups), rather than approach relatedness from the view of a strategic platform.

In pursuing a strategic platform for the corporation, the center needs to ensure that this strategic relatedness occurs, and to allocate resources, both financial and human, consistent with this vision. Portfolio and corporate strategy must do a better job of defining and exploiting these corporate shapes.

SUMMARY

We have discussed a number of stages in the progression or evolution of corporate strategy. In the process, we have also defined corporate strategy as a multidimensional task, with a changing mix of those tasks depending on the situation of the particular company. These tasks include:

(1) *Corporate strategy.* There is a continuing need to create or adjust the vision for the corporation, and use resources to take advantage of its available or emerging strategic platforms.

(2) *Finance and financial policy.* Funding strategies, portfolio diversification, and portfolio balancing are elements of corporate strategy that have generally diminished in importance with well-developed capital markets. However, restructured companies and companies in markets with less well-developed capital markets must continue to pay relatively more attention to this role of the corporation.

(3) *Human resources management.* In business environments in which cash is not the primary constraint, the corporation can gain strategic advantage by focusing on 'softer' skills, with human resources a critical asset. In many situations, the corporation may have access to a larger and higher quality talent pool than the individual s.b.u.s and can afford to take a longer term and less parochial view of attracting and developing superior people.

(4) *Business unit strategies.* The corporation needs to reassert its role in the divisional strategy process, by strategically challenging individual business unit plans and bringing a broader, external perspective to bear.

(5) *Business unit operations.* The corporation can usually encourage additional performance from the strategic business units by stretching the boundaries of the possible through setting higher operational performance hurdles than the business unit might set for itself.

ACKNOWLEDGMENTS

I would like to thank Anthony W. Miles and Thomas G. Lewis, vice presidents in the San Francisco and Munich offices of the Boston Consulting Group, respectively, for their helpful comments.

4

THE GROUP COMPETITIVE INTENSITY MAP: A MEANS OF DISPLAYING COMPETITIVE POSITION

Patrick McNamee and Marie McHugh

Centre for Research in Management, University of Ulster

SUMMARY

This chapter is based upon empirical work into competitiveness in the clothing industry. It draws together and extends two major themes which have dominated strategic thinking and practice in recent years: matrix displays and the work of Michael Porter. The chapter fuses these themes and develops a new strategic device: the Group Competitive Intensity Map (GCIM). The map quantitatively displays, in the form of a matrix using ellipses, the locations of an industry's strategic groups and the competitive intensity which they face. It also shows the relative risks which different groups face. Finally, this chapter illustrates how these maps were used in a study of the clothing industry and points to their future potential. The concept of the group competitive intensity map has evolved out of an empirical investigation into the Northern Ireland clothing industry. Brief details of the study are given in the appendix to this chapter.

INTRODUCTION

The objective of this chapter is to draw together and extend two major themes which have dominated strategic thinking and practice in recent

International Review of Strategic Management.
Edited by D. E. Hussey. © 1990 John Wiley & Sons Ltd

years: the use of matrix displays and the work of Michael Porter (1980) on competitive strategy. The authors attempt to fuse selected aspects of these two themes and develop a strategic device which will add an extra quantitative dimension to current work being carried out in the area of competitive strategy.

MATRIX DISPLAYS AND STRATEGIC PLANNING

The extra clarity which matrix displays, or two-dimensional maps, can bring to strategic thinking has been well documented. Prominent among the most successful applications of this approach are the works and publications of Henderson (1970), Patel and Younger (1978), Robinson, Hichens and Wade (1978), Hofer and Schendell (1978) and Haspeslagh (1978).

The seminal work on matrix displays is usually regarded as the Boston Consulting Group's Growth Share Matrix (Henderson 1970) and is outlined briefly below.

The approach asserts that for a firm which has a portfolio of products* it is possible to display its overall strategic position by means of a product market portfolio matrix. This matrix relates each of the firm's products to the product's position in its market. The overall strategic position of the *firm* is represented by the sum of the strategic positions of each of the products. The fundamental determinants of each product's strategic position are as follows:

* The growth rate of the market for the product.
* The product's relative market share.
* The monetary value of the product's sales.

When each of these factors is known for each product, it is then possible to draw up a product market portfolio, such as is shown in Figure 4.1. This type of matrix quantitatively displays the strategic position of the firm.

Although the product market portfolio is an excellent means of gaining insights into the overall strategic position of a firm, and the strategic positions of particular products, when measured by criteria such as:

* the balance of the firm's portfolio of products;
* the likely cash position of the firm;

---

*Although this exposition has been set at the level of the 'product', it could also have been set at the s.b.u. level.

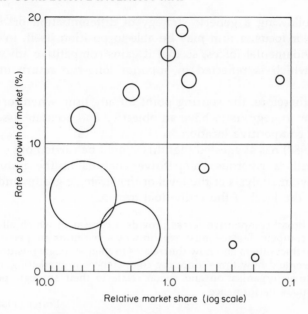

Figure 4.1 A product market portfolio

• the overall market position of the firm relative to its competitors;
• the relative market and cash positions of individual products;

it should be noted that the matrix relies, almost exclusively, for its construction and the consequent decision rules, upon *marketing* data.

The work of Porter (1980) indicates that for many firms (and industries) a more informed judgement about relative strategic position is likely to be achieved if the locus of strategic position is determined by a broader set of criteria. These criteria are outlined briefly below.

THE PORTER CONTRIBUTION

The core of the Porter approach to strategic planning is that the competitive climate of any industry is determined by five fundamental competitive forces:

(1) The threat of entry.
(2) The threat of substitutes.
(3) The power of buyers.
(4) The power of suppliers.
(5) The intensity of rivalry of existing competitors.

Through following a generic strategy of differentiation or overall cost leadership or focus, a firm may be able to position itself, in relation to the five fundamental forces, so that it gains competitive advantage over its rivals which is reflected in superior long-run return on invested capital.

Clearly, therefore, the starting point for any firm, when formulating a competitive strategy, is to have an objective and accurate assessment of its current competitive location.

Porter (1980) has suggested that this should be carried out sequentially starting with a rigorous competitive analysis at the industry level, followed by an analysis at the level of the strategic group, and finally an analysis at the level of the individual firm.

> The five broad competitive forces provide a context in which all firms in an industry compete. But we must explain why some firms are persistently more profitable than others and how this relates to their strategic postures. We must also understand how firms' differing competences in marketing, cost cutting, management, organisation and so on relate to their strategic postures and their ultimate performance.
>
> Porter (1980, page 127)

The device which Porter uses to analyse competition at the sub-industry level is the strategic group map (henceforth known as the Porter strategic group map). He suggests that any industry may be mapped into a number* of strategic groups where a strategic group is defined as 'the group of firms in an industry following the same or similar strategy along the strategic dimensions'.

In this definition the 'strategic dimensions' are the different competitive strategies that the firms employ. These competitive strategies include approaches such as: specialisation, brand identification, channel selection, product quality, technological leadership, etc.

When the major firms of an industry are categorised along their strategic dimensions, taken two at a time, then strategic groups will naturally emerge and the industry may be mapped as shown in Figure 4.2.

APPLYING THE PORTER STRATEGIC GROUP MAP TO THE CLOTHING INDUSTRY STUDY

In the clothing industry study (brief details of this study are given in the appendix to this chapter), although the *industry analysis* was carried

---

*This number may, of course, be just one in the case of an industry in which all the competitors are following the same strategy.

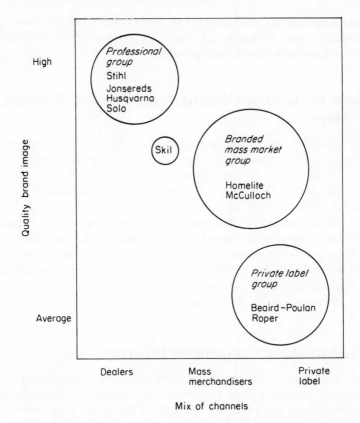

Figure 4.2 Illustrative map of the US chain saw industry

out using a conventional Porter-type approach, when the *strategic group analysis* commenced, it became apparent that it would be possible to develop further the concept of the strategic group.

Thus, although the Porter strategic group map aims to enable its users to:

- identify key mobility barriers,
- identify marginal groups,
- chart movements,
- analyse trends, and
- predict reactions,

in the clothing industry study it was not possible, using this device, to achieve all these aims. More specifically, although the map did enable key *mobility barriers* to be identified, it did not fulfil the other aims. There were two main reasons for this: firstly, the potential lack of objectivity that could arise in the construction of the Porter strategic group map, and secondly, the difficulty in assessing competitive intensity, or competitive pressures, from such a map.

The Need for Greater Objectivity in Drawing Strategic Group Maps

When the initial Porter strategic group maps for the clothing industry study were drawn, it was felt that their explanatory power and generality would be enhanced if it were possible to draw them with a greater degree of standardisation. In the Porter strategic group map the sizes of the circles (or other shapes) in which strategic groups are enclosed appear to be at the discretion of the researcher. For example, in Figure 4.2, although the 'Professional Group' has a smaller circle than the 'Private Label Group', it is not clear why this should be the case. There is no explicit indication of what the areas of the circles represent. Consequently, if *chart movements* and *trends* are to be plotted over time it is difficult to see how consistency is to be achieved.

The Need to Show Competitive Intensity

Although the Porter strategic group map shows the *competitive location* of a particular group, it does not reveal the *competitive intensity* that is faced by the group. For example, in Figure 4.2 it is not clear whether the competitive pressure (i.e. the competitive intensity) faced by the 'Professional Group' is greater than, equal to or less than that faced by the other groups. Because the degree of competitive intensity is not clearly revealed it is difficult to deduce from the map which are the *marginal groups* and what are the likely *competitive reactions*.

THE CONCEPT OF THE GROUP COMPETITIVE INTENSITY MAP

The concept of the Porter strategic group map was extended and has led to the development of a display known as the group competitive intensity map (GCIM). The development of this map is outlined below.

The starting point for the map is the assumption that the distinctive characteristics which the members of any strategic group display are a function not just of the *strategies* that they follow but also the *structures* that they possess, and consequently the competitive location of any firm should evolve from coordinates based on both *strategy and structure*.*

Therefore, the axes which are used in the group competitive intensity map, although similar to those used in the Porter strategic group map, are more comprehensive: the Porter strategic group map's axes are the strategic determinants, taken two at a time, while the group competitive intensity map's axes are the *strategic and structural determinants* taken two at a time.

The strategic and structural determinants comprise those elements of a firm's strategies and structure that delineate the strategic groups into which it falls.

The range of *strategic determinants* is similar to that advocated by Porter (see Porter, 1980, pages 127–129) and among the principal ones used in the clothing industry study were:

● Product category specialisation (i.e. shirts and blouses, night attire and lingerie, menswear, ladies outerwear, children's wear, leisurewear, knitted garments, and workwear/uniforms).
● Geographical market specialisation.
● Customer type specialisation.
● Pricing strategy.

The principal *structural determinants* that were used included:

● Size.
● Type of ownership (i.e. locally owned managed company, locally owned limited liability company, and UK owned subsidiary),
● Main activities (i.e. production unit only, production design R & D but no sales or marketing, own branded, cut make and trim for others).†

This is the first major extension of the Porter strategic group map: the axes of the group competitive intensity map explicitly reflect group mobility barriers that are based on *strategy and structure*. This is illustrated in Figure 4.3 which shows the axes of a hypothetical group competitive intensity map for the clothing industry.

It should be pointed out that it is not necessary for the axes of a group competitive intensity map to have both strategic *and* structural

---

*The debate on the relationship between strategy and structure has, of course, a long and distinguished history (see Ansoff, 1980; Chandler, 1972).

†Since this chapter has been written, other GCIMs based on new sets of strategic and structured determinants have been constructed.

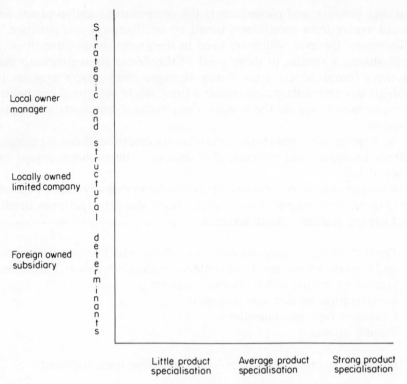

Little product   Average product   Strong product
specialisation   specialisation   specialisation

The strategic and structural determinants

Figure 4.3 A hypothetical group competitive intensity map for the clothing industry illustrating the axes

determinants. For example, a GCIM could have two structural determinants as its axes (e.g. type of ownership for one axis and main activities for the other), or two strategic determinants (e.g. customer type specialisation for one axis and pricing strategy for the other), or, as shown in Figure 4.3, a combination of strategic and structural determinants.

The second major extension of the strategic group map is the measurement of the competitive intensity that prevails in any strategic group.

In the clothing industry study, competitiveness was assessed through the use of three measures: sales per employee, sales per pound of assets and net profit before tax. The rationale behind the adoption of these measures is given in the appendix to this chapter.

If it is accepted that those *firms* which have the highest scores on the measures of competitiveness are likely to be the most competitive, then it is suggested that those *groups* which enjoy the highest scores on each of the measures of competitiveness are either the most competitive, or face the least serious competitive pressures, or both.

Therefore the *average* value for each of the measures of competitiveness for each of the groups was chosen as the primary index which would express the relative competitive intensity faced by each group: the higher the average value of the measure of competitiveness, the less the relative competitive intensity likely to be experienced by a group (when assessed by any of the three measures). For example, Figure 4.4 is a hypothetical group competitive intensity map for the clothing industry which uses average annual sales per employee (£000) as the measure of competitiveness. From this map it is assumed that the strategic group formed by the intersection of the strategic and structural determinants 'Locally owned limited liability company' and 'Strong product specialis-

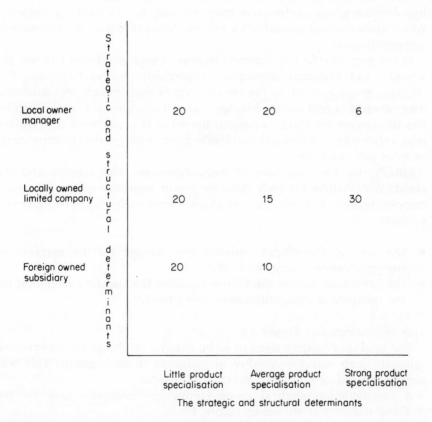

Figure 4.4 A hypothetical group competitive intensity map for the clothing industry illustrating the average sales per employee (£000)

ation' faces the least competitive intensity because its average sales per employee of £30 000 are greater than the average for any other group.

Although the average measure captures the overall level of relative competitive intensity that obtains in a strategic group, it may not truly reflect the nature of the competitive terrain that prevails *within* a strategic group. The variation in the measures of competitiveness of the individual firms within a group was assessed by using the standard deviation computed from the values for each member of the group. The standard deviation would, it was believed, indicate both the variety of competitiveness and the degree of risk that prevailed within a group. The measure was taken to be correlated with risk in the sense that it was assumed that those groups which had the largest standard deviation would contain the greatest degree of risk relative to other groups, while those with the smallest standard deviation would contain the lowest degree of risk relative to other groups. This is illustrated in Figure 4.5 which is a hypothetical group competitive intensity map for the clothing industry, which uses average annual sales per employee (£000) as the measure of competitiveness.

In the map, the first and second figures in each bracketed pair are the average and standard deviation, respectively, for each group. The strategic group formed by the intersection of the strategic and structural determinants 'Local owner manager' and 'Little product specialisation' has the largest standard deviation, therefore it is assumed to have the relatively highest level of risk and also to possess the greatest heterogeneity in sales per employee.

Finally, for each measure of competitiveness, the average and the standard deviation for each strategic group were drawn on the group competitiveness intensity map as ellipses with each ellipse being scaled so that:

• the area of the ellipse equalled the average for the measure of competitiveness being used, and
• the horizontal axis of the ellipse equalled the standard deviation for the measure of competitiveness being used.

This is illustrated in Figure 4.6.

The final quantitative element to be entered on the group competitive intensity map was the number of members in each group. This was simply entered as a number beside each ellipse.

A complete hypothetical group competitive intensity map for the clothing industry is shown in Figure 4.7.

This section has outlined the second major extension of the Porter strategic group map: ellipses which are located at the coordinates

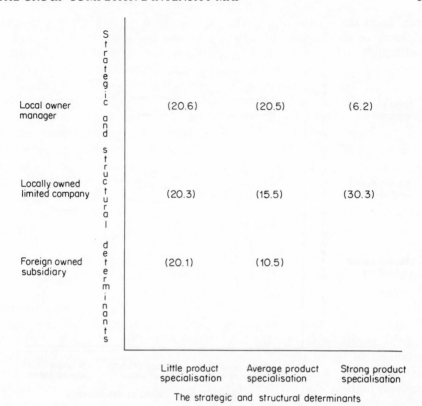

	Little product specialisation	Average product specialisation	Strong product specialisation
Local owner manager	(20.6)	(20.5)	(6.2)
Locally owned limited company	(20.3)	(15.5)	(30.3)
Foreign owned subsidiary	(20.1)	(10.5)	

The strategic and structural determinants

Figure 4.5 A hypothetical group competitive intensity map for the clothing industry illustrating the standard deviation and average sales per employee (£000)

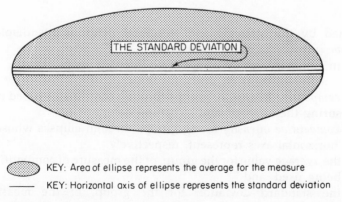

KEY: Area of ellipse represents the average for the measure

KEY: Horizontal axis of ellipse represents the standard deviation

Figure 4.6 The rationale behind the ellipses on the group competitive intensity map

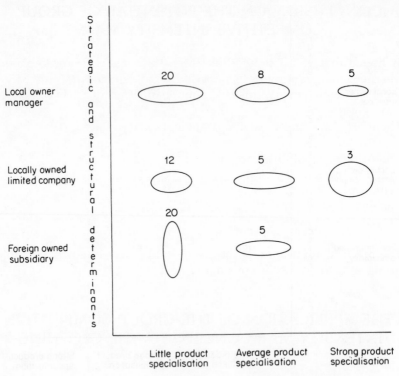

The strategic and structural determinants

Figure 4.7 A complete hypothetical group competitive intensity map for the clothing industry, based on sales per employee, (£000) (not to scale)

determined by the strategic and structural determinants display the *competitive intensity* faced by each group.

Thus, in summary, group competitive intensity maps show:

(1) The *competitive location* of groups through coordinates based on axes measuring the strategic and structural determinants,

(2) The *competitive intensity* facing groups through ellipses whose areas and horizontal axes represent, respectively:

    (a) the average value for the group, of the measure of competitiveness being used, and

    (b) the standard deviation for the group, of the measure of competitiveness being used.

(3) The *number of competitors* in each group.

CONCLUSION ON THE POTENTIAL OF GROUP COMPETITIVE INTENSITY MAPS

It is hoped that group competitive intensity maps will enable planners to locate strategic groups objectively, to identify the intensity of competition which the groups face, and the numbers of direct competitors for the groups.

Therefore, by using these maps planners may:

- identify key mobility barriers,
- identify marginal groups,
- chart movements,
- analyse trends, and
- predict reactions.

The practical application of the group competitive intensity map to the clothing industry study is considered next.

THE APPLICATION OF THE GROUP COMPETITIVE INTENSITY MAP CONCEPT TO THE CLOTHING INDUSTRY STUDY

Three GCIMs (one for each measure of competitiveness, i.e. sales per employee, sales per pound of assets and net profit before tax) were developed for each of the following pairs of strategic and structural determinants:

- Company structure by company activity.
- Company structure by product category specialisation.
- Company structure by geographical market specialisation.
- Company structure by most important customer type.
- Company structure by pricing strategy.
- Company activity by product category specialisation.
- Company activity by geographical market specialisation.
- Company activity by most important customer type.
- Company activity by pricing strategy.
- Pricing category specialisation by geographical market specialisation.
- Product category specialisation by most important customer type.
- Product category specialisation by pricing strategy.
- Geographical market specialisation by most important customer type.
- Most important customer type and pricing strategy.

- Geographical market specialisation by pricing strategy.
- Company size by product category specialisation.
- Company size by geographical market specialisation.
- Company size by most important customer type.
- Company size by company structure.
- Company size by company activity.
- Company size by pricing strategy.

Thus a total of 63 GCIMs were drawn up.

In this chapter, however, just two sets of GCIMs developed in the clothing industry study are displayed. These maps were chosen because they are representative of all maps developed and also because they effectively display the nature of the GCIM. Each set is drawn on a different pair of strategic and structural determinants. The GCIMs are presented as follows: each set comprises three GCIMs which are based on the three measures of competitiveness.*

ANALYSIS OF TWO SETS OF GROUP COMPETITIVE INTENSITY MAPS FROM THE CLOTHING INDUSTRY STUDY

Introduction

The analysis of each set of GCIMs is presented as follows:

(1) The axes (i.e. the strategic and structural determinants) for the set of GCIMs are defined.

Individual GCIMs are then displayed and commented upon in the following fashion:

(2) The GCIM is displayed.
(3) Features of the GCIM. This provides a commentary on the distribution of competitive intensity that prevails on the GCIM.
(4) Groups facing relatively severe competitive intensity on the GCIM. This attempts to identify those groups that appear to be experiencing most competitive intensity.

---

*It should be noted that in the analyses that were carried out many of the GCIMs that were drawn using the measure of competitiveness net profit before tax had smaller numbers of strategic groups than GCIMs constructed using the other two measures. This was because only 36 respondents declared their net profit before tax figure.

THE FIRST SET OF GCIMs: GCIMs BASED ON COMPANY STRUCTURE AND PRODUCT CATEGORY SPECIALISATION

(1) The Axes for the Set of GCIMs

Three group competitive intensity maps were constructed using the strategic and structural determinants company structure and product category specialisation. Each of these maps is analysed below.

(2a)

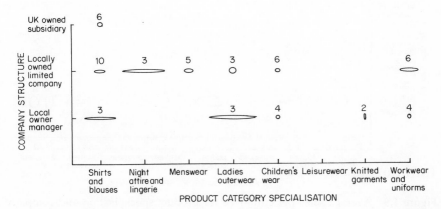

Figure 4.8 Average sales per pound of assets for product specialisation and company structure

(3a) Features of the GCIM (Figure 4.8)

Locally owned limited companies that specialise in the manufacture of night attire and lingerie and locally owned/managed companies that manufacture ladies outerwear experience the highest average sales per pound of assets. However, both of these groups had large standard deviations which suggests that although members are likely to experience the least competitive intensity they must cope with relatively high degrees of relative risk.

A large variation is evident in the average sales per pound of assets experienced by manufacturers of shirts and blouses: UK owned subsidiaries appear to be under the greatest relative competitive pressure while locally owned/managed firms seem reasonably successful although a degree of relative risk is present.

(4a) Groups Facing Relative Competitive Intensity in Figure 4.8

The groups which appear to be experiencing relatively strong competitive intensity are: locally owned/managed companies specialising in the manufacture of children's wear, knitted garments or workwear and uniforms. Other groups which fall into this category are locally owned limited companies specialising in the manufacture of children's wear and UK owned subsidiaries which produce shirts and blouses.

(2b)

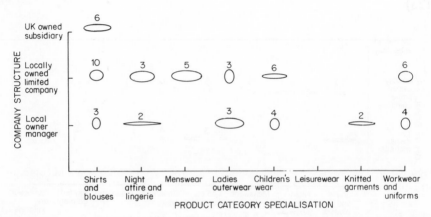

Figure 4.9 Average sales per employee for product specialisation and company structure

(3b) Features of the GCIM (Figure 4.9)

Company structure does seem to strongly influence the relative competitive positions of firms specialising in the manufacture of particular products. Generally, although locally owned limited firms appear to enjoy superior average sales per employee, with the manufacturers of night attire and lingerie and menswear achieving the highest figures, there are two other product categories that deserve some comment. The performance of shirt and blouse manufacturers appears to be affected by the structure of the firm—UK owned subsidiaries experience much higher average sales per employee than those firms that are locally owned. There are also differences in the relative positions of ladies outerwear manufacturers: although locally owned/managed companies experience higher average sales per employee than locally owned limited companies it is perhaps worth noting that the degree of relative risk, shown by the width of the ellipse, is much higher for the former group.

(4b) Groups Facing Relative Competitive Intensity in Figure 4.9

Although there is little evidence of any particular group experiencing severe competitive pressure, there are some which appear to occupy relatively weak competitive positions. The most obvious group is locally owned limited firms specialising in the manufacture of shirts and blouses.

(2c)

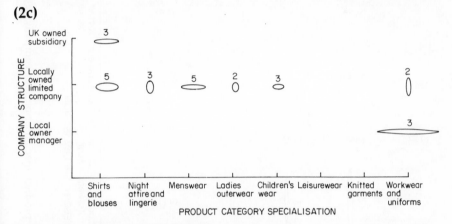

Figure 4.10 Average net profit before tax for product specialisation and company structure

(3c) Features of the GCIM (Figure 4.10)

It appears that locally owned/managed companies specialising in the manufacture or workwear and uniforms enjoy the highest average net profit before tax, although the large standard deviation would seem to indicate that these firms also experience the greatest degree of relative risk. When the performance of this group is compared with that of fellow manufacturers which are locally owned limited companies, the latter seem to occupy a comparatively weak competitive position.

Although there is relative homogeneity in the amount of competitive intensity experienced by locally owned limited companies, some product categories appear to be more exposed to risk than others. To illustrate, menswear manufacturers experience substantially greater levels of relative risk than manufacturers of workwear and uniforms.

(4c) Groups Facing Relative Competitive Intensity in Figure 4.11

Although there is little evidence to suggest that any particular group is experiencing strong competitive intensity, there are some which occupy

(2a)

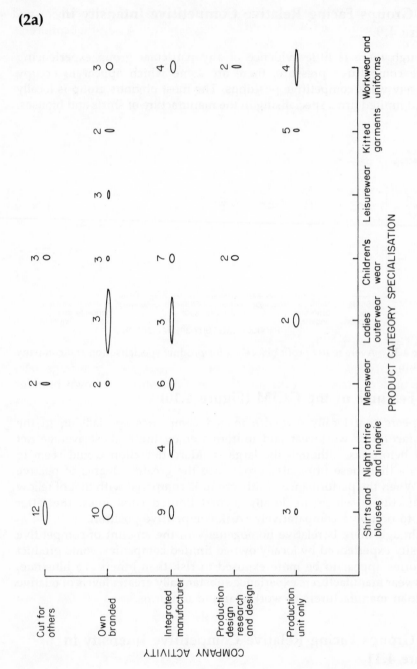

Figure 4.11 Average sales per pound of assets for product specialisation and company activity

relatively weak competitive positions. Such groups include: locally owned limited companies which specialise in the manufacture of either children's wear or ladies outerwear.

THE SECOND SET OF GCIMs; GCIMs BASED ON COMPANY ACTIVITY AND PRODUCT CATEGORY SPECIALISATION

(1) The Axes for the Set of GCIMs

Three group competitive intensity maps were constructed using the strategic and structural determinants company activity and product category specialisation. Each of these maps is analysed below.

(2a)

See facing page.

(3a) Features of the GCIM (Figure 4.11)

Manufacturers of ladies outerwear tend to enjoy superior average sales per pound of assets with the most successful group being own branded manufacturers. However, it should be pointed out that this group also had the largest standard deviation indicating the greatest degree of relative risk.

With the exception of shirts and blouses and ladies outerwear most of the groups of own branded companies seem to be facing relatively greater competitive intensity than other groups. This is particularly the case with the product category 'Children's wear'.

(4a) Groups Facing Relative Competitive Intensity in Figure 4.11

Groups which appear to be experiencing relatively strong competitive intensity are production units which specialise in either the manufacture of shirts and blouses or knitted garments, own branded firms which specialise in the manufacture of menswear, children's wear, leisurewear or knitted garments and firms involved in CMT for others who are manufacturing menswear.

(2b)

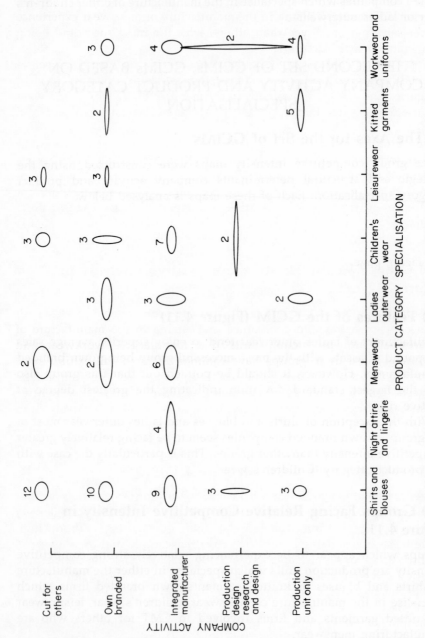

Figure 4.12 Average sales per employee for product specialisation and company activity

(3b) Features of the GCIM (Figure 4.12)

In general, firms specialising in the manufacture of menswear experience higher sales per employee than others, with the most successful being own branded manufacturers.

While there appears to be little variation in the average level of competitiveness exhibited by integrated manufacturers across product categories, those firms specialising in the manufacture of ladies outerwear had the smallest standard deviation. This suggests a relatively lower level of risk.

One product category which deserves comment is that of workwear and uniforms. Although the map suggests that own branded companies, integrated manufacturers and production, design, research and design units experience similar average sales per employee, there are significant differences in the degree of relative risk experienced by each of these groups.

(4b) Groups Facing Relative Competitive Intensity in Figure 4.12

Those which appear to be under pressure are firms involved in CMT for others and own branded companies specialising in the manufacture of leisurewear, and production units that manufacture workwear and uniforms. These three groups have common features—all exhibit *small* average sales per employee and have *large* standard deviations. This suggests that as well as experiencing relatively strong competitive intensity, members of such groups have to cope with relatively high degrees of risk.

(3c) Features of the GCIM (Figure 4.13)

In general, manufacturers of workwear and uniforms which are either own branded companies or production units tend to experience relatively higher average net profit before tax than other groups. Production, design, research and design units which are specialised in the manufacture of shirts and blouses also appear to occupy a relatively strong competitive position. Not only does this particular group exhibit superior average net profit before tax but the degree of relative risk experienced by members is small.

Although there is similarity in the competitive positions occupied by other groups plotted on this GCIM, there are differences in the degree of relative risk experienced. To take an example, the two groups of own

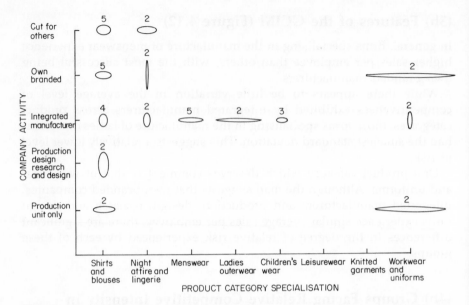

Figure 4.13 Average net profit before tax for product specialisation and company activity

branded companies seem to experience similar average net profit before tax. However, the degree of risk experienced by firms specialising in the manufacture of night attire and lingerie is much less than that experienced by the manufacturers of shirts and blouses.

(4c) Groups Facing Relative Competitive Intensity in Figure 4.13

The map indicates that although no particular group is experiencing relatively severe competitive intensity, integrated manufacturers which specialise in the manufacture of children's wear occupy a slightly weaker position than all others.

CONCLUSION ON THE GROUP COMPETITIVE INTENSITY MAP AND ITS FUTURE DEVELOPMENT

It is hoped that this chapter has demonstrated that the group competitive intensity map is part of a continuum in the development of tools to aid competitive strategy. The chapter has shown the added objectivity that can be applied to the delineation of strategic groups and also the added quantitative assessment of competitive intensity that can be incorporated into the Porter strategic group map.

The chapter has been both theoretical and practical in that, firstly, it traced the theoretical roots from which the map was developed, and, secondly, it showed its practical application to a major study in competitiveness. This chapter has described the first application of the GCIM, and on page 85 it was shown that the map may be used to identify:

- key mobility barriers, and
- marginal groups.

It is hoped that the clothing industry study will be repeated over a number of years so that a longitudinal dimension can be added to the work. This dimension will enable the map to reveal its power to:

- chart movements,
- analyse trends, and
- predict reactions.

A hypothetical illustration of how this might be achieved is shown in Figure 4.14.

In Figure 4.14 the groups' competitive positions for the previous year are indicated by the shaded ellipses (the previous year's competitive positions are shown in Figure 4.7), while the current competitive positions are indicated by the unshaded ellipses. How the trends can be interpreted is considered below at the industry level and also at the level of the strategic group.

At the industry level it can be seen that in the past year the total number of firms in the industry has increased from 78 to 83 (this can be seen by comparing Figure 4.7 and Figure 4.14). More specifically, the previously empty strategic group formed by the intersection of the strategic and structural determinants 'Foreign owned subsidiary' and 'Strong product specialisation' now has five competitors. Additionally, while the group formed by the intersection of 'Local owner manager' and 'Average product specialisation' has increased the number of members in its group by two, the group formed by the intersection of 'Local owner manager' and 'Strong product specialisation' has reduced its numbers by two. Thus the map can capture structural dynamics at the level of the industry.

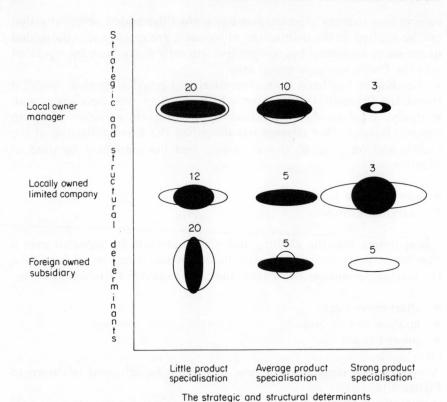

The strategic and structural determinants

Figure 4.14 A complete hypothetical group competitive intensity map for the clothing industry, based on sales per employee (£000), illustrating how trends may be charted over time

Trends at the level of the strategic group are illustrated through two cases:*

Case 1. The strategic group formed by the intersection of 'Local owner manager' and 'Little product specialisation' has performed relatively well as:

- the number of firms in the group have stayed the same at 20 firms, and
- the average sales per employee have increased.

*It should be noted that in both of the cases described here, the standard deviation has not been included because it does not appear to have a strong influence in assessing change in either case. However, if changes in the group formed by the intersection of 'Locally owned limited company' and 'Strong product specialisation' were being considered, then the standard deviation would be relevant.

Case 2. In contrast, the group formed by the intersection of 'Local owner manager' and 'Strong product specialisation' appears to have been subject to greater competitive intensity because:

- the number of firms in the group has fallen from five to three (see Figure 4.7), and
- the average sales per employee has decreased.

Thus the map can capture structural dynamics at the level of the group.

It is hoped that this group competitive intensity map has illustrated the power of the map to chart changes over time, both in terms of the overall structure of the industry and individual groups.

In conclusion it is hoped that the group competitive intensity map will prove to be a device that will contribute to more effective strategic and competitive thinking because of three major characteristics. These are:

(1) *Generality.* The map is a general approach and the quantitative measures used in any study may be employed.
(2) *Objectivity.* The sizes of the shapes delineating the strategic groups are defined objectively: they are no longer at the discretion of the researcher.
(3) *Comprehensiveness.* The map has the power to show five determinants of group competitive position in a two-dimensional form. The five determinants being:
    (a) Two strategic and structural determinants.
    (b) The average value for the measure of competitiveness for each strategic group.
    (c) The standard deviation for the measure of competitiveness for the individual firms in each strategic group.
    (d) The numbers of firms in each strategic group.

REFERENCES

Ansoff, H. I. (1980) *Strategic Management.* Macmillan, New York.
Chandler, A. D. (Jr) (1972) *Strategy and Structure.* MIT Press, Cambridge, MA.
Haspeslagh, P. (1978) Portfolio planning: Uses and limits. *Harvard Business Review*, May/June, pp. 95–102.
Henderson, B. (1970) The product portfolio. *Perspectives.* The Boston Consulting Group, Boston, MA.
Hofer, C. W., and Schendell, D. (1978) *Strategy Formulation: Analytical Concepts.* West Publishing, St Pauls, Minnesota.
Patel, P., and Younger, M. (1978) A frame of reference for strategy development. *Long Range Planning*, **11**(2), April, pp. 6–12.

Porter, M. E. (1980) *Competitive Strategy: Techniques for Analysing Industries and Competitors*, The Free Press, New York.
Robinson S. J. Q., Hichens, R. E., and Wade, D. P. (1978) The directional policy matrix—tool for strategic planning. *Long Range Planning*, 11(4).

APPENDIX: COMPETITIVENESS IN THE NORTHERN IRELAND CLOTHING INDUSTRY

Objectives of the Project

The objective of the project was to analyse, using a Porter (1980) approach, the nature of competition in the Northern Ireland clothing industry and the structural forces which are shaping it. The analysis had two major components: an analysis at the *industry level*, and an analysis of *strategic groups* within the industry. These analyses formed the basis of policy recommendations. The project was published by Centre for Research in Management of the University of Ulster in 1987 and 1988 in the form of An Industry Report and A Strategic Group Report.*

Nature of the Project

In the project a total of 76 clothing firms (this is 75% of all the clothing firms in the region) were personally interviewed by a team of interviewers using a structured questionnaire, and from the results a competitive profile of the industry was developed. In terms of numbers of firms questioned and depth of questioning, this is the most comprehensive survey of the clothing industry ever undertaken in this region.

Measuring Competitiveness

One of the core issues in research into competitiveness is how to measure it. The rationale behind the measure used in the clothing industry study are set out below.

The traditional view of competitiveness which economists often advance is that it is largely determined by *costs* and *prices* relative to competitors. Although this view often admits to the existence of non-price factors, they are often excluded from the economic analyses.

---

*Although this exposition has been set at the level of the 'product', it could also have been set at the s.b.u. level.

The increasing importance of non-price competition has been stressed by many writers since the 1930s. Product changes and advertising have become the main competitive weapons. Despite this development, economists have largely ignored product changes and have concentrated on models of *pure price equilibrium*, in which the product is given and price is adjusted by the firm in its attempt to maximise profit or attain other goals. Economic theory has predominantly been *price theory*.

Koutsoyiannis (1982)

For the clothing industry study attributing competitive prowess to costs and prices alone was considered to be too narrow a perspective.

Consequently, a broader view of competitiveness was adopted which started with the following assumptions:

(1) The competitiveness of an industry or sector is *the sum of the competitiveness of the individual firms* that comprise the sector. Consequently, insights into competitiveness will only be gained through understanding competitiveness at the *level of the firm*.

(2) Competitiveness is complex and is determined by factors other than price. Factors such as: relative product quality, degree of capital intensity, degree of vertical integration, power of buyers, power of suppliers, the availability of substitutes and the threat of new entrants, all, in some way, help determine how competitive a firm is.

(3) Although, theoretically, an accepted effective measure of competitiveness is 'the ability to gain market share profitably' (see Carroll, 1985; Schoeffler, 1980), pilot investigations revealed that in practice this measure would be difficult to apply to the clothing industry as it became apparent that respondents frequently:

(a) did not know their own market shares;

(b) did not know the market shares of their competitors;

(c) did not know if they were gaining from their competitors or losing;

(d) were not always able to measure market share because they were not sure that they were comparing like product with like product;

(e) were not always willing to disclose their level of profitability.

The measures used in the project

Because of the potential difficulties involved in using the above measure, it was decided that competitiveness should be judged on the basis of three complementary measures: net profit before tax, sales per employee, and sales per pound of assets. Three measures were chosen because it was believed that for most analyses a *set* of measures would provide a more comprehensive and accurate estimate of competitiveness than a *single* measure. Thus it was anticipated that competitiveness would not always be reflected in all the measures 'moving' in similar directions. For example, if a respondent firm were engaged in a strategy which involved a period of relatively high capital investment combined with the shedding of labour, it might be the case that during this period the measures net profit before tax and sales per pound of assets could be moving in a negative direction while the measure sales per employee could be moving in a positive direction. The three measures attempt to accommodate such movements. The measures that were used were selected on the basis of the following:

(1) Their potential utility in measuring competitiveness: each of the measures is a standard index which is used extensively in industry analyses (see for example ICC *Business Ratio Report* (1985)).
(2) Their availability: it was felt that most respondents would have the data required for the measures readily available.
(3) Their objectivity: for two of the measures—sales per employee and sales per pound of assets—it was believed that respondents would be willing to disclose the true figures.

REFERENCES

Business Ratio Report: An Industry Sector Analysis: Clothing Manufacturers (Major) (1985) ICC Business Ratios, IPC Information Group Ltd., London.

Carroll, C. (1985) *Building Ireland's Business: Perspectives from PIMS*. Irish Management Institute, Dublin.

Koutsoyiannis, A. (1982) *Non-Price Decisions: The Firm in a Modern Context*. Macmillan Press, p. 9.

Porter, M. E. (1980) *Competitive Strategy: Techniques for Analysing Industries and Competitors*. The Free Press, New York.

Schoeffler, S. (1980) Nine basic findings on business strategy. *The PIMSletter*, No. 1, Strategic Planning Institute, Cambridge, MA.

5

MANUFACTURING STRATEGY FOR COMPETITIVE ADVANTAGE

A. John Pendlebury

Coopers & Lybrand

In today's changing environment, the role of manufacturing in an organisation's competitive positioning is becoming more and more important. While in the past the existence of suppliers' markets led many managements to focus on cost-related issues, the change to consumer orientation has required other elements of performance to merit greater attention, including service performance and product quality.

Western business has generally been slower than the Far Eastern competition in recognising the new realities of competitive life. Corporate strategists and planners, through knowledge, experience and inclination have assumed either that manufacturing was totally compliant to the requirements of marketing or finance, or that its contribution to new thinking would be relatively limited.

Perhaps the sole exception to this generally reactive assessment of manufacturing capability was the frequently exercised option of closing a segment of excess costs or capacity. To be fair, this down-sizing or rationalising approach has done much to improve manufacturing efficiency in the organisations in which it has been applied, although we have to say that the process is more indicative of previous strategic failure than current competitive success.

The fact is that positioning a company today correctly to exploit the opportunities presented in national and international (even global) markets is a complex affair because it is necessary to consider such a large and complex group of interconnected activities, including: marketing, sales, design, engineering, service, purchasing and supply, quality, manufacturing and distribution, and how a whole range of external and internal factors impinges upon them. Paradoxically, the positioning of

International Review of Strategic Management.
Edited by D. E. Hussey. © 1990 John Wiley & Sons Ltd

the company must itself be expressed in simple terms because it has to be communicated without difficulty to shareholders, management, employees, suppliers and a variety of governmental and other institutions. This implies a degree of distillation and précis to draw out the vital few items from the trivial many.

In this chapter we shall examine how the process of determining a manufacturing strategy can be best undertaken so as to cope effectively with competitors and with the complexities experienced in the external and internal environments. But first two definitions are presented below:

(1) *Business strategy* is a course of action over a future time period, which defines the goals of the business and how it intends to meet its fundamental obligations to stakeholders, customers, management and personnel, in the face of anticipated political, social, economic, technological and competitive developments which will enable an organisation effectively to determine its overall future, fix its plans and allocate its resources. (For a similar definition of business strategy see Koonz and O'Donnell, 1976.)

(2) *Manufacturing strategy* is a path over a future time period which defines how the manufacturing and related functions such as design, engineering, service, purchasing and supply, distribution, quality, information technology and human resources will be developed, organised, planned and managed to be effective overall in supporting the business strategy and in creating and then sustaining competitive advantage.

The time period for deliberation will vary in each case but will be long enough for the path taken to be strategic in nature with regard to product life cycles, process lives and requirements regarding payback on investment.

What is so important now is that the two strategies are mutually interdependent since the advance of the various technologies deployed in manufacturing has raised their importance in setting future direction and in the allocation of resources (Figure 5.1).

A good example of the linkage between business and manufacturing relationships being exploited comes from Cadbury's in the United Kingdom. While the manufacturing concept was arranged to bring the manufacture of primary materials nearer to sources of supply, finished products were transferred to more focused factories close to market. At the same time, brands were rationalised down to half their previous number. The manufacturing strategy was supported by a major investment in new technology. The end result was five years of Japanese-style double digit annual productivity growth.

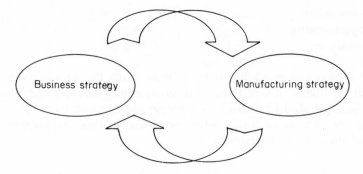

Figure 5.1 The interdependence of manufacturing and business strategies

In many cases manufacturing methods or technologies will be the dominant force in a company's strategic thinking. A fine example of engineering capability providing a business advantage was Honda's fight back against Yamaha's attempt to take over leadership in the world motor cycle markets. When Yamaha declared 'war' on Honda, Honda responded by rapidly increasing the rate of change in its product line, using variety to hurt Yamaha. Eventually Yamaha was forced to end hostilities, since pricing tactics could not compete with Honda's strategic advantage in fast new product introduction (Stalk, 1988).

The result is to make business strategy itself much more visionary, compelling and aggressive, requiring substantial inputs from a variety of technical managers if a leading position is to be developed.

Given that business strategy can be developed in a way that is meaningful in this new world, we continue by describing the processes which may be used to develop a manufacturing strategy, leading ultimately to competitive advantage. We shall examine later how the business strategy may then subsequently be modified in the light of expected changes in manufacturing capability. This iterative process is essential if a proactive manufacturing approach is to be introduced.

It must be emphasised that the development of manufacturing strategy must not be seen as cumbersome, heavy handed or taking up the input of a big staff group. More apposite is a more rapid, more intense process in which the following broad steps are undertaken as far as possible by line managers, but with the input of specialists in their fields:

- Understanding
- Vision
- Direction setting

- Committing
- Implementing
- Sustaining

The aim anyway must be to be flexible with the capability to adapt quickly to changing external and internal needs much in the manner so actively supported by America's General Electric Company.

It is the purpose of much of the remainder of this chapter to examine each of these steps in more detail.

UNDERSTANDING

Our understanding is developed by becoming aware of the forces which are driving product markets and assessing how well equipped is the organisation to respond to them:

> If you know the enemy and know yourself, you need not fear the result of a hundred battles.
>
> Sun Tzu on the Art of War
> circa 500 BC

Understanding the strategic role of the manufacturing and related functions rests on the requirements of the owners expressed through the business strategy on the one hand and on external and internal factors on the other, as shown in Figure 5.2. The existing capability is measured through the present situation with regard to external and internal factors, measuring for example cost characteristics, product performance, service levels, lead-times, and turnover of working capital. Other elements of Figure 5.2 are described below.

Business Strategy

From the definition of business strategy given previously we would expect to receive a wealth of data on the positional and other requirements of the business as a whole over some foreseeable distance into the future. A good strategy will set a firm framework for manufacturing, covering requirements such as the definition of the main business areas and critical success factors in each, product/market combinations, geographical spread, the likely logistics arrangements for finished products, service requirements in the product offering and target costs and prices.

Among factors of decisive influence will be the policy to be followed regarding human resources, the requirements on financial parameters, such as profitability, and return on capital employed, investment and

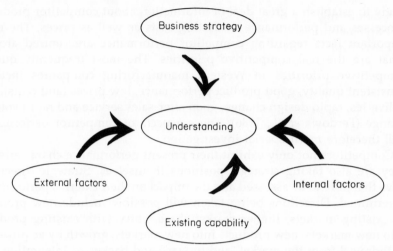

Figure 5.2 Gaining understanding of the manufacturing environment

working capital constraints, and the need to reward owners in a progressive way.

These elements can be treated initially as external inputs to the manufacturing strategy. The nature of the other external inputs is described below.

External Factors

External influences on the business are among the most important to manufacturing strategy. They include the dynamics of industrial markets, the requirements of customers, the positioning of competitors, the development of suppliers, technological advances, and changing political, social and economic conditions.

Customers and competitors

Clearly, both customer requirements and competitor positioning are relative in nature and advance with the passage of time. There is little excuse for not knowing the requirements of customers, although it is common enough to find examples of organisations neglecting or ignoring the voice of the customer. In recent times the measurement of customer satisfaction has become increasingly common as part of efforts in introducing total quality.

The positioning of competitors enables companies to determine how best to modify their own existing position. It is possible through careful study to establish a great deal of information about competitor products, processes and performance, including costs as well as prices. The most important facts regarding competitor performance are centred around what are the real competitive priorities. The most frequently quoted competitive priorities in Western manufacturing companies include: consistent quality, good product performance, low prices (and costs), fast deliveries, rapid design change, good after-sales service and rapid volume change (Ferdows *et al.*, 1986). These aspects of competitor performance will therefore merit special investigation.

Competitors not only exhibit their present performance characteristics, they are also taking strategic positions themselves. Strategic directions have therefore to be assessed and the impact on their external performance determined. Directions being taken will possibly include new products in existing markets, higher market share, entry with existing products into new markets, new products into new markets, growth by acquisition, withdrawal from the market, and forward and backward integration (see Ferdows *et al.*, 1986).

Product characteristics

The characteristics of the products themselves and their position in the market relative to those of the competitors must be studied in detail in the effort to create competitive edge.

There are really two aspects to the problem: perceived product quality and ease of manufacture, which in many cases are mutually reinforcing, although from time to time the very difficulties in manufacture create the opportunity to keep competition out.

The concept of relative perceived product quality (RPPQ) was developed by the Strategic Planning Institute in Cambridge, Massachusetts, and gives a measure of a product's quality and service–delivery traits in comparison with competitors. It has been demonstrated by SPI from survey data that companies achieving superior RPPQ are in the long run likely to show better financial performance than their competitors. Superior manufacturing strategy must therefore address quality and service as a major issue.

Ease of manufacture is something which can in the case of competitors be measured on the basis of the product produced and by undertaking design reviews on products made in-house. Value engineering and parts rationalisation are of crucial importance. A recent example from a major American machine tool manufacturer, in which a particular line of machine tools was examined in a design review, revealed an immediate possibility to cut manufacturing costs by 10% (Comments made by Dan Meyer, President of Cincinnati Milacron at the 1988 World Manufacturing Conference of Coopers & Lybrand, Napa Valley, California).

The complete study of the product was completed in a few months. The extension of these attitudes to continuous improvement, year-in-year-out has time and again created competitive advantage in areas such as domestic appliances, air conditioners and commercial vehicles.

Success in manufacture is another important piece of information in situations where the same product is made in more than one place. Two most interesting examples come from the motor industry on the one hand and aerospace on the other. The Ford Motor Company noticed that gearboxes made in Japan with the same equipment and specifications as those made elsewhere actually performed better. A similar observation was made by the US Department of Defense regarding the production of a US fighter under licence in Japan.

Clearly, alternative sourcing of the same product gives opportunities to make manufacturing processes more competitive. In the two cases cited above, the response was to introduce new techniques of performance measurement and quality management.

Development of suppliers

As important as the customer relationship is that which holds with suppliers. Since suppliers are majoring in the components which they manufacture, it is perfectly reasonable to look to them to help in both new product development and in identifying product improvement opportunities. We shall return again to the matter of suppliers in the section devoted to internal factors contributing to strategy.

Advancing technology

It is interesting to note that the managing director of a leading Japanese company once ascribed half of his company's productivity improvement to the efforts of shopfloor operators and half to the management effort centred around the introduction of new technology. Technology advances continuously with regard to both products and processes and many an organisation has fallen behind through failing to assimilate new technologies, particularly from contiguous areas not previously thought to be important.

Again we can look to Japan for an interesting case, that of machine tools. It was the Japanese who perhaps most successfully exploited the linkage between mechanical and electronic technologies to make available to world markets 'intelligent' machine tools. Mechatronics is the word the Japanese themselves often use in this connection. Clearly, other major industries have also benefited in the same way as the ubiquitous microprocessor has carved out new product and process opportunities. Yet it was not so long ago that the engineering profession found it difficult to determine how the microprocessor with all its great innovative possibilities would find practical application.

Advances in product and process technology clearly represent innovative capability. Experience has accumulated that the creation of an innovative culture is not so easy in traditional organisational forms (Peters and Austin, 1986). The need has been identified for a less structured way of allowing innovators to work since most great innovations have come into being in spite of organisation rather than because of it. The Japanese companies, in their efforts to stimulate higher flexibility and great innovative capacity, are now increasingly preoccupied with creating more individualistic company cultures, to some extent at the expense of their well-known and respected group-oriented culture.

The process of interpreting technological trends and their impact on products and processes is therefore important in the determination of manufacturing strategy but is still relatively little understood. The very least that must be done in the context of global competition can be summarised as follows:

(1) Core technologies must be reorganised and then kept and developed in-house to acquire distinctive competence.
(2) The technologies of competitors must be fully understood.
(3) Contiguous technologies must be identified, followed and kept under review.
(4) New developments must be tracked in all major industrial economies.
(5) Innovative cultures must be allowed room to develop.
(6) Technological competence must be represented in the company at the highest organisational levels.
(7) Customers and suppliers must be looked to for a maximum contribution.

Globalisation

No sector on external impact would be complete without consideration of the impact of globalisation on manufacturing business, since in many sectors such as computers, pharmaceuticals, automotive and bulk chemicals the process has already occurred.

A company serving global markets has to take into consideration a number of additional factors impacting on manufacturing strategy. The process of 'going global' can be said to occur in four distinct phases:

(1) *The national company* servicing mainly national markets.
(2) *The international company* servicing international markets through a predominantly national (country of origin) structure.

(3) *The multinational company* in which decision making has become more diffused but which does not service global markets in a truly consistent manner.

(4) *The global (or transnational) company* which services global markets with a consistent strategy and approach.

The key point is that for manufacturing companies making this transition, additional factors come into play, including:

- focused factories with global mission;
- global engineering so as to meet product requirements in a multitude of countries;
- de-centralised R&D facilities, probably with specific targeting;
- balanced asset and sales portfolios to minimise exchange rate exposures;
- utilisation of international economic comparative advantage (for example, by carrying out assembly operations in low wage cost environments);
- developing competence centres to deal with specialist technical issues;
- establishment of international logistics structures to cover the movement of goods;
- transportability of manufacturing processes and systems, particularly those reflecting the company's 'distinctive' competence (e.g. fractional horsepower motors at Black & Decker);
- institution of global purchasing and supply concepts.

While there is not space within this chapter to cover these issues in full detail, from time to time reference will be made to the special needs of the global enterprise. For an interesting discussion of the characteristics of emerging global enterprises the reader is referred to Porter (1986).

Financial and operating performance

One of the most important external investigations is concerned with assessing the financial and operating performance of competitors, both in the manufacturing arena and more generally. The revolution in manufacturing attitudes in the West in recent years owes as much as anything to the comparison of measures such as output per employee, turnover of long-term and working capital, return on capital employed, space utilisation, per cent defectives, direct/indirect ratio, etc., which provide the real 'bottom line' on manufacturing performance.

The establishment of competitive objectives on all these ratios, and others appropriate to each case, is an important exogenous input to the determination of strategy, which often determines whether a business sector is worth staying in or not. Clearly, if there is no early prospect of good performance, it will be better to liquidate or sell-off this facility, unless rationalisation and improvement can be achieved through greater scale via a suitable acquisition. Countless industry sectors have suffered this fate over the last ten years in areas such as fork-lift trucks (Coventry Climax-Kalmar, Lancing Bagnall-Linde), trucks (Leyland-DAF), telecommunications (Alcatel-ITT) and many others, all seeking economies of scale, wider spreading of development costs, or improved market access.

Human resource management

Improving productivity in manufacturing industry is greatly dependent on the labour environment, either in the industry sector concerned or in national or global markets. The massive shift of capacity to the Far East was caused initially by a low cost labour environment in which labour-intensive activities were greatly favoured. Location decisions are often most significantly impacted by the availability of good quality labour, so that the importance of people-related issues will always be high. Efforts by governments to attract manufacturing investment often amount to job subsidies, creating a low entry cost.

Apart from the price factors associated with labour there is increasing awareness that labour practices and educational and training levels have a high impact on the manufacturing mission. There is no doubt, for example, that Japanese manufacturers benefit greatly from the attitudes and conditioning of their labour force. The ability of Japanese companies to maximise the contribution of *all employees* in the continuous improvement process is a major competitive edge which cannot be quickly eliminated by companies outside Japan. In Germany, senior managers will readily ascribe their manufacturing edge to the durable and dedicated qualities of their craftsman grades. Hayes, Wheelwright and Clark (1988) attribute much of the relative decline in American manufacturing capability to the loss of the appropriate blend of artisan, engineering and scientific skills.

Other political, social and economic conditions

Aside from the issue of globalisation, financial performance and human resource management, there remain a plethora of conditions which in any one single instance can exert an important or even dominant influence on the manufacturing mission. It is not possible in this chapter to pick out all those that might be relevant, we content ourselves here with listing just a few:

- Grants to encourage the establishment of facilities at a particular location (the UK's system of selective assistance under the Industry Act).
- Grants in support of product or process initiatives.
- Tax holidays applied to joint ventures (e.g. in the Soviet Union).
- Non-tariff barriers applied to products (e.g. the protection afforded by the EEC to automobile and electronics manufacture, and the US Government's protection of its semiconductor industry in recent times).
- Difficulties in achieving product conformance with standards (homologisation in the telecommunications industry in France).
- Difficulties in laying off workers (the use of the Case Integrazione in Italy).
- National requirements to improve value-added activities (Australian requirements to create R&D capability).

Clearly these factors vary greatly by country and must be picked up in the context of individual circumstances. The famous Japanese 'screwdriver' plants in the UK reflected a certain minimal view of what is a suitable entry strategy. The need to conform to local sourcing requirements to adapt to EEC rules is typical of a non-tariff barrier, designed to improve local industry conditions. Obviously, such conditions can rapidly become very political and quite complex. Local sourcing requirements will probably become more stringent in the post-1992 market.

Internal Factors

While attention to external factors is absolutely essential to competitive success, it is most often through neglect of internal factors that a business suffers. This is so because many of the different business functions (such as marketing, sales, distribution, purchasing, quality, R&D) are in regular outside contact, as well as the manufacturing and engineering functions, but relatively few people really understand in a *strategic* sense the workings of the internal environment and its internal relationships—a clear case of not being able to see the wood for the trees. This is reinforced by the protectionist nature of many managers who react adversely to criticism, real or implied, or suggestion of change, even when well intended, in their existing organisation.

It is only too easy to underestimate resistance to change which will most certainly escalate rapidly to alarming proportions in the vast majority of organisations trying to undertake it. So many organisations we have seen know *what* they must do; they fail to see *how*.

In this section we describe some of these internal problems that need examination in the context of defining manufacturing strategy. The path taken when moving manufacturing forward first *links* external requirements for competitivity to changes required in internal factors; hence the importance of understanding the existing status of internal factors.

Organisation structure

The best way to understand company organisation structures is that they are a sad and inevitable fact of life and must therefore be adjusted for by encouraging a real effort in 'personal responsibility and concern' (Herrhausen, 1988). This is so because in the one-man business there is not usually a communication problem—there is no need to communicate. But thereafter, as the numbers involved increase, the need to organise becomes more apparent, and so we create hierarchical, peer-to-peer network and other structures through the formal and informal systems, which we are compelled to introduce as the scale of activity increases.

What we forget though is the need for economy in such structures because, once created, they feed on themselves and become ever more hierarchical and complex—actually inhibiting efficient performance while they simultaneously enhance inefficiencies.

The seriousness of the problem came to light when companies such as GM and Ford began to compare their structures with the much flatter structures in use at Toyota and other Japanese competitors.

Larry Sullivan, President of the American Supplier Institute, said at the Coopers & Lybrand World Manufacturing Conference 1988 that Professor Ishikawa, on visiting Ford in the United States some years ago, was asked to comment on the Ford organisation chart. He pointed out that it was too vertical with insufficient attention to horizontal communication, using a nice analogy of the warp and weft in weaving cloth. The product passes *horizontally* not vertically through an organisation; if this fact is neglected both quality and productivity suffer. There needs therefore to be considerable horizontal interaction between people at similar levels in a hierarchical structure.

No, we are not going to do away with organisation structure *but* it must be economical and encourage peer-to-peer communication. Total quality control (TQC) is an attitude or tool which encourages effective peer-to-peer relationships.

In conclusion, manufacturing strategy cannot be decoupled from organisation and changes may be needed as part of a new approach.

Cultural attitudes

Every organisation, particularly the better ones, has a very powerful cultural tradition which needs careful examination before change can be contemplated. If we require such traditions to be abandoned, how can we justify this? And what is to replace them? Can we educate and train enough people fast enough to make change stick? One Swedish company found the problem insoluble and had over a period of time to replace its entire workforce at one plant with younger people with no experience of prior malpractices (viewed in terms of the new requirements).

We shall be describing later how these cultural problems can be tackled, although it has to be said that without fine leadership the task is impossible. In *A Passion for Excellence* (Peters and Austin, 1986) the components of good leadership are discussed in some detail. What is of greatest interest is the clear need now emerging from all sorts of enterprise of the need to move away from the purely 'command and control' mentality to more visionary compelling, and dynamic concepts.

Strength of management

Much has been talked of the recent Japanese miracle of responding effectively to much higher exchange rates of the yen against the dollar and competition coming from the newly industrialised economic states (NIES).

Clearly miracles do not happen, rather that the Japanese companies systematically re-examined their businesses in the light of changing conditions and made the necessary re-adjustments.

The novelty though was the speed of change at which the Japanese companies have changed their management style. The slow step-by-step, upward consensus style is being replaced by a more rapid approach involving the top–down leadership of an aggressive, younger, technologically minded, breed of management. It is this new group which is increasingly supervising the reconstruction of Japanese business (Volpi, 1988). If Western companies are to establish and sustain competitive advantage they must be capable also of demonstrating such remarkable capability of adapting to changing requirements in their management.

Management strength must be sufficient to provide leadership during the current period of rapid change, recognise when changed approaches are required and then have the courage, leadership and drive to *make it happen.*

Labour practices

There is no doubt that labour practices can impose severe limitations on a company's ability to make progress. On the other hand changed working arrangements in BMW in Germany resulted in much higher productivity from existing facilities. Future plans there include annual hours agreements which allow for greater period-by-period flexibility. In a similar way Ford of Europe has substantially reorganised its working practices, seeking essentially to create higher flexibility.

Other organisations throughout the West have sought to eliminate bonuses paid on output quantities so as to promote a different operating mentality. Cincinnati Milacron springs to mind in this context as do certain parts of Lucas in the United Kingdom. Major organisations such as IVECO have energetically sought to bring down their break-even point.

All of these changes in their different ways reflect a response to merging strategic priorities associated with higher flexibility and productivity and better use of working capital.

Yet the renowned inflexibility of European labour markets and workforces is still a great inhibitor of performance improvement. Individual companies must open up the labour question if they are to move to a leadership position in comparison with Japanese and US competitors.

Quality

We have seen already that customers' perceptions of quality have a remarkably strong influence on the price that can be asked for and on long-term profitability. No less important is the internal impact of quality, since in total, quality-related costs can account for as much as 20% of product cost and even company turnover.

The beneficial impact of attention to quality has been seen at major corporations such as Hewlett Packard, Ford and AT&T. Ford in particular has demonstrated time after time that improvements in quality can be achieved with simultaneous reduction in costs.

Improvements in a company's delivered quality can therefore simultaneously improve performance in the market while cutting manufacturing costs, they also help to establish a greater unity of purpose, a sense of team-play and higher self-esteem.

Time to market

An important source of competitive advantage, impacting not only on cost but also on market share, is the time it takes an organisation to bring a new product from design into production and then into the market.

The product development phase is important also because it is the period during which as much as 80% of product costs are determined. Development costs themselves are clearly affected by the time taken in development so there are obvious opportunities when speeding up development time to cut costs and therefore raise the productivity of the development teams themselves.

For these reasons it is only to be expected that a great number of organisations are taking steps to reduce the length of the product development cycle—indeed IBM has it as one of its principal strategic priorities.

Fast times are achieved through task orientation and early manufacturing involvement (EMI). The latter is a major factor in successful globalisation of manufacturing, providing the opportunity to design for manufacturability. A significant ratio in this regard is the ratio of design to manufacturing engineers. The ratio in Japan shows a significantly greater involvement of manufacturing engineers in product development activities.

Focused factory concepts

It is well known among production personnel that an increasing variety of products manufactured will normally have a deleterious impact on productivity and on production lead-time. The more variety, the more complexity in the production process and the greater the difficulty in securing least-cost conditions on a particular product being manufactured.

European companies have in the main resorted to a country-based manufacturing approach in which each national facility produced the broad range of products required for its markets.

The situation is now changing as European and global manufacturers realise that more of a focused approach by product line, in which particular facilities make a narrower range of products for world markets, leads to higher productivity, albeit with some degree of sacrifice in other cost areas (distribution, for example).

Within single factories the same principles can be applied by creating manufacturing cells dedicated to particular products or product groups. The principle is best applied to higher volume items, as revealed by Pareto (ABC) analysis, leaving lower volume variety to be picked up on more general purpose and functionally (rather than product) oriented equipment.

Focused factory concepts are in fact the first stage in achieving higher productivity from existing facilities. The second is to make progress on handling variety, conceivably by making use of more advanced technology (e.g. flexible manufacturing systems) and by creating greater flexibility of labour and management systems.

Companies making use of focusing concepts in the recent past have included SKF in ball bearing manufacture, where factories have become more focused on particular product ranges, and Cincinnati Milacron in machine tool manufacturing where some real cost and productivity advances have been achieved, reporting substantial improvements in lead-times, work in progress, set-ups, backlogs and machining times.

Demand management

One of the most critical internal constraints to improving manufacturing performance is the way in which customer demand is managed. It is in fact a deeply interesting and absorbing question not really addressed by the majority of companies which simply let the situation degenerate to some kind of uneasy truce between the sales and manufacturing functions.

Yet it is in demand management that we actually reveal our real flexibility and integrity in front of the customer. We really want to be in a position to structure our flexibility and service concept so that performance is optimised and repeatable.

By structuring the performance concept we are then able to examine its acceptability in the market and actually set out a strategy for improvement in the future. The strategy for demand management is both an input to and an output from the manufacturing strategy itself. Examples abound of superior demand management creating major competitive advantage. In the motor industry, for example, the manufacturers are working hard to reduce the time it takes for a customer to be delivered a fully personalised motor vehicle from receipt of his order. The supply of spectacles is a good example of how market requirements are beginning to dictate a one-day delivery service from the original eye test—something unthinkable a few years ago.

Distribution

As the possibilities for reducing lead-time are realised by competitors it becomes necessary for companies engaged in distribution to take more control of the total lead-time offered to the customer along the entire supply chain.

It is not always possible for suppliers to take this control since for the very same reason their customers may also have the same interest, but this depends on the circumstances which hold in each particular sector. In the motor industry, for example, the assembly plants are looking for economic higher delivery frequencies and have been trying various ways of changing the economics by parcelling up suppliers, either through new in-bound warehousing concepts (in which the supplier might share the costs) as with the Rover Group in England, for example, or in using milk-round concepts for in-bound freight.

The changes made by Toyota to out-bound distribution in 1982 were phenomenal after it was decided to merge the previously independent manufacturing and sales companies, the motivation being that the improved manufacturing performance resulting from the company's just-in-time philosophy was not being reflected in distribution, therefore threatening the whole concept. The supply cycle time was originally targetted to be reduced from six weeks to two weeks. Now the cycle time in Japan is just a few days, including both manufacturing and distribution (Stalk, 1988).

Purchasing and supply

For many industrial sectors, increasing specialisation of manufacturing activities has resulted in the relative contribution of bought-in materials to increase in manufacturing costs to the point where it is usually 50% or more of total product costs. At the same time the labour proportion of product cost has shown a steady decline in importance.

So with material costs five times as important as labour, relations with suppliers merit prime importance. The natural consequence is that there has been an evolution in the attitude towards suppliers, who have evolved from providing products through providing solutions to becoming business partners. Partnerships require a long-term commitment to mutual goals, it is through this type of interaction that the effectiveness and productivity of both parties can be improved.

By coming together with suppliers, significant costs can be avoided, including specification time, design time, quality assurance, in-bound inspection, financial administration, counting and weighing, working capital, and other quality related costs. Savings of as much as 25% of common product costs have been achieved in this manner. Manufacturing strategy must therefore pay fullest consideration to supplier capability.

Factory layout

Factory layouts are often inappropriate to the purpose for which they were originally intended, yet there is often considerable inertia either in thinking about the problem or in being prepared to make changes. If we are to create higher volume flexibility in our factories, we must design them for this purpose. If we wish to focus activities then we must move away from the tendency to put similar groups of machines together. If we are to make inventories visible then we must move the storage points to places adjacent to where they are to be used. If we are to change our inventory and production management concepts, then we must re-think the way we record material movements. If we are to eliminate working capital, we must shrink as a matter of policy the space allocated to the production facilities and dispose of the surplus.

Cost management systems

It is more than likely that company management will be firmly wedded to costing concepts that have ceased to be effective in their representation of product costs. This can lead to mistaken conclusions about the profitability of products and product ranges. It is beyond the scope of this chapter to enter into the details of what is a lengthy discussion and debate. The interested reader will find more information in the book edited by Berliner and Brimson (1988). Symptoms of the problem are management being unprepared to support reductions in working capital because 'profits' will be adversely affected, or a reluctance to move to greater flexibility because 'efficiency' will be reduced, or difficulties encountered in justifying investment.

Investment justification

Much of industry suffers from the fact that improvement efforts in manufacturing cannot apparently be justified on conventional justification criteria. There really are three elements to this debate:

- Is the method used the right one?
- Are the parameters correctly set?
- Is the project scope sufficiently wide?

Undoubtedly some form of discounted cash flow is the appropriate tool for investment appraisal work, although care must be taken to understand the difference between current and constant money. Equally the question of economic return or the return after considering the mode of financing must also be addressed. Cost data emanating from company cost management systems must also be treated with a degree of caution.

Parameters set too tough will prevent the company investing at all. Highly set hurdles sacrifice future performance to the benefit of current results. This process is very risky with the impact of shorter and shorter product and process life cycles, together with competitive market conditions. The process becomes institutionalised if companies fail to measure and reward their managements on the basis of strategic as well as short-term 'command and control' capability. It can be a useful analysis to measure the impact of not investing on the basis that market share and market prices will be crucially impacted as a result; in other words, by thinking of a more 'strategic' base case for comparison.

Thus it is clear that there are numerous internal factors, entirely under management control, that can be influenced in the process of setting future strategic direction. Some of these factors can be used to respond to changes needed in the external environment and some stimulate the strategic thinking process in their own right.

We have understood the situation when we have come to grips with the interplay of external, competitive and internal factors to be aware of our real position. Being aware of this position we will know what are our strengths and weaknesses and how our position is likely to be threatened in the future. If we are really good we will have obtained a large number of measures on different aspects of these qualities, both external and internal. Opportunities for improvement emerge to the extent that obvious remedies may be available.

That is not to say we know consistently and completely how to address the problems that our understanding reveals, this is the subject of the next section.

VISION

It has often been said that there can be no strategy without a vision of the future; this is just as true in manufacturing as in anything else. But what is vision and how may it best be arrived at?

> Vision, the act or sense of seeing, sight: anything seen: anything imagined to be seen: a supernatural appearance, an apparition: anything imaginary: imaginative perception: foresight.
>
> *Chambers Dictionary*

Vision implies sight, clarity and distance. It also suggests rare appreciation and the ability to recognise a pattern out of uncertain images. It requires intelligence, understanding and profound experience. Beyond this it requires a certain degree of imagination to fill in gaps, eliminate inconsistencies and develop new dimensions and parameter sets. But there is also a certain flavour of impracticality or of difficulty of putting ideas into effect (see Figure 5.3).

Without a precise understanding of the existing environment our vision will be unreliable, as it will be also if not anchored to the surrounding environment. Without this anchorage it is only a dream, likely to vanish when normal conditions return.

An example from the US electronics industry will serve to make the process more clear. A leading manufacturer of telephone equipment determined that he could not compete cost-wise on world markets against Far East competition. He looked at his manufacturing processes and determined that they were unsatisfactory in terms of a whole range of performance measures. He was aware that new tools and techniques in

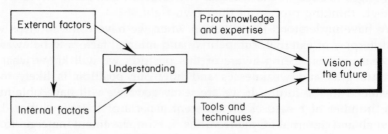

Figure 5.3   The development of visionary concepts

design and manufacture could close the gap because there was still much good in his operation, particularly regarding the capacity of his workforce to adapt to change. His vision was to become the lowest cost manufacturer from his US base, with industry-best quality and delivery characteristics. Subsequently his vision was realised as production costs were reduced by over 25%.

In order to create such visionary ideas, in an area with so many interdisciplinary connotations, it is essential to find a mechanism for involving a broad range of company competence in the thought process. We may refer to this process as functional balancing as we try to obtain the input of all business functions in the development of new concepts.

We know, however, that there will be considerable resistance to change (see Pendlebury, 1987) and it will be necessary for a champion of change of some status to push the development through the company top–down (both Western and Japanese experience support this view).

The second issue is that it may not be easy for existing management to be creative in the development of visionary concepts, it depends so much on the chemistry of the team, and their exposure to outside influences. For this reason the catalytic input of outside specialists might be useful in developing new directions of development.

The output of the visionary process is likely in many cases to be something so fundamental as to be called 'paradigm shift', an expression denoting a profound change in the rules under which a particular business is conducted, such as 'top–down' rather than 'bottom–up', make to order rather than make to stock, lifetime employment giving way to contract labour, or third party supply.

The vision gives us the broad strategic options we should be considering, without as yet making the determination as to which is the most suitable to follow. It would be unfortunate if our vision could only find one possible path, because this makes life too easy for the competition.

DIRECTION SETTING

In the visionary process we were concerned to identify the need for radically new strategic priorities and rules of the game to be identified, but we were not in the initial stages overly concerned with the ultimate practicality of the proposals. It is in the process of direction setting that we select the direction to be followed from among those available to us from the visioning stage. Effectively we make our strategic choice.

The choice can only be made in the light of the following conditions:

- A description of each possible scenario.
- An assessment of the implications of each scenario for business strategy and for all the functions impacted by it.
- Quantification of the costs and benefits of each scenario so that the different alternatives can properly be compared.

The clear implications are that each scenario must be internally consistent, that manufacturing objectives can be developed from each, that the various functions can determine how those objectives are to be achieved and that they will know what tools will consequently be required.

Example: A specialist engine manufacturer sees the world market for his product shrinking with increased cost-based competition making it most unlikely he will see significant increases in volume from manufacturing his existing product range. He needs a new vision and direction for the worldwide business.

After careful study he concluded that the existing model range could be protected through massive improvements in manufacturing efficiency as typified by just-in-time techniques in both design and manufacture. Furthermore, he would enter developing country markets through special licensing agreements, offering engineering assistance. At the same time he would invest in new technology products to create higher performance engines capable of developing broader ranges of use and therefore higher sales volumes and value added for the product.

By comparing the different scenarios on the basis of their usage of tools, resources and the business case (i.e. how they meet the requirements of the business strategy) it is possible for the various company functions to agree on the best direction to take (see Figure 5.4).

Pausing for a moment at this point, we can see that we have taken maximum account of the customer, competitive, external and internal factors, the desires of the various business functions, and the requirement to conform with the dictates of business strategy. We have built a visionary top–down manufacturing concept and are therefore less likely to miss the opportunity to exploit major changes in the market.

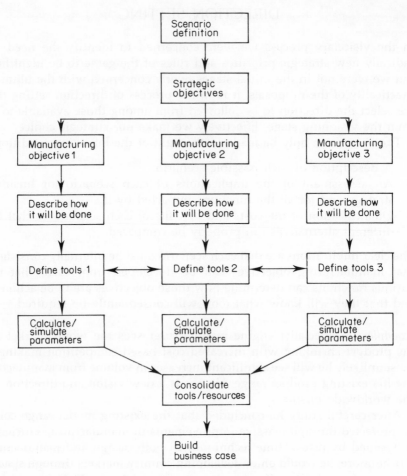

Figure 5.4 Developing vision into direction statements

In some cases we will want to carry out sensitivity analysis. This is important when the choice between different scenarios is relatively finely drawn, as for example with location decisions on where and how to manufacture and distribute. Sensitivity analysis is used to examine the robustness of decisions to changing circumstances, often making use of supporting computer analysis.

COMMITMENT

It is a fair summary of the experience of many companies in implementing a manufacturing strategy that the good ideas of top management on determining the direction they must go in the future cannot actually be implemented in the organisation because in some deep sense the organisation as a whole is unable to do so. How can this be and what can we do about it? Below we summarise some of the issues that surround the ability to introduce change and then what needs to be done to minimise the problem.

(1) *Lack of communication.* If people are not involved with a process of change they are unlikely to support it when it finally hits them. Their first reaction will most often be opposition, unless they can see some advantage to themselves from the new ways being proposed. In the absence of efficient communication from the company, their views are likely to be based on uninformed opinion and their reaction at best unpredictable and at worst resolutely against *on principle.*

(2) *Bottom–up processes.* We have seen earlier that bottom–up processes in which employees act as the original source of ideas have a correspondingly high chance of success of being implemented. However, such approaches tend to be incremental in their nature and somewhat slow in their ability to make change. They very rarely lead to strategic (as opposed to tactical) shifts. There is no doubt that top–down methods have to be used to develop competitive manufacturing strategies, although bottom–up concepts are at the heart of continuous improvement processes.

(3) *Leadership.* Since we have to recognise that strategies set in competitive conditions require a top–down emphasis, the ability of an organisation to adapt to change depends very much on the quality of its leadership. The leaders of the business must have the ability to communicate with and relate to the management and employees on the basis of common goals. The leader will not be able to carry his workforce along with him if he has not beforehand made the effort to make them of the same mind as himself. This explains why the really good organisations put so much time and trouble into company beliefs and culture, management development, and education and training.

(4) *Pride.* Paradoxically, it is in some of the very best companies that resistance to change can be at its highest. Past successes tend to create deep roots among those who were responsible. Why change now, they ask, when we have been doing so well? The argument comes even stronger from those who have held a single position for a considerable period. Top management will most likely have had shorter occupancy than these solid and experienced managers. Yet their pride is also a good quality which we would wish to harness

in the future. We can do so if we can convince them one by one that change is essential to the company's future. We will probably need to demonstrate with outside examples why new concepts are the only road forward in the future. In other words we must maximise education and involvement among the experienced management group.

From the above comments it can be seen that the commitment process is all about people and their ability to learn about, contribute to and then manage the change process. In company structures they are organised in different divisions and departments and may well have developed a tendency to think along narrow departmental lines.

The first step therefore is to involve the various functional areas as fully as practicable in the visioning and direction-setting processes and then, when the preferred scenario has been developed, interpret the scenario in terms of the requirements to be placed on each function. It is not easy to achieve functional balancing because in most organisations there is a tendency for functions to act in a suboptimal fashion, maximising their own performance without much regard for the deleterious effects they may have on others. Examples of local suboptimisation include:

Marketing: product proliferation for marginal business.
Design: proliferation of similar designs, unmanufacturable products.
Finance and accounting: inaccurate and inappropriate cost management.
Purchasing: excessive purchased quantities to obtain supplier discounts.
Sales: unrealistic promises on delivery price and lead-time.

To reconcile these conflicts we need a method in which agreed overall (i.e. strategic) objectives can be driven into the various functional contributors, as well as into the manufacturing function itself. Figure 5.5 shows how the commitment process can be initiated, following closely a procedure defined by Tom Gunn, Vice President, Unisys at the 1988 Coopers & Lybrand World Manufacturers' Conference.

On the basis of this detailed breakdown of activities it is possible to start the process of talking to the various functions about the changes being considered and their likely contribution.

Clearly all functional departments must buy into the programme before it is embarked upon, if we are to maximise our chances of success. Equally, the various functions must begin to identify and then commit the resources that will be needed to implement the strategy as intended.

An important part of the commitment process is to create the 'inter-functional glue' that will ensure that we 'weave the cloth', working as much horizontally through the organisation as vertically up and down the functions. A good idea is an away-day type of conference at which all the different function heads meet in the presence of a facilitator to go right through the ramifications of the programme. At the end of the session (or series of sessions) the company leader asks for 'sign off' from all concerned. The company therefore makes commitment of the functions to a formalised and group activity at which they all participate with roughly equal status, once they have committed, the leader himself declares his own personal championship.

Experience in several group commitment sessions would suggest that the method is helpful to the group and particularly helpful to the leader. The process can be repeated with different company constituencies to obtain commitment, for example, from suppliers (Ford worked in this way back in 1980 and 1981 with regard to its AJ campaign), labour unions, distributors and even customer groups.

The output from the commitment phase is a detailed statement of strategy, covering the manufacturing and related functions, the changes they have agreed to make, the objectives they will meet and the benefits they can deliver to the organisation as a whole. Resource requirements are identified and committed and a full schedule of costs and benefits prepared.

Economic analysis of the strategic plan is undertaken, probably making use of discounted cash-flow techniques. Sales and marketing data are agreed with those responsible for their preparation. Any modifications needed to the business plan have been re-cycled through so that the manufacturing strategy has been able to modify the company's approach to business.

The proactive nature of the process should not be underestimated. It is noticeable, for example, that shorter design lead-times, simpler, new generation products and fast and efficient manufacture open up new market opportunities or the opportunity to take market share. Fast manufacturing puts new pressures on distribution and allows for a greater degree of customisation of products to meet customer requirements. Old-fashioned competitors become potential takeover candidates once a company's management sees opportunities for making industry best standards of return on capital employed. If you can win at home why not abroad by taking command of your stricken competitor's capacity?

IMPLEMENTATION

Once the direction has been set, there remains the major task of implementation. Since strategy is the subject, it is likely that the implementation plan is set for a period of three or four years or more, and so it usually proves to be the case.

Manufacturing objective and how it will be done	COMPANY FUNCTIONS → ... etc.				
	Design	Manufg	Purchasing	Marketing	MIS
Reduce cumulative lead-times by 50%	EMI new CAD/CAM link	Introduce GT cells	Reduce number of suppliers	Reduce product proliferation	Select CAD/CAM system
	Broader classification of engineer	Focused factories	Eliminate quality check	Set new order lead-times	Update M/C capacity
	New project management methodology	JIT work	Agree new target lead-times	Implement preferred system concept	Modify MRP system for JIT scheduling
	Sub-contract project X	New layout	Create new co-operative agreement	Change pricing structure	Introduce bar coding
	More use of supplier capability	Eliminate incentive system		Eliminate bulk order concessions	Development engineering database
		New flexible labour system			
		Sub-contract non-core activity			
etc.	etc.	etc.	etc.	etc.	etc.

Figure 5.5   Obtaining functional commitment

The organisation of company-wide activity over time frames such as this requires that the activities be built up into a programme which typically will consist of 12 to 20 different projects, each with its own timetable, resources, benefits, costs and start and end points. Individual projects will be coordinated with others via the overall programme.

Differences of opinion exist on the extent to which projects should be placed in special task groups as opposed to being passed into the normal line organisation. Clearly there are pros and cons associated with each, depending upon the speed required and the extent to which a variety of business functions are involved.

In any event it is wise to oversee implementation through a steering committee, consisting of senior representatives of the main functions involved, under the chairmanship of the change champion, who might be a senior executive with manufacturing responsibility or the chief executive himself.

The programme should be under the management of a programme manager who for obvious reasons needs to be well experienced in the different business functions and who is endowed with the personal characteristics to introduce change successfully.

In the change process we are normally trying to balance three complementary components, both across the enterprise and within the different functions involved: people, technology and management systems. The project manager should be experienced in all three dimensions so as not to make the mistake of attaching too much weight to any single one. In view of the sensitivity of the various business functions to the changes being imposed, he should have an easy familiarity with the operations of those functions most heavily impacted.

Individual project managers need to be dynamic and hard-working, able to sustain and manage a heavy transient workload. Their skills must reflect the particular project being undertaken but they must retain a capacity at all times to take a broader view.

Little wonder that many companies find it very difficult to staff such programme and project activities, since the necessary staff are either unavailable or already committed to ongoing management activity. Although some of the load can be taken on by outside consultants it is wise to retain the majority of effort within the organisation to engender the necessary feeling of ownership.

Programme and project teams often require some instruction in project management techniques, since multidisciplinary, task oriented activities impose different management requirements on team members. These techniques should not be confused with computer-based project management tools, the techniques are more general in nature and addressed more particularly to resource management and gaining and retaining motivation and commitment.

Achievement of the programme against objectives is best measured every five or six weeks because it is a remarkably constant fact that management expectations of improved performance or progress towards objectives usually functions over a six-month horizon. If the progress meetings do not take place over a six-weekly meeting cycle, it is difficult to control the programme to satisfy management expectations.

A not inconsiderable part of the programme must be devoted to education and training. Education creates a generic sense of awareness and well-being, while training specifically relates to solutions being developed, whether people, technology or systems oriented. The difference between education and training is most graphically brought out in the case of a man who, while wishing his daughter to have a sex education, was not so keen she should be fully trained.

When projects are complete, they must be closed down and ongoing activities transferred and secured in the functional organisation. Allowance may need to be made (particularly with high levels of investment in technology) for the project team to reinforce the line organisation for some considerable period after hand-over, although the whole idea of good project management is to minimise the requirement.

Figure 5.6 is a summary of the complete process of strategy development from the initial analysis to implementation in the various functions.

SUSTAINING

Competitive advantage, once created, has to be sustained so that the improvements obtained through strategic re-positioning are not dissipated afterwards. There are four respects in which sustainment can be encouraged:

- Continuous improvement, in which everybody in the company is trained and then encouraged to participate in the improvement process.
- Total quality programmes, in which at higher levels of attainment, sustained competitive advantage results (clearly connected to the first point).
- Re-addressing the strategic decision-making process, cycling round marketing, business and manufacturing strategies to examine their sensitivity to changing circumstances.
- Ensuring there is no slippage in the functional areas away from global priorities. We have seen already that many organisations show incremental tendencies towards suboptimisation which may or may not be good for the business.

The ability to sustain a competitive position is reinforced by the original demonstration of developing a strategy and then implementing it, because by implementing a profound change in a rapid and controlled manner, the capability and confidence exist to do so again. What is so impressive about companies who have achieved major change is the way they then proceed to apply this competence time and time again. Thus the capacity to create major change is itself a competitive advantage which can be used to address an even more ambitious series of strategies.

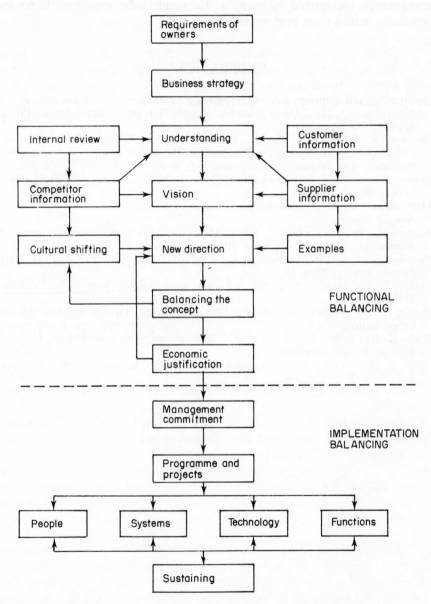

Figure 5.6   Stages in developing manufacturing strategy

The end result is a markedly more flexible and superior management competence, recognised by many as *the* single most important factor in achieving world-class performance.

REFERENCES

Berliner, C., and Brimson, J. A. (eds) (1988) *Cost Management for Today's Advanced Manufacturing. The CAM-I Conceptual Design.* Harvard Business School Press, Boston.

Ferdows, K., Miller, J. G., Nakane, T., and Vollmann, E. (1986) Evolving global manufacturing strategies: Projections into the 1990s. *International Journal of Operations and Production Management* **6**(4), 6–16.

Hayes, Wheelwright, and Clark (1988) *Dynamic Manufacturing.* Free Press, New York p. 56.

Herrhausen, A. (1988) *Leadership for Today's Complexities.* The Conference Board, Annual Report.

Koonz, H., and O'Donnell, C. (1976) *Management, A Systems and Contingency Analysis of Managerial Functions,* 6th edn. McGraw-Hill, Kogakusha.

Pendlebury, A. J. (1987) Framework for a balanced manufacturing strategy. *Long Range Planning,* **20**(6), December.

Peters, T., and Austin, N. (1986) *A Passion for Excellence.* Warner Books, New York.

Porter, M. (ed.) (1986) *Competition in Global Industries.* Harvard Business School Press, Boston.

Stalk, G. (Jr.) (1988) Time—the next source of competitive advantage. *Harvard Business Review,* July/Aug.

Volpi, V. (1988) *Ora il dollaro punisce i grandi manager.* Lettera da Tokio. Corriere della Sera, 25/26 October.

6

MAKING THE
TECHNOLOGY–STRATEGY
CONNECTION

John P. Henry, Jr

Senior Vice President
International Business Consulting Group
SRI International

Technology, proprietary knowledge increased by the application of science, is a corporate asset. Its dimensions and sophistication vary— from the 'cleverly innovative' to the 'dramatically new', from 'fundamental breakthroughs' to improvements that 'enable' a major technology to enter the marketplace. However, placing a corporate value on technology is an elusive exercise and one that entails evaluating its linkage to business strategy.

Strategic approaches for implementing technology to achieve competitive advantage vary considerably. For example, Northern Telecom Limited achieved a very strong position in digital central office switching by, in effect, 'betting the company'. At the same time, technology management can also prove a serious liability if ill-timed or wrongly conceived as it was for those engineering companies whose strategies centered on the perceived promise of synthetic fuels and the nuclear power industry.

Scientists and engineers once used technology as a barrier to keep management at bay, and technology as such was both revered and feared by corporate leaders. In reality, however, technology should be viewed as only one business asset among many: its importance rests in the degree to which it can be linked to other elements of a corporate strategy. In assessing the linkage between technology and corporate strategy, it is important to understand the difference between 'technology push' and

International Review of Strategic Management.
Edited by D. E. Hussey. © 1990 John Wiley & Sons Ltd

JOHN P. HENRY

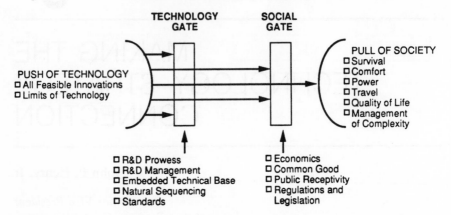

- Realism
- Often, Changes in Attitude
- Linkage to Corporate Mission or Strategy

TECHNOLOGY GATE   SOCIAL GATE

PUSH OF TECHNOLOGY
□ All Feasible Innovations
□ Limits of Technology

PULL OF SOCIETY
□ Survival
□ Comfort
□ Power
□ Travel
□ Quality of Life
□ Management of Complexity

□ R&D Prowess
□ R&D Management
□ Embedded Technical Base
□ Natural Sequencing
□ Standards

□ Economics
□ Common Good
□ Public Receptivity
□ Regulations and Legislation

Figure 6.1 What is needed in technology management? *Source*: ATT-Bell Lab; SRI International

'market pull' (see Figure 6.1). The market effectiveness of any technology, and thus its value to any corporation, is governed by its ability to pass through two gates—a technical and social gate. In the society of the industrialized world, which is driven more by 'want' than by 'need', the value of technology takes on dimensions of quality and complexity that differ significantly from such important historical criteria as availability and cost.

Thus, a technology-related strategy today is likely to be driven by social and market forces, with technical and performance aspects collateral issues. At the same time, consumers are often oblivious to technology's role in meeting their real or perceived 'wants'. Therefore, technology should be viewed as only one of several corporate assets (albeit an often critical one) that enables a company to meet corporate objectives of financial security, and growth, as well as others that management deems important. As a result, it is critical that R & D managers and planners communicate with corporate executives through 'application-related' dialogs so that the true value of the technology to the company's future is understood all along the route from fundamental research to commercialization.

Before addressing the technology–strategy linkage, it is useful to review the other major forces that affect a company's business (see Figure 6.2). Changes in the world economy affect industries and industrial resources; they, in turn, can alter the national conditions that make for corporate success or failure. Because companies both provide goods and services

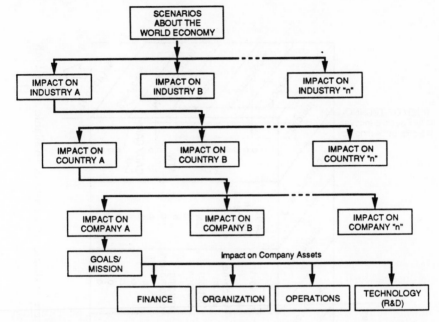

Figure 6.2 A company's strategy is necessarily driven by world forces that can be analysed...

to individual national markets and also engage in world trade, economic and demographic evolution strongly affects business portfolios. Such changes take place virtually continuously, and a company's responses to them determine corporate strategies for dealing with a dynamic and increasingly competitive environment.

The corporate strategy constitutes the corporate 'game plan' for using today's assets to meet future goals. Principal company assets can be grouped as follows:

- Manufacturing or systems assets (operations, including marketing).
- Financial capability.
- Technology and knowledge—the information base.
- Organizational strengths (people).
- Image—customer and reputation base (this can also be viewed as a part of operations and is considered part of system assets in the discussion that follows).

Linking technology with strategy can be critical. It is thus useful to expand our definition of 'technology' to include anything from an innovative device or system to a venture, which in itself might not be

134

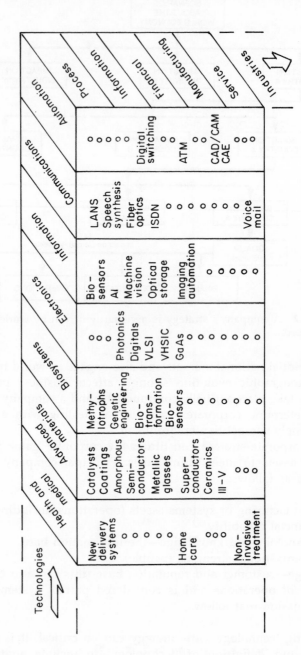

Figure 6.3 The dizzying array of new technologies that are available or soon-to-be available offers both threats and opportunities to world business

novel but which might be entirely new to the corporation seeking a different business dimension or direction. The term can vary from a fundamental breakthrough, such as the recent advances in superconductivity, to needed enabling technologies that make such advances really useful. New devices or systems are usually associated with instability, and entail such issues as:

- High risks/rewards for inventors and entrepreneurs.
- Short product life cycles.
- Rapid growth or decline in a business maturity curve.
- A high ratio of technologists and dreamers to the historical staff distribution.

Given the anxieties these issues can cause in chief executives, corporate environments are often unable to support new technology directions long enough to derive potential advantage from them.

As Figure 6.3 indicates, no single, generalized technology strategy can include all or even most of the devices and systems available. Moreover, even though the figure is complicated, it still does not address the time or time-of-decision variable, which differs for each strategy combination; nor does it take account of those *system* variations that affect the value of an application for end users (e.g. artificial intelligence can be applied to process production and control in manufacturing or to market analysis in certain industrial segments).

Given an intensely competitive future business environment, we assume that most aggressive companies worldwide will have to deal with such issues in detail to be successful. To illustrate further why a generalized technology management strategy is so elusive, Figure 6.4 focuses on the complexity of just one of the positions shown in Figure 6.3, the advanced materials/ceramics business. From 'function', through 'properties', to 'applications', the opportunities for using ceramics technology are both broad and deep, and the strategies for application— from laser diodes, to artificial bones and teeth parts—are vastly diverse. If a company chose to pursue this field, its ceramics strategy would thus need to be designed to cut across a wide variety of industrial niches, each with its own risk profile and profitability perspective. In fact, by making the technology–strategy linkage, R & D in ceramics properties could afford a new business entry from an existing technical base (e.g. turbine blade coatings to precision instrument parts).

Although, when viewed together, these issues may seem overwhelming, certain ideas are fundamental and should help corporate executives link technology assets and strategic objectives.

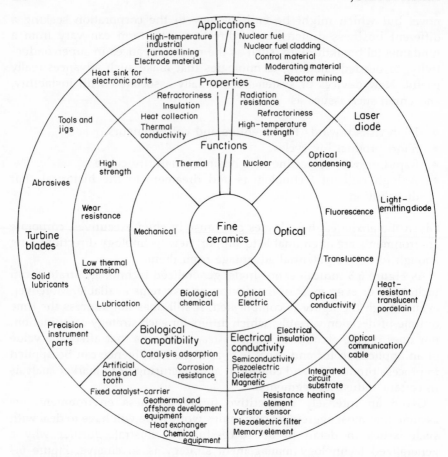

Figure 6.4 Technology applications in the ceramics business offer numerous opportunities

First, as noted, consumers, are interested in goods and services—not technologies per se. In a few cases, however, a good technology reputation can be an asset, or at least a perceived asset. However, a recognized technology advantage can also prove a financial disappointment. For example, many consumers feel that the Sony Beta video recorder system (the first system widely available) is superior to the more popular VHS format. However, Sony may, in fact, be forced to abandon the Beta format because the company does not seem to be able to capitalize on this asset.

Figure 6.5 provides a simplified picture of the likely linkages between a consumer and the basic resources from which products and service are derived—material or natural resources, labor and capital. The critical issues for a corporation are understanding (1) where *its* business links

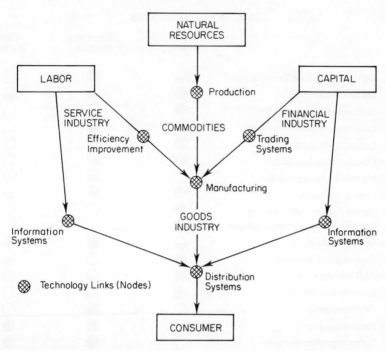

Figure 6.5   Technology is an asset that enables companies to leverage resources to meet market needs

are positioned in the 'consumer chain'—the chain of business steps from raw material acquisition, through manufacturing and distribution, to marketing and the ultimate consumer illustrated in Figure 6.5 and (2) how important its unique technological strengths are to its current business and to its hoped-for business. In each step or link (combined and described as nodes in the figure) between the deployment of available corporate resources and the consumer (market), technology has a 'value-added' role. Realistically assessing that role is critical to linking technology to strategy.

A number of formal methodologies can be used to establish the linkage between technology and corporate strategy. Figure 6.6 lists most of them and denotes their applications, whether in developing corporate strategy itself or in enabling technology to be linked to the rest of the corporate asset base. Those methodologies listed under 'strategy' are used in the corporate analyses directed principally toward strategic planning; those listed under 'Technology position' are applicable to detailed analyses of corporate technology positioning and needs. The 'both' column lists

FOCUS ON METHODOLOGIES

	The Strategy	Technology Position	Both-The Link
Artificial Intelligence/Expert System	◒	●	○
Competitive Analysis	●	◒	◒
Consumer Behavior/VALS™	●	○	○
Decision Analysis	●	◒	○
Economic Forecasting	●	○	○
Environmental Scanning	●	◒	○
Information Management	○	◒	◒
Innovation Search	●	●	◒
Market Evaluation/Forecasting	●	○	○
Mathematical and Financial Models	●	○	○
Operations Analysis	◒	●	●
Organizational Analysis	●	○	◒
R&D Management	●	◒	●
Scenario Development	●	○	○
Tech Monitoring	○	●	○
Technology Audit	○	●	●
Technology Management	○	●	●
Value-Added Analysis	○	◒	●

● = Important
◒ = Relevant
○ = Unimportant

Figure 6.6 Formal methodologies are used to develop business strategies and to link technology assets to them

methodologies that can be used to link technology assessment and management with strategic objectives once such are developed.

Every company has a strategy in place that is based both on its history and on its business aspirations; the strategy may be as simple as survival. None the less, each company needs to ask two questions about the technology–strategy linkage. 'Is the company's stated strategy the right one to achieve corporate objectives?' and 'What is the most effective way to use the corporate technology asset to meet those objectives?'

To link effectively the existing or potential technology asset with strategic objectives, once they are known, four steps are necessary (see Figure 6.7):

(1) Conduct a technology audit.
(2) Analyze the strategic implications of the corporate technology portfolio.

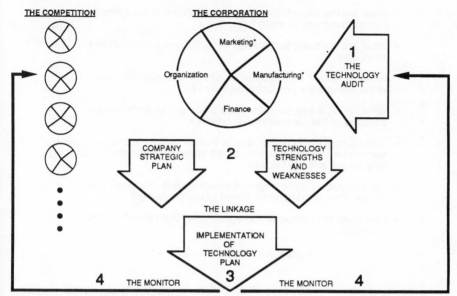

Figure 6.7 The technology–strategy connection can be made analytically

(3) Develop an implementation plan for using technology assets to advantage.
(4) Establish a monitoring system to keep the analysis updated.

The four steps are discussed below.

THE AUDIT—STEP 1

A technology-asset audit focuses on determining the real or perceived value that any technology node, or its individual technology links, has in the business benefit/cost chain—from raw material acquisition, to the supply of the product or service, to the customer. The technology audit focuses on the current and near-term asset value of the company's technology position vis-à-vis its competitors. Figure 6.8 lists typical types of questions related to this analysis. For example, a Japanese high-technology manufacturing firm may have achieved a unique technology position in automotive engine assembly through robotics. The ability of European and US competitors to leverage local production in local markets may pose a challenge to that company, which views increased technology exports as a critical element of its future strategy.

- **What are the basic technology assumptions in the company's current business strategy?**

- **What are the basic technology assumptions in competitors' strategies?**

- **Is the customer's perception of the technological qualities of the company's products important?**

- **What value, if any, do customers place on the technological qualities of the competitors' products?**

- **Is corporate R&D contributing to improvements in the company's current technology position, or are improvements starting to take longer and cost more?**

- **Are competing technologies becoming cost-effective? Are competitors making gains ahead of the company?**

- **How does the company manage information related to these questions?**

Figure 6.8   Basic question set

In conducting an audit (see Figure 6.7), a project team systematically examines each current business line and identifies the technology links or 'nodes' (see Figure 6.5 for an example). The team then does the same for competitors, critically evaluating the asset value of each node. Doing so establishes whether a node is critical or merely useful; thus such an evaluation helps management decide how to position technology in its business asset portfolios more competitively.

The output of the audit, then, is a technology model for the corporation that details the current and expected value of its asset base in the face of competition.

STRATEGIC IMPLICATIONS OF THE TECHNOLOGY PORTFOLIO—STEP 2

Step 2 of the analysis is conducted with a view to ascertaining how best to leverage the company's technology assets to meet tomorrow's business objectives as defined by the current strategic plan. It is likely that the audit will show dynamic trends in competition that reinforce the importance of some technical linkages or indicate that others should be abandoned. New R & D directions may well be suggested, and even new business products or service lines may become apparent. In addition, changing economic conditions (see Figure 6.2) may suggest that current technology strategies are only 'cash cows' in so far as true future development is concerned. On the other hand, strong 'seed technologies' that the R & D department is now developing may lead to entirely new business linkages; and may even require re-evaluation of the strategic plan itself.

The outcome of this second step, therefore, is an analytically sound understanding of the value of the current and future roles of technology in the corporation, and an assessment of the technical vulnerabilities of each business line—both current and expected.

THE TECHNOLOGY IMPLEMENTATION PLAN— STEP 3

The first two steps provide the basis for answering two important questions:

(1) Given our company's strategic vision and the roles that technology will play in it tomorrow, how can we improve our corporate technology portfolio (including R & D) so that it effectively meets these actual and perceived needs?

(2) Would it be more effective to go outside our organization to improve our chances for success by acquiring needed technological links elsewhere, for example as a result of:
    (a) partnerships, joint ventures, or a global alliance;
    (b) licenses;
    (c) acquisitions?

The implementation plan—a time-dependent action process (see Figure 6.9 for an example)—is specific, and the degree of realism it embodies helps determine the success of the outcome. (In this light, most corporate implementation plans are highly optimistic, often overestimating in-house technological capabilities while underestimating competitors' prowess.)

Of equal importance, but one of the least understood issues in implementation and thus one that is all too infrequently dealt with directly and analytically, is managing the 'people' issues related to building new business thrusts, especially those based on new technologies. Moreover, the technology focus of the asset base must be attuned to customers' as well as to internal corporate needs and must be managed accordingly.

To inspire ongoing creativity in new technology-driven business lines, personnel policies thus often have to be tailored, with new types of rewards offered for knowledge workers and new mechanisms installed.

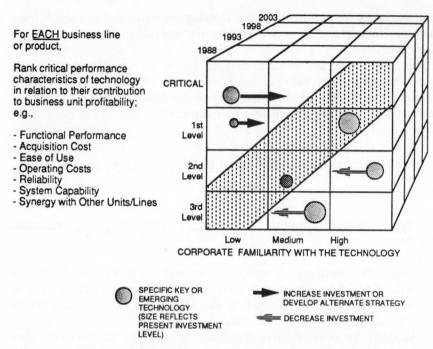

For **EACH** business line or product,

Rank critical performance characteristics of technology in relation to their contribution to business unit profitability; e.g.,

- Functional Performance
- Acquisition Cost
- Ease of Use
- Operating Costs
- Reliability
- System Capability
- Synergy with Other Units/Lines

CRITICAL

1st Level

2nd Level

3rd Level

Low   Medium   High
CORPORATE FAMILIARITY WITH THE TECHNOLOGY

2003
1998
1993
1988

SPECIFIC KEY OR EMERGING TECHNOLOGY (SIZE REFLECTS PRESENT INVESTMENT LEVEL)

INCREASE INVESTMENT OR DEVELOP ALTERNATE STRATEGY

DECREASE INVESTMENT

Figure 6.9   Technology-based resource allocation competitive product profiling

Furthermore, the entrepreneurship needed to implement new business directions does not have to take the form of professional free spirits as it often does. Rather, discipline linked to a suitable reward system is required to channel the entrepreneurial spirit productively.

Consequently, personnel, organizational cultural, and technology issues all have to be considered in careful detail (see Figure 6.10) as the company implements its technology plan. In most cases, effective management thus requires careful re-examination of the traditional corporate organization.

THE TECHNOLOGY MONITORING PROGRAMME— STEP 4

Establishing the technology–strategy connection is a dynamic process (see Figure 6.7). Given ongoing changes in the world economy and in consumer buying patterns, strategic planning processes have to be designed to accommodate to multiple future scenarios, rather than to single-point forecasts based on history. The technology-oriented marketplace is littered with overly optimistic corporate forecasts. Fortunately, many of the corporations were not mortally wounded, but recovery often necessitated painful reductions in their asset base and constrained future options for growth and profitability.

Drawing on the findings of Step 1, the audit and Step 2, the business strategy link, a dynamic analytical follow-up model, can be established to represent and position the technology component in the company's value-added business chains. The risks associated with the development of technology or failure to do so can thus periodically be assessed so that Step 3, the implementation plan, can be continuously updated. Obviously, these endeavors are iterative and need to be carried out over the life of the corporation.

SUMMARY

As a concept, technology can often intimidate corporations and corporate leaders because the 'strategic link' issue is complicated and entails business implications that appear to be risky. Technology, however, can be successfully managed, even given our expectations for increasingly unpredictable and volatile markets. To do so, understanding market pull and its impact on business is critical.

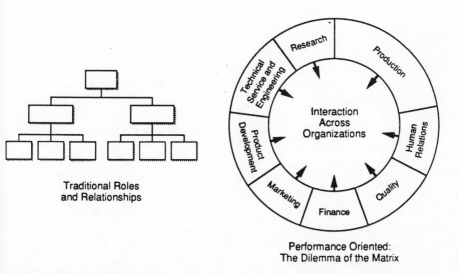

Figure 6.10 Orchestrating the organization's needs for managing new technology presents a real challenge

In this context, technology management as a subset of corporate management is a custom business. It requires innovation on every business front: from definition, to organizational design, through production, to marketing. Techniques exist to help corporate executives evaluate their technology asset bases and leverage them into a dynamic strategic planning process.

The keys to that leverage are a comprehensive evaluation of technology's role in each current and expected corporate business line, and a realistic value-added analysis of that role. A thorough audit will provide confidence for executives as the corporation implements a dynamic technology-related strategic plan to achieve future profitability at minimum risk.

7

USING INFORMATION SYSTEMS (IS) TO BUILD COMPETITIVE ADVANTAGE AND COPE WITH CHANGE

Ed Tozer

Independent Consultant

INTRODUCTION

Everyone these days feels obliged to seek competitive advantage. Assuming you know what it is for your business, and that you are really convinced that you need it, then this chapter is here to show how information systems, and the underlying technology to support them can help you achieve it.

Competitive advantage cannot be assumed to follow automatically from investing in information technology—or in anything else for that matter. Rather, it is gained as a result of single-minded pursuit of carefully selected goals by business management who know where they are, where they want to go, and why.

That being said, for most organisations, a significant contribution to competitive advantage can be obtained through development and proper use of the right information systems, and through enlightened and systematic exploitation of information technology (IT) to support them. But success will be rare and haphazard unless normal business judgement and common sense are retained and applied in the search for it. As always, success requires the right blend of systematic method, business flair and sheer bloody-mindedness.

International Review of Strategic Management.
Edited by D. E. Hussey. © 1990 John Wiley & Sons Ltd

This chapter sets out guidelines for focusing and moderating your business flair so as to maximise your chances of effectively exploiting information technology to the best advantage of your business, not that of your computer vendor's account representative.

Terminology

The IT world is notorious (but not alone) for its jargon and misleading terminology. We will try to avoid that in this chapter. However, we will need to introduce a substantial amount of specialised terminology, which is not the same thing at all. As far as possible, terms will be defined when first used, and will be used consistently. Terms which look like jargon, but which are not defined should be read in the common English sense.

Firstly, a definition of the overall subject. The phrase *information technology* (common shortened to IT) really concerns technical solutions to particular needs, i.e. the 'hardware' (boxes and wires) and systems software that form the environment on which information systems run.

The term IT is commonly misused to refer to all aspects of the provision of information systems for a business; we will not do that, as it can be seriously misleading. This reinforces the mistake commonly made by those enamoured of technology, of designing the solution before they have understood the problem.

Instead, we will refer to the need to provide an *information systems strategy* (commonly shortened to IS strategy) for an organisation. The IS strategy concerns application systems, the stored data and the user interfaces, and the manner in which they serve the needs of the business. It also includes the IT strategy as a subset.

Chronic Problems with Information Systems

The history of use of information systems within business organisations has not been all sweetness and light. Over-ambitious plans and expectations have all too often come crashing to earth, and management scepticism has grown.

The blame must be shared about equally between the technologists and management. IT has time and again failed to deliver, and management has consistently failed either to ensure that the real problem has been defined, or to apply normal management controls to the IT/IS function. Of course it is not all bad—there are notable exceptions. But this chapter assumes that you have some of the problems set out below, and need help with them.

The most important of the failings of IS/IT include the following. Problems only are defined at this point—it is intended that some of the answers will emerge from the remainder of the chapter:

(1) *Development takes too long.* The lead time from initial request to delivery of a correct operational system is just too long. The business needs will have moved on, and the users either solved the problem some other way or lost interest.

(2) *Changes take even longer.* The same time delay problem applies to modifications or extensions to operational systems.

(3) *Excessive spend on 'maintenance'.* A variety of studies have indicated that the total spend on maintenance of a system after initial development is three to five times as great as the initial cost of developing it. The variation is large, and depends whether true enhancements as well as amendments are included, but the message is clear—the most productive target for cost savings is not initial development, but the 'evolution' phase as it is coming to be called.

(4) *Systems functions as delivered are out of date.* It follows inevitably that, if delivery is late, the functionality of a system will tend to be out of date, especially in a fast moving, competitive industry. Further, the initial maintenance backlog to fix the out of dateness will already be significant.

(5) *Forbidding replacement costs for inflexible, out-of-date systems.* Many organisations which made extensive, courageous investment in core systems in the 1960s and 1970s are now paying an unfair penalty. They need to replace these very old, inflexible systems, which are cramping business development. However, it is difficult to develop a convincing business case in conventional terms when the new system, built at high cost, will offer no immediate increase in business functionality. Rather, the change over will cause significant disruption. It looks like another case of 'jam tomorrow' promises from IS/IT as far as management is concerned. So what is the rationale for replacing these systems, and where does the business case come from?

(6) *Inadequate IS support impedes rapid response to market needs.* For all of the above reasons, the business may not have the right portfolio of information systems to enable it to rapidly formulate, develop, launch and support the products which it needs to compete in its marketplace. Products get launched without the right support—support costs are too high, customer service levels are too low, and the competition romps away once again. Perhaps the market analysis systems are so poor that you don't even get to know it happened!

(7) *DIY solutions get out of control.* Dynamic management will not stand

for this. They declare UDI, and start DIY systems development, or hire a systems house direct to build systems for them. Sometimes this works, and is the right thing to do. More often, they run into the same road blocks a little later, and the organisation's portfolio of systems becomes even more fragmented and muddled.

(8) *IS/IT investment is out of phase/focus with business priorities.* Looking at the above, it is hard to see how this can fail to happen. A clean start is needed to communication both ways, as well as rectification of the development and maintenance delay problems, before the information systems development cycle can be properly linked to the business planning cycle.

(9) *IS/IT staff don't understand business needs.* Like all technical specialists, IS/IT staff can become very isolated and arrogant. They can lose touch with business realities through not getting involved, and also because they become victims of the mushroom theory of management, which means being kept in the dark and periodically sprayed with manure.

(10) *Senior management doesn't understand IS/IT constraints.* This is the converse—management wants results, and quite rightly is impatient with excuses as to why something is impossible, or will take too long. Often, the systems developer gives in and agrees to a timescale which he knows is impossible—with predictable results soon afterwards.

WHAT IS ON OFFER?

Senior management is really seeking a true contribution from IS/IT to business effectiveness and competitive positioning. This can be translated into a set of objectives for IS/IT.

Information Systems—Overall Objective

The overall objective for IS/IT must be something along the lines of *meet the information and support needs of the business in the optimum manner.* This can be 'layered' in the following manner:

(1) Avoid late, inaccurate or missing information being a constraint on business performance.
(2) Contribute to improved efficiency and effectiveness of business operation:
  (a) closer control;
  (b) lower stocks;
  (c) better customer service.

(3) Improve quality of management decisions by providing better information support.
(4) Support development of new business areas through effective IS/IT support of products and their delivery systems.

There is a hierarchy of ways in which information systems can contribute to company well-being. Usually, this forms a logical progression, in which a sound basis established in earlier layers is a prerequisite to success in the later layers, although this may not always be so. The types of contribution are:

(1) *Efficiency*: doing the same but cheaper—the old 'headcount displacement' basis. Systems designers often inadvertently take this approach through lack of vision, when far more effective solutions are available. For example, in manufacturing industry, many production line jobs can be replaced by flexible machines inaccurately called 'robots'.

(2) *Effectiveness*: achieving the same end, but in a more effective manner, possibly in a fashion radically different from the traditional way of doing things. For example, after 'Big Bang' in 1986, the London Stock Exchange found that the screen-based trading facilities were so much more effective for its members that the old trading floor fell into disuse, except for some specialised market areas. This led to a totally unexpected benefit, that they could consider making this valuable space available for other purposes. Other examples include the use of online information to improve customer service in all types of industry, and the 'hole in the wall' banking cashpoint terminals.

In manufacturing industry, the whole 'just in time' philosophy is based on a violation of the old principle that there should always be sufficient buffers of work in progress, and stocks of raw materials close at hand to cover any inaccuracies in manual scheduling.

Once computer-controlled integrated manufacturing passes a 'critical mass', then the safety margins can be trimmed right down, with large savings in floor space and materials holding costs.

(3) *Proactive*: doing different things, or the same things in a radically different manner, because IT makes it possible. Here, the IS/IT people can offer constructive input to business/product planning. Exploiting 'technology push' as well as responding to market pull, information systems become intimately involved in the business planning cycle, and in the product/service life cycle. A penalty is that systems based on this approach become totally dependent on the automation systems.

One example is the 'fly-by-wire' systems used in modern high performance aircraft, where the airframe is inherently unstable, and is unflyable manually. Another example is the real time process control of chemical plants, nuclear reactors and oil refineries. The dependence on automated control systems here is very great; therefore, reliability requirements are extremely high. The benefits are far higher operating efficiencies. It is beyond the scope of this chapter to debate whether the benefits always justify the price.

(4) *'The system is the product is the service'*: in the most extreme examples of types 2 and 3 contributions, it becomes impossible to determine where the information system leaves off and the product or service starts.

Examples include the services of information providers, such as Reuters and Telerate, who sell or hire terminals through which their service is delivered to those needing up-to-date financial information. Travel agents are heading in this direction with their viewdata-based services; one is often better to ask directly what holidays are available meeting certain criteria, than browsing through the glossy brochures.

The manner in which this progression is followed, and the degree of penetration of the higher layers varies by industry and over time. Also types 3 and 4 contributions pose a challenge as regards business justification. The traditional 'headcount displacement' type of justification totally misses the point here. Typically we need to consider impact on items such as market share (or even the chances of opening up a whole new market), rather than marginal costings or headcount displacement.

We can take the progress in certain industries in the later layers as indicative, however, that increasingly, IS/IT contribution will move to types 3 and 4, as the potential for levels 1 and 2 gets used up. It is a challenge for your industry to see if you are yet positioned to exploit types 3 and 4 opportunities.

WHAT HAS CHANGED IN TERMS OF THE POTENTIAL OFFERED BY INFORMATION SYSTEMS?

The Rate of Change is Changing

In most business sectors the very pace of change is itself accelerating. Even Japan, the consumer goods star of the 1970s, is now finding Taiwan and Korea breathing down her neck. This phenomenon mirrors, but is by no means due to, the rate of change of costs and opportunities offered by information technology. Given that, in the West, we are not prepared to drop our labour costs to the lower levels of some parts of the Far East, exploitation of these IT opportunities may be a critical factor in survival.

Business Climate and Market Forces

Why can we not develop a solution and let it run, sitting back and reaping the rewards? Firstly, competitors have an annoying habit of noticing our greatest success areas and trying to muscle in—cutting prices, offering better products or services, and generally trying to seduce our favourite customers. So we have to change in order to keep one step ahead.

Secondly, customers themselves, due to business pressures of their own, boredom, changes in fashion, or changes in the economic climate, change their behaviour, switching to new products or options. So we have to change or go out of business.

Better Management Techniques

New approaches have been developed, e.g. those of Porter (1980, 1985, 1987), which help us to analyse market forces and competitive position. These can be used to help to identify opportunities to exploit and extend existing product lines and expertise into new market areas.

Typically, in the past, organisations built information systems that were specialised by product. A new product line would necessitate a new set of systems. Today it is increasingly realised that systems based on the support of functions, across products offer far greater flexibility.

Figure 7.1 illustrates a simple three-dimensional analysis of a typical business environment, where the old product-oriented systems were like

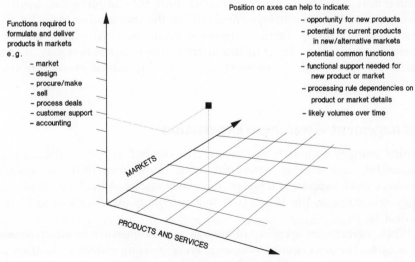

Position on axes can help to indicate:
- opportunity for new products
- potential for current products in new/alternative markets
- potential common functions
- functional support needed for new product or market
- processing rule dependencies on product or market details
- likely volumes over time

Functions required to formulate and deliver products in markets e.g.
- market
- design
- procure/make
- sell
- process deals
- customer support
- accounting

MARKETS

PRODUCTS AND SERVICES

Figure 7.1 Business dimensions

pieces of toast in a toast rack, each with its own set of functions, databases, etc. There are, of course, many more dimensions, but three are sufficient to illustrate the principle. By building instead functionally oriented systems—in effect horizontal planes in the diagram, we gain a far greater chance of being able to support a new product or market venture with little or no disruption to existing systems. So we can do it fast, and follow our established business principles. Also our key databases, especially customers, are integrated, so we can offer the all-important but in the past hard to achieve profitability reporting across customer and product type.

Customer Sophistication

Our customers themselves are experiencing all of the same pressures to change. Customers get better at assessing the performance of their suppliers, and commercial necessity requires that they react quickly to any problems.

Customers have real choice, and information systems to help them exercise it. Increasingly, information and material flows may need to be integrated across company boundaries. This imposes constraints in terms of the interfaces we need to meet with the systems both of our customers and our suppliers.

For example, in the financial markets, dealers need to interface, often in real time, with the information services of information providers, other finance houses, and the systems of the exchanges. There are often quite stringent regulatory requirements concerning the completeness, accuracy and permissible time delays involved. In the automotive industry, the main manufacturers impose rigorous production schedules on their component suppliers. In retail and distribution, major outlets may become closely involved with the production and quality control systems of their suppliers.

Management Awareness/Expectation

Senior management notices that certain competitors are outstandingly successful, and tries to determine why. Sometimes (but not always) effective IS/IT support is a factor. They may also read books such as this! They will come to the conclusion that *sometimes* excellence in IS/IT is a critical factor.

While investment level is not always a good measure of effectiveness, it is often the only guide—major players in competitive industries do not seek publicity for their failures.

Investment in information systems (per cent of revenue by industry)

Banking & finance	4.5
Electronics	3.7
Industrial & automotive	2.7
Insurance	1.7
Food & beverage	1.6
Process industries	1.6
Petroleum & petrochemicals	1.3
Transport	1.3
Metal & metal products	1.1
Utilities	1.0
Health care & pharmaceuticals	0.6
Retail	0.2
Sample average	1.8

In this context, the above data from a survey of 120 major US corporations, conducted by the US magazine *Datamation*, published in September 1987, is of interest.

The Ability of IS/IT to Deliver

Overview

Increasingly, information systems are delivering more complete and responsive services and support to the business. The improvement is not uniform, and sometimes it is hard to understand the reasons behind the successes and failures, but overall, things are improving.

Some examples already cited bear this out. In the finance sector, many products or services are themselves totally embedded in the IT delivery systems. A major power failure in the City of London would literally stop business, except for those who had installed 'no break' stand-by power supplies, or who had 'hot stand-by' computers located elsewhere.

Traditionally, wholesale banking has made the distinction between the 'front office' where the deals are done, and the 'back office' where, off-line, the deals are processed. This has left often to serious reconciliation difficulties, when the disparate allegations concerning big deals are matched and reconciled. What was said in good faith in the heat of the moment by each party may not agree in the cold light of day. The ideal solution, which is becoming increasingly possible, is to relax the distinction between front and back office. The more of the stages of the deal which can be agreed on the screen in real time, and validated on the spot by both parties, the less scope there is for misunderstanding and grief afterwards. This also helps the regulators—it is better to advise someone who may in all innocence be about to carry out a deal which contravenes a regulation, than it is to recognise the problem after the fact and deal with the resultant bad publicity.

For these reasons, most major players in the financial markets have an objective to do away as fast as technology and regulation allow with the distinction between front and back office. Now that it is becoming actually cheaper, easier and safer to process transactions in real time on current generation computers, this objective is a real possibility, not a 'Holy Grail'.

The effectiveness of the 'just in time' approach in manufacturing industry is another example, as is the improvement in delivery scheduling achieved by major retail chains.

Specific advances which are significant include the following.

Perception by IT professionals

Increasingly, systems providers are becoming convinced that they can improve their performance. Until a few years back, members of the traditional data processing department often exhibited a 'stockade' mentality. Resulting from this, they acted as a law unto themselves, and were among the most conservative of users, failing to believe or accept that they needed to change. This now at last is changing.

Speed of development/change of systems

Modern rapid development techniques are making it possible to build and deliver certain classes of system much faster. However, there are a few words of caution here:

- The techniques usually only work well on limited, well-defined classes of system. Used outside of their range, they can be counter-productive.
- Benefits in maintenance and evolution will not be realised until the systems being maintained are themselves written in the up-to-date vehicles. It is easy, and misleading, to observe a productivity gain of, say, five-fold, and assume that this applies to all current maintenance also.

Accurate categorisation of systems types

It is becoming recognised that there are significantly different classes of information system, and that these different classes need to be treated in quite different ways.

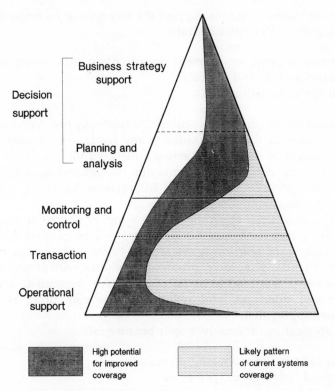

Figure 7.2   Information systems classes: current and potential coverage

It is recommended that organisations undertake a systematic assessment of the degree of coverage of each class, and the potential for raising that cover. This will lead to a clear indication of where to place strategic emphasis for your business. Figure 7.2 illustrates the approach, and a process for achieving this is set out on page 163.

Classification of information and systems.   In planning the overall information systems architecture for an organisation, it is possible to lay down some general principles concerning classes of system, and the ways in which they relate. With reference to Figure 7.2, business information applications can broadly be divided into five layers:

- Operational support.
- Transaction processing.
- Monitoring and control.
- Planning and analysis.
- Business strategy support.

Operational support systems support the day-to-day business administration functions. Examples include:

– automated support for payment chasing operations, using auto-dial;
– command and control systems;
– true office automation (OA).

Transaction processing systems process the relatively high volume routine business events of the organisation. They tend to be predefined and relatively simple in nature, and access structured files or databases.

Monitoring and control systems monitor the routine operation of the business and produce management information based on predefined criteria (e.g. rules, guidelines, limits, etc.)

Planning and analysis applications have a higher degree of volatility. It is more likely that further ad hoc processes will be generated, resulting from the recipient's reaction to the answer to the previous query. These applications tend to have lower processing volumes, with greater volatility of requirements, but tend to be far more heavily dependent upon good presentational interfaces, and require heavier computing power per request to support them.

These applications themselves split broadly into:

– numerically based modelling processes;
– text-based 'intelligence' processes.

Business strategy support applications may be of almost any type, with any mixture or combination characteristics. Their inherent characteristics are that they are mostly concerned with external information, the user interface is highly critical to their success, to the extent where considerable human intervention is required in most cases, and the requirements for them are almost entirely unpredictable and extremely volatile.

Figure 7.2 illustrates these classes as layers, with an indication of the likely current coverage and potential for development.

The role of decision support systems. The planning and analysis and business strategy support categories are together commonly referred to as 'Decision Support Systems', or DSS. Loosely, decision support systems are those applications described above which provide a basis for improved management decision making. They thus make a proactive contribution to business operation for competitive advantage. The potential for contribution to business success from decision support can be illustrated clearly by reference to Figure 7.2 where the largest gap between current coverage and needs can be seen to lie at the decision support level.

Definition of decision support systems

OBJECTIVE Improvement of the speed and quality of senior and middle management decision making, through provision of better information, up to date, at the right time, in the right format.

APPROACH Provision of more interactive, more flexible planning and analysis facilities, which provide access to:

- up-to-date, integrated operational databases;
- external information sources;
- the results of previous actions by the user.

CHARACTERISTICS Ad hoc, rapid interaction; ability to formulate new requests 'on the fly' in response to results of previous query. Ability to handle less 'structured' problems.

Sub-classification of DSS request type

(1) *MIS.* Relatively predefined, at least in general form and scope, but with high variability in selection and summarisation needs.
(2) *Operational DSS.* Essentially predefined in nature, but of many possible classes.
(3) *Intelligence.* Heavily text oriented, with extended 'speculative' analysis and search. Dealing with a degree of uncertainty and probability. Likelihood of associated strings of queries, during an extended session.
(4) *Numerical analysis.* May range from simple spreadsheet, through complex modelling, to OR/LP type needs.
(5) *Unstructured.* Composed of any combination of the above, but with a significant degree of uncertainty, and the need to cope with the ability to relate to human/judgemental approaches.

Cost/performance of IT

The underlying trend in computer hardware cost/performance is steadily and relentlessly *down*, by around 30% compound per annum. This is so unusual that it has raised many suspicions, but it has been checked very carefully, and found to be accurate, and reliable. This is the explanation for the personal computer explosion.

The consequences are far reaching. The most obvious is that replacement of people roles with computer processing in the systems development process itself offers enormous payoffs.

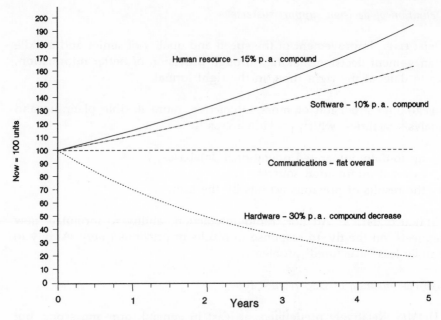

Figure 7.3   Basic IT cost trends (cost per unit of capacity)

Figures 7.3 and 7.4 compare the cost per unit trends of the primary IT costs drivers, and derive the implications for the typical IS/IT budget as a trend over time.

Reliability and security

New approaches to building hardware and new operating system techniques are meaning that the concept of 'fault tolerant' or 'non-stop' computer systems has already become a reality, at little or no extra cost. In these systems, extensive redundancy is coupled with monitoring techniques, so that no single point of failure can stop a computer system. In this way, mean time between failures for whole computer configurations can rise to several years.

Closely related techniques are making computer systems much more secure, in the sense of resistance to unauthorised penetration, and/or loss or corruption of data or messages. That is not to say that security is guaranteed; all security systems can be broken, given time, resource and motive. But the newer generations of systems are orders of magnitude more secure than manual files—which are after all the only alternative.

It used to be thought that such reliability and security levels would

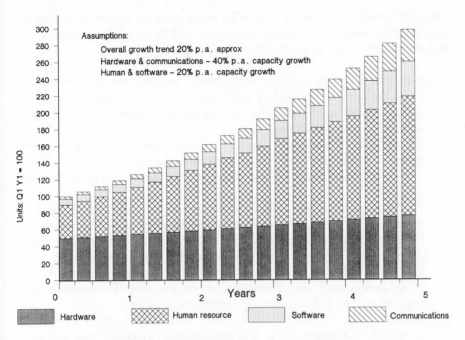

Figure 7.4 IT budgets growth and make-up

be very expensive. It now appears that this will not be so—the features can be made sufficiently intrinsic that their costs will be marginal.

Implications

The consequences of all these changes taken together are that the products and services of the business are always changing; the economic and competitive climate in which the business operates is always changing, and the cost/benefit of what IT can do for it is ever-changing also.

But the prize for getting it right is true competitive advantage for the business—at least for a while.

So, what can possibly go wrong? . . .

WHAT CAN GO WRONG?

Introduction

As has been shown so far, there are a series of well-defined problems which have limited the effectiveness of IS/IT in supporting business competitiveness. But there are specific developments which offer significant promise that these can be overcome. In this section we summarise and comment on some of the risks to this success.

(1) *Failure to welcome and cope with change.* As the rate of evolution of business approaches and IT opportunities for their support accelerates, so it becomes ever more critical to treat change as an intrinsic feature of the landscape.

(2) *DP diehards.* A particular facet of change resistance is the inability often of traditional DP shops within organisations to cope with changing needs and deliver truly flexible and accurately targeted solutions.

(3) *The cart can drive the horse.* Development can often be allowed to focus on 'IT strategy', rather than getting to grips with the underlying business thrust and environment. IT strategy is a misleading term, even by the jargon-ridden standards of the information industry. Successful information systems must be built on a sound foundation of understanding and prioritisation of business information and support needs and supporting strategies.

(4) *Loss of nerve by senior management.* This can happen at critical moments. Attention spans and management horizons can get very short when times are hard. Surviving this month is strategic too!

(5) *'Me too' mimicry of competitor activities.* This can lead to replication of competitors' mistakes—a common pattern in London-based securities houses in the run-up to Big Bang.

(6) *The pendulum can go too far.* Excessive and misdirected investment in IT can occur, usually followed by grief, burned fingers, retrenchment and senior management disillusion. Strangely enough, spectacular success in early, simple developments can actually increase this risk.

(7) *Competitive complacency.* Another risk which is exacerbated by success. Don't forget that the competition is smarting after your last success, and will try even harder.

(8) *Missing the market need.* This can also be achieved by pricing yourself out of it. Quality is having the right product on the market at the right time at the right price, and offering the right support service, and developing the product along with the market.

(9) *Failure to achieve critical mass.* Some market sectors offer no such thing as a minority market share, e.g. the world's best telephone system will not get used if it has a minority market share.

(10) *Lack of vision on the part of IT specialists.* The IT specialists can be remarkably reactionary. The impression that IT drives the business, while palpable nonsense, is remarkably prevalent within IS/IT

departments. They must be shaken out of this viewpoint, and a genuine two-way communication concerning strategic business priorities and needs, and the best way of serving them with IS/IT, must be substituted.

WHAT HAVE WE GOT TO GET RIGHT TO GAIN THE BENEFITS?

Overview

An approach to planning for information systems is needed which will enable the information systems department to get involved with business planning and position itself so as to continue to meet, or facilitate the meeting of, the primary business needs.

Some of the critical factors governing success are as follows:

(1) Management commitment and sponsorship.
(2) Proper linking of the business plans and the information systems strategy. Tuning-up information systems for competitive advantage imposes stress on the business planning disciplines and cycle—fuzziness won't do.

   The business and product planning cycle and the IS/IT planning cycle must be coupled together. Typically, a new business venture will require specific IT support, and a decision concerning it will depend heavily upon such questions as:

   'How quickly can we support this? What will it cost to build, run, change? Can we handle rapid growth in business? Can we remain economic in support costs if business grows slowly or peaks out?'
(3) Exploitation of 'technology push' inputs. The IT specialists may have suggestions to contribute as to how IS/IT support can be more proactive, or offer unforeseen product features. They should be sufficiently closely in touch with business strategy to be able to offer significant insights as to how IS/IT can contribute.
(4) Controlling the level of detail and resources spent on planning. A little bit of planning goes a long way. It's like garlic in cooking—the right amount is almost undetectable, except for its effect on the whole. Because planning is quite a pleasant occupation, it is seductive to over-indulge when you should be getting out and running the business instead.
(5) Ability to manage the impact of change on the organisation. Any plan needs to allow for organisational inertia. Don't expect miracles all at once if yours is a non-planned culture—changing company

culture can take several cycles. Go for key achievable improvements each cycle.

(6) A sound basis for the business cases for the investment in information systems is essential, and not always easy to deliver. We showed earlier that the more creative types 3 and 4 contributions do not lend themselves to traditional justification. Remember that IS/IT projects have to compete with funding for all the other capital spending projects. They have to be evaluated on a risk/reward basis along with all of the others.

(7) A sufficiently sound and complete basis of operational systems is needed to serve as a platform on which to build MIS, decision support.

(8) Up-to-date methods are necessary for efficient application systems development. This is especially true of opportunities for 'short cut' or rapid development, which is increasingly relevant to certain classes of need, and critical to effective exploitation of appropriate rapid development tools.

(9) Effective planning and prediction of the needs for manpower skills/resources and IT facilities.

A limited selection of these critical factors is discussed in the remainder of this section.

The Need for Management Commitment and Sponsorship

Business needs must be specified by businessmen; so must be business solutions to business problems. Management should specify its own information needs and priorities (although we can offer techniques to help to refine them). Business negotation over business priorities is best conducted by the business line managers. It follows that they should develop the business cases for the IS developments that follow, negotiate across functional divisions for funding and other resource, and provide the overall project managership where possible. This approach helps to get the IS division out of the firing line for business case development and prioritisation. It avoids many of the problems that have arisen in the past, where the DP department, having devised solutions to apparent problems, then attempts to sell them to unreceptive users.

Links to the Business Planning Cycle

To be effective, the information systems plan must be linked directly to the business planning cycle. This link is two way, in that significant changes in business direction or priority must be reflected quickly, but also, existing DSS may provide valuable planning assistance for future business cycles.

In a growing number of cases, what is done in business terms may be constrained by what is possible in information systems terms. In the extreme, we may see 'technology push' from IS—e.g. electronic funds transfer—directly influencing the choice of new product or new market directions. Figure 7.5 illustrates the different types of planning cycle, and how they interlock.

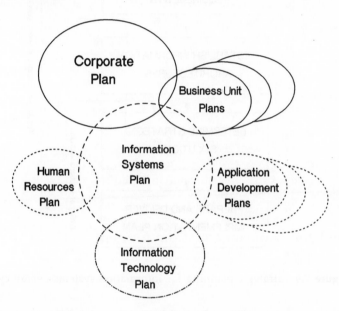

Figure 7.5   Interdependent planning cycles

An Effective Planning Method

Overview of the method

The Information Systems (IS) plan must be practical and feasible. It must cover the evolutionary process of moving from current status to the desired goals, and it must show attractive business benefits in doing so. Increasingly, the feasibility and costs of IS development will depend on specific technical developments. Therefore, the IS plan must be supported by a fully worked out technology plan.

Planning is not a once-off process—the plan is there to serve as a basis for future actions and plans. Therefore, it must be laid down how the

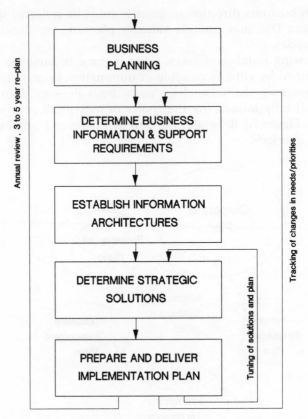

Figure 7.6 Strategic planning for information systems overall cycle

plan is to be maintained, and how this maintenance is to mesh with the business planning cycle. An effective planning method is outlined in Figure 7.6.

Objectives of the method

The planning method set out here is intended to produce an information systems plan which reflects the business information needs, operational support needs and priorities, and which forms a basis for subsequent evolution.

In particular, it will:

- align and focus information systems and IT strategies of the organisation so as to best support and reinforce the business mission and goals;

- link the business, systems and IT planning cycles so as to ensure continuing focus on strategic priorities;
- secure and retain senior management commitment to the planning process, and to sponsoring the implementation;
- identify and exploit opportunities offered by information technology (IT) to help the organisation gain and hold a competitive edge.

Scope of the method

The approach starts with the business planning process, and makes clear the logical links with and dependencies on corporate and divisional business plans. It covers all aspects of business information, service and support needs. It sets applications development priorities, and develops the technical skills and organisational strategies needed to support the information systems development and operation. All classes of application are covered, including office automation and voice and data communications.

It follows through into the development of a complete, practical, business-oriented information systems plan encompassing a definition of what must be done, along with estimates of costs, timescale, organisation needs and skill/resource requirements.

Key products from the method

The planning method delivers the following:

- A consolidated and agreed statement of business information and support needs and priorities.
- An assessment of current information systems and coverage of needs achieved.
- An assessment of current IT and applications status, including their match to business requirements.
- Definitions of target applications and database architecture.
- A definition of the target IT technical architecture required to support the information systems recommended.
- A recommended target organisation IS/IT and skills/resource strategy.
- Urgent actions plan for interim 'quick fixes'.
- Phased development plans for:
  - application systems and databases;
  - IT development projects;
  - staff skills upgrade.
- A phased migration plan for an orderly transition from the current status to the target.

- A linked set of business cases for the transition.
- Criteria for re-evaluation of the plan.

Key features of the method

The approach is pragmatic. It recognises that there is great variation in the level of detail and formality normally found in corporate plans. It is oriented to delivering a practical, approximate plan within a reasonably short timescale. It tempers formality with business expediency, in that it is recognised that there is a level of planning, varying by industry and management style, beyond which it is not worth while to proceed.

Because of the concentration on priorities and critical success factors, it is possible to conduct the study within a limited timescale, and also to select an appropriate tradeoff between precision/detail and business expediency/urgency, according to prevailing need.

The planning process advocated is:

- Business/priority driven—'tuned in'.
- Top/down, focused—'rifle bullet' approach.
- Open architecture
  - flexible, continuing to evolve;
  - framework is distinct from techniques.
- Estimatable, controllable.
- One in which process and results are understandable, verifiable.
- One in which process is proven.
- Complete—delivers implementable plans.
- Efficient in elapsed and management time.
- Iterative.
- One in which key analytic tasks are amenable to automation.

Techniques used

The method recognises and takes practical account of contemporary trends in business and information strategy planning (for example the work of Alloway and Quillard (1981), and of Bullen and Rockart (1981) at the Sloan School of Management). It positively encourages the active use of up-to-date approaches to information systems development, typified by the terms 'end-user computing', 'fourth generation language' and 'rapid development'.

It is 'open' with regard to extension/enhancement of the techniques embodied, and specifically avoids taking a doctrinaire stance over details of the methodology to be followed.

Timescale and resource needs. The approach is economical in its use of management resources, and can lead to a reasonably short development timescale, because of the 'rifle bullet' approach to business priorities. The planners are strongly encouraged to keep their eye on the strategic priorities, and to defer attention to detail which is not material at the strategic level to its proper place during detailed analysis and design.

Provenness. It has been used successfully in major corporations over a period of five years. It continues to be used, and in consequence is continuing to develop.

Visibility and reproducibility. The results of the planning cycle are documented in the form of a working model, in which the logical derivations of the planning outputs based on stated business needs and priorities are clear. This facilitates communication with the senior management control group during the study, helping to foster and maintain confidence. It also permits subsequent review in the light of changed business plans or priorities, enabling it to be determined whether the plan needs to be revised on an exception basis.

Summary of phases and products

There are four main phases:

(1) *Determination of business information needs.* What does the business really need, now and in the future?
(2) *Developing information architectures.* The framework for flexible, long-lasting systems:
    (a) databases;
    (b) applications;
    (c) technology base.
(3) *Determine strategic solutions.* Match what there is today with what is needed. Establish key priorities and analyse dependencies. Derive optimal groupings and delivery sequences.
(4) *Assemble and deliver the plan.* Fine tuning, matching with business cases, presentation of the resulting plans.

The above phases are now examined in somewhat more detail.

Determination of Business Information Needs

The approach must be business driven. From the top–down, senior management must be really committed, and get 'hands-on' in the decision making. Formulation and assessment of business strategy are essential prerequisites for accurate definition of business information and support needs. This in turn drives the formulation of information and systems strategy, and governs the priorities applied in their implementation. Information systems strategy is subordinate to all of these.

It is essential to recognise change as a fundamental requirement, not a nuisance to be suppressed. Plan for change, as it may be your most important single requirement. Can you really forecast your industry, and hence product and services and hence systems needs for five years? If you can't, what are you going to do instead? One approach to this is 'scenario planning'.

Scenario planning

OBJECTIVES   The objectives of scenario planning are:

- To force consideration of a realistic range of contingencies.
- To identify positioning/strategies which ensure survival under all contingencies.
- To avoid being super-optimised but unstable.

APPROACH   The approach to scenario planning is along the following lines:

- Generate contingencies in 'brainstorming' mode.
- Develop scenario(s) for each contingency.
- Explore on a 'what if' basis for:
  – business threats/opportunities;
  – appropriate strategies for avoidance, exploitation or survival.
- Prune and select strategies on the basis of probabilities—risk assessment.

USEFULNESS OF GENERATED SCENARIOS   The scenarios generated can:

- Reveal or help articulate strategically significant uncertainties.
- Flush out critical success factors or potential causes of failure.
- Provide different interpretations of the present (not just medium/high/low projections of a single model).

The analysis of business plans. Analysis of the business plan, and the derivation from it of a set of integrated, prioritised information needs can track the business planning process itself closely. Thus the analysis and interview process is based on the assumption that there exists in some form the following thought process:

(1) Determination of overall strategic business objectives, in terms of markets, products, operations and support needs.
(2) Development from these of a set of specific, quantified goals.
(3) For each function which must be performed, the development of a related set of sub-goals.
(4) Propagation of this thinking down through as many levels of the function as are appropriate.
(5) At each level, the identification of those factors which are critical to success or failure, using critical success factor (CSF) concepts.
(6) For each of these, the determination of specific information which is needed to monitor the critical factors, and also any information relating either directly to the performance of the function, or to monitoring of performance against agreed goals.

The resulting business information needs are assigned priorities, based upon the underlying priority of the function served.

Implications for systems. The final stage of analysis of business needs, termed *information needs analysis*, concerns the inference of the characteristics of information systems and stored database contents needed to support and deliver the stated information needs. In brief, it is assumed that each *information need* is supplied by some form of *delivery process* (not necessarily automated or automatable), and that such delivery processes need to be fed by hierarchies of *feeder processes*. All such processes need to access information about *data categories* or *entities*, which ultimately comes from some *data source*, be it operations of the business, external sources, or the minds of management, through some forms of decision-making process.

The approach is self-checking, in that the resulting set of information processes and stored data needs can be cross-checked against stated operational needs for support systems and also against the 'textbook' view of what is needed to run an organisation of this type, in this industry.

Developing Information Architectures

Information architectures provide the base framework for flexible, long-lasting systems. The important classes are:

- functional structure of the business;
- data architecture—for guiding the logical structure of the core databases;

BUSINESS FUNCTIONAL AREA

INFORMATION LEVEL	MARKETING	PRODUCT DEV'T	BUYING	DISTRIB-UTION	SALES	PROPERTY	FINANCIAL CONTROL	ADMIN SERVICES etc . . .
STRATEGIC								
PLANNING & ANALYSIS								
MONITORING & CONTROL								
TRANSACTION								
OPERATIONAL SUPPORT								

Figure 7.7 Application systems map—overall structure

- application systems architecture, being the overall idealised portfolio of application systems which you would *like* to have to run the business. An outline structure for an application architecture is shown in Figure 7.7;
- the technical architectures on which the systems and databases should run.

Data architecture is of especial relevance to strategic planning, because it has been found that the inherent data structures of a business are often the most stable things about it. Get those right, and base information systems on them, and those systems will survive for a very long time. You need to change the business a lot to lose the concept of 'customer' or 'product', for example.

Functions are somewhat less stable, especially in detail—e.g. new products may have quite different processing rules to the old. Functions need to be distinguished carefully from organisation units, which are far more driven by the needs of the moment, the personalities and egos involved and the skills mix available. Organisation units can change on a whim, but the underlying functions are mostly only re-grouped.

Determine Strategic Solutions

This aspect falls into two divisions:

(1) Assessing the match of what you have already with what you really need. This match may turn out to be surprisingly poor if you are honest. Figure 7.8 illustrates the overall matching process.
(2) Deciding what to do about the results of that assessment. This is concerned with identifying the ideal business delivery sequence for new or revised systems, and then examining how close it is possible to get to this sequence in practice.

Circumstances will always drive you away from the apparently optimal delivery sequence and rate for the business. Where you are starting from can be the greatest handicap in achieving the desired target. This is made respectable and called 'migration planning'.

The art is to identify the minimum necessary departures from the ideal plan for reasons of:

- application and data dependencies/sequencing constraints;
- technical dependencies;
- technology gaps/risk management;
- getting value for money from current investment;
- having a good business case for each step;
- containment of skills/resource/culture shock.

It is important to give careful thought to the real meaning of quality for each system. It is vital to get the right tradeoff between:

- development speed;
- accuracy and completeness of meeting businesses' need;
- stability/operability/integrity;
- changeability.

Investment should be focused on key payoff areas. Develop the bland 'hygiene' systems using utility packages, with minimum hassle. Reserve the key effort and focus for 'mission critical' (awful term) key competitive systems. Build these specifically and very carefully.

There is a jargon term which is much used in this context: 'mission-critical' systems. This is only jargon for systems on which the business depends. If the business really doesn't need a system, save money and don't build it, or switch it off! The real issue is the degree of criticality of the system—how long can the business continue if the system is

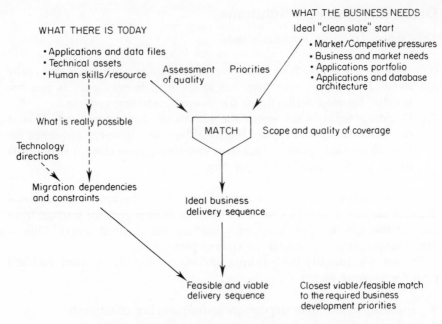

Figure 7.8   What there is versus what we need

disabled? Will the business be breaking the law if it runs without the system? Will the business done without the system be profitable and safe—e.g. aircraft loading, trading in financial instruments? Maybe it is better to stop trading until the system is fixed.

Look especially for short-term tactical ways to improve matters also. There is nothing in the rules that says strategic is only long term. It will often turn out to be possible to initiate early action on certain key areas. This is a very good thing to do. There is nothing so good for credibility as a strategic planning project which pays for itself during its own timescale.

Much more can be done using rapid development techniques than you ever thought. There are always things you can and should do straight away, with calculated risks. Figure 7.9 illustrates a useful approach to rapid development and change of suitable systems.

Assemble and Deliver the Plan

This stage involves integration and fine tuning of the plans for applications, databases, technical architectures and human resources/ skills upgrade. The business cases need to be assembled, with a clear indication of how the costs will be offset by the benefits.

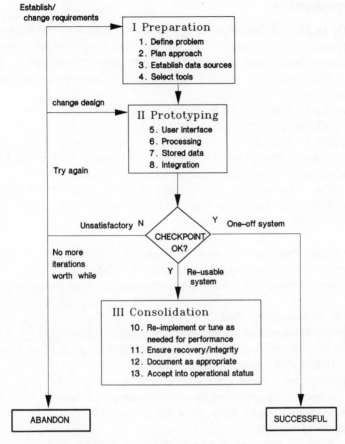

Figure 7.9 The rapid development cycle

HOW ARE THINGS LIKELY TO CHANGE IN THE FUTURE?

Business and Competitive Climate

There appears little hope that the competitive climate will become easier. The worst case assumption must be that there will be constant pressure on established markets and margins in them. This will place a premium on continuing to search for new markets and product/service opportunities, as well as the need to be able to exploit them rapidly.

This in turn places pressure on the ability of IS/IT to deliver effective, efficient support to new or changed products and services, as well as to assist management in the analysis of market and competitive position, in order to find the new opportunities before the competition.

IT Opportunities

Generally in IT and information systems development, the lead times to bring products of promise to market are far longer than hoped. This phenomenon has given rise to the jargon term 'vapourware' (usually spelt the American way, as the United States is the primary world source of products of this class).

In practice, it can take 10 to 20 years for a key innovation to come to market, and the dropout rate is very high.

The point of this sorry tale is that there will be nothing available, proven in the marketplace, for the next five years which we have not seen already announced and described in the press.

Some relevant examples, taken from developments which have been publicised heavily for some time, but which are only now becoming significant include the following:

- *Relational database management systems (DBMS).* First theoretical papers: 1970; experimental systems 1978–82; first usable but slow commercial products 1984; high performance, high integrity products 1988.

  Will be a success after 20 years.
- *Expert systems and object-oriented programming systems.* Developments of the late 1970s; much hyped, but little penetration of real products; have influenced mainstream products.

  Fate still undefined after 10+ years.
- *The lag of operating systems for personal computers behind the technology.* (The examples refer only to a single, widely used family in the interests of brevity.)

  1981: IBM PC released, using 1978 technology chip—8088.

  1984: first PCs based on more advanced chip, 80286, of 1981 vintage; operating system (PC DOS/MSDOS) still oriented to 8088 technology.

  1987 (April): operating system at last announced (OS/2) which will utilise features of 80286 chip.

  1987: first shipments of PCs based on more advanced 80386 chip (announced 1985). These are still crippled by having to run operation systems built for 10-year-old 8088 chips.

  1988 (end): First complete form of OS/2 shipped, now able to exploit seven-year-old chip technology.

  1989: Promises (no dates) of OS/386 able to exploit 1985 technology 80386 chips.
- *Automation of application development methods.* Because of cost pressures, this area has received most attention and publicity. Correspondingly, it exhibits the largest proportion of false claims and disappointments.

It has been recognised for many years that large projects are difficult to manage, and that computers are more efficient than people in carrying out exhaustive cross-checking when building and making changes to complex systems. It has also been recognised that 'seamless' end-to-end coverage of the systems development life cycle is necessary, and that complex designs are best managed in diagrammatic form. However, it has taken 18 years so far to develop from the earliest commercially available data dictionaries such as LEXICON, to computer assisted software engineering (CASE) tools, which today are still probably three to five years from being able to manage large shared design databases properly, complete, fully compatible with DBMS, and suited for most applications.

IT rates of change of cost/performance

The underlying rates of development of cost/performance of raw IT power are more satisfactory. The trend of 30% p.a. indicated in Figure 7.3 has been verified over more than 20 years and several major changes of technology. It still holds good today, which means that over the two years which it takes hardware advances to get into small computers, and the five years which it takes for large computers, this rate will hold good in general.

Discontinuities

This section may appear to the reader as complacent—we have said that there are no IS/IT surprises in store. Of course, by definition, we cannot predict surprises. All we can say is that there *will* be some, and that they will offer competitive advantage in surprising ways. Also, many organisations will burn their fingers trying to exploit unproven developments in inappropriate ways.

Some examples from the past may suffice to indicate the range of possibilities.

Personal computers

In the early 1950s, industry experts assessed the total world demand for computers at *less than 20 in all*! First large, then medium corporations found that the benefits of running a computer justified it—and the world demand ran to many hundreds of thousands.

Personal computers started as toys of hobbyists in the late 1970s—as exemplified by the names of the early market leaders Apple and Pet. The corporate standard PC of the 1980s was designed by IBM as a games machine for home use!

It now appears that many people work more effectively in front of a screen, using a very cheap local box, rather than tapping the mighty resources of their corporate mainframe computer. This may seem like bad news for the major computer vendors, until the total value is calculated of one PC per desk in a large corporation, plus the networking and support overheads, plus the administrative overheads they cause on the corporate mainframe when they do check in to it.

We have no idea what will be the next 'personal computer' type phenomenon, but it is certain that there will be one.

Screen-based trading

The London Stock Exchange (now known as the International Stock Exchange) designed and built in the mid-1970s a small, simple experimental system, based on viewdata principles, for displaying the market prices of equities in the offices of its members. It was thought that it might become quite popular—most members might take it up, so the system was designed to support up to 200 terminals.

By 1986 at the time of the City of London de-regulation 'Big Bang', there were over 8000 terminals on the system, with an embarrassingly large backlog. It turned out that the very simple principles lent themselves very well to the 'off-floor trading' which was evolving in London, and user demand exploded.

The financial world is still waiting to see what happens to trading patterns and volumes in the longer term after Big Bang and the October 1987 crash, but it is certain that computer screen-based trading is here to stay.

REFERENCES

Alloway, R. M., and Quillard, J. A. (1981) *Top Priorities for the Information Systems Function*. CSIR No. 79, September, Sloan School of Management, MIT, Cambridge, MA.

Bullen, C. V., and Rockart, J. F. (1981) *A Primer on Critical Success Factors*. CSIR No. 69, June, Sloan School of Management, MIT, Cambridge, MA.

Porter, M. E. (1980) *Competitive Strategy*. Free Press, New York.

Porter, M. E. (1985) *Competitive Advantage*. Free Press, New York.

Porter, M. E. (1987) From competitive advantage to corporate strategy. *Harvard Business Review*, May/June.

8

NEW DYNAMICS OF STRATEGIC MANAGEMENT IN THE GLOBAL CONTEXT OF THE 1990s

Gen-Ichi Nakamura
Chairman, SMI 2I Co. Ltd.
Principal, Gen-Ichi Nakamura Associates

THE NEW DYNAMICS

The fundamental trend of global environment in the foreseeable future towards the twenty-first century may be an underlying stream of 'new detente' between the two biggest countries on this planet. A commonly agreed and growing recognition is that a 'new detente' has been brought about by a concurrent decline of Pax Americana as well as Pax Sovietika, particularly since the mid-1980s. It will be logical, in this connection, to expect a number of inexperienced phenomena in the global environment of the 1990s.

Firstly, as far as environmental forces are concerned, a higher priority will be given to economic/technological forces than to ideological/defensive ones. Secondly, on the political economic front, a new tendency will be towards democracy with wider amplitude of pendulum between free trade and protectionism at national/regional/global levels. Thirdly, these new phenomena/tendencies will be perceived specifically in each of several major regions in a more remarkable fashion.

The United States of America

- Shift from Pax Americana to Pax Consortis.
- Measures to overcome economic twin deficits.

International Review of Strategic Management.
Edited by D. E. Hussey. © 1990 John Wiley & Sons Ltd

Figure 8.1 Outlook of the world economy towards the year 2000

GNP of Selected Countries and Regions

	Actuals					Estimates				
	GPN–1980		1980–1986 Growth Rate (%)	GPN–1986		1986–1993 Growth Rate (%)	GPN–1993		1983–2000 Growth Rate (%)	GPN–2000	
	US $ 100 Mil.	Percent of World tot.		US $ 100 Mil.	Percent of World tot.		US $ 100 Mil.	Percent of World tot.		US $ 100 Mil.	Percent of World tot.
USA	27 320	23.0	2.4	42 085	25.2	2.5	50 000	23.8	3.0	61 500	23.2
EC	27 811	23.4	1.4	30 930	18.6	2.0	39 400	18.7	2.5	46 800	17.7
Japan	10 589	8.9	3.7	19 628	11.8	4.0	28 200	13.4	4.0	37 100	14.0
ANICS	1 397	1.2	7.2	2 152	1.3	6.5	3 400	1.6	7.0	5 400	2.1
ASEAN	1 599	1.3	3.1	1 765	1.1	5.5	2 300	1.1	7.0	3 700	1.4
China	1 917	1.6	9.0	3 935	2.4	7.0	6 300	3.0	7.0	10 100	3.8
(Sub total)		(13.0)			(16.6)			(19.1)			(21.3)
USSR	14 216	12.0	2.4	22 059	13.2	2.5	26 200	12.5	2.5	31 200	11.8
Other	33 998	28.6	1.9	44 149	26.5	3.0	54 300	25.8	3.5	69 100	26.1
World total	118 917	100	2.3	166 703	100	2.9	210 100	100	3.4	264 900	100

Sub-total = Sub-total of Western Pacific Basin Countries
Source: Economic Planning Agency of Japan

- More focus on rejuvenation of the US economy with higher dependence on highly advanced technologies as competitive edge.
- A pendulum between free trade and protectionism.
- Pressure on Japan and some rapidly growing countries including ANIEs (the Asian Newly Industrialised Economic states) for higher appreciation of local currencies.

Western Europe

- A pendulum between free trade and protectionism.
- Discussion is underway for a realization of market unification in 1992.
- Trends toward de-regulation and privatization of state-owned enterprises.
- Landslide restructuring of industries leading to more frequent use of merger and acquisition (M&A).

Japan

- Trends toward affluent and post-industrial society.
- Rise of corporate cash-abundant society.
- Reluctance at governmental/industrial levels to restructure her long-cherished political/economic/societal systems in accordance with international interdependence.
- Growing frictions with the rest of the world due to her overpresence in overseas investments as well as her export/import imbalance.
- More focus on highly advanced technologies as competitive edge.
- Increased pressure for higher appreciation of Japanese yen.

Western Pacific Basin Countries Excluding Japan (ANIEs + ASEAN + China)

- A new driving force for world economy development (Figure 8.1).
- Shift from medium-tech to high-tech in ANIEs.
- Shift from low-tech to medium-tech in ASEAN.
- Increased pressure on ANIEs for higher appreciation of local currencies.
- Trends toward democracy.

The USSR/Eastern Europe

- Good-bye to Marx.
- Wider penetration of perestroika.
- Trends towards democracy/economic open door.
- Trends towards growing tie-ups with Western countries.

With all these new phenomena/tendencies coming up in each major region, a global basic stream of corporate environment in the 1990s within the context of strategic management may be represented by two key words of 'Restructuring' and 'Dynamics'. In connection with the former, the decade of 1990s will see a dramatic development of global restructuring at all levels. With regard to the latter, a new wave of global dynamics at all levels will give a massive impact in two different directions to a number of companies irrespective of nationality, industry or size—growing opportunity to well-prepared companies versus increasing threat to ill-prepared counterparts.

In other words, only those companies willing to restructure themselves for a new wave in the corporate environment of the 1990s will be able to capture a new dynamics as strategic opportunity.

The above discussion leads us to the next issue of how to construct/reconstruct strategic management, because the author's definition of strategic management is 'a corporate self-restructuring mechanism for survival/growth in the turbulent environment'. According to his further definition, strategic management is made up of three Ss such as strategy, system and structure.

Firstly, when the author talks about strategy, he talks about corporate self-renewal/self-restructuring as opposed to extrapolative management of daily operations. Secondly, when he talks about system, he talks about corporate system of involving people through participation, interaction and consensus-making including a corporate planning system as opposed to one-man ad hoc management. Thirdly and lastly, when he talks about structure, he talks about organizational capability of people as opposed to the separation between a small number of decision makers (planners) and a majority of implementers (doers).

This chapter, therefore, will deal with the topic of the new dynamics of strategic management in the global context of the 1990s using the above-cited three ingredients of strategic management.

NEW DEVELOPMENTS OF INTERNATIONALIZATION/ HIGH-TECH/DIVERSIFICATION STRATEGIES

The author's understanding is that corporate strategy in terms of corporate self-renewal/self-restructuring has three essential dimensions such as logistics, technology and business. It may be self-explanatory that the vectors of three different strategies to be developed along these three

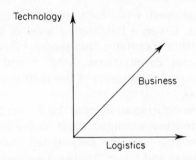

Figure 8.2   Technology, business, logistics

essential dimensions are towards internationalization, high-tech and diversification strategies respectively. Figures 8.2 and 8.3 illustrate this statement.

By way of logic, the above three essential strategies make up the corporate strategy cube as illustrated in Figure 8.4. It may be worth while to note here that these three different strategies can be divided typically into the three segments such as familiar, partially familiar and unfamiliar as illustrated also in Figure 8.4. To look back at the decades of 1960s or 1970s just for the interest of the reader, some distinguished and fully fledged companies at this moment found themselves in a small cube located at the corner as illustrated by a small black box in the corporate strategy cube of Figure 8.4.

Figure 8.5 describes three aggressiveness levels of three essential strategies to be developed along three essential dimensions of the corporate strategy cube. As easily understood, each of three aggressiveness

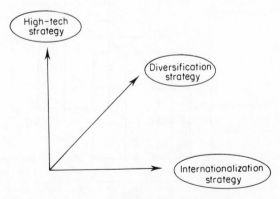

Figure 8.3 High-tech strategy, diversification strategy, internationalization

levels of strategy is aligned with each of three turbulence levels of corporate environment. Given a heightened level of turbulence as well as of dynamics in the 1990s, as briefly discussed previously, an increasing number of multinational corporations (MNCs) will be requested to redevelop their own strategies in terms of the shift from medium to high levels of aggressiveness.

To cite the internationalization strategy of the Toyota Motor Corporation as an example, the company indulged itself at the low level up to the year of 1983. In accordance with the heightened level of trade friction between the United States and Japan, Toyota developed a tie-up strategy with General Motors to establish a joint venture company for the local production of GM cars in an old and inefficient factory at Flaremont, in the state of California. Toyota started to supervise local manufacturing operation at the Flaremont factory by bringing in major parts/components manufactured in its own and subsidiary plants in Japan.

With its first Japanese car position in the US market being replaced by Honda Motor Company in the first half of 1985, Toyota decided to establish an independent manufacturing plant in the United States. The result has been an independent factory located at Georgetown, in the state of Kentucky, which started its manufacturing operation in 1988. It is reported that Toyota will export engines and/or final products produced there to some overseas countries including Japan and Taiwan in accordance with an expected higher appreciation level of local currencies in those countries.

One of the most important points here is that Toyota restructured itself at an incredibly accelerated speed to shift from the low to the high levels

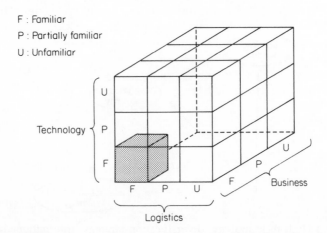

Figure 8.4   Corporate strategy cube after late 1980s

within a short time period of five years. The same or similar can be applied to two other strategies of high-tech and diversification.

To cite a more sophisticated industry as an example of integration between the above three essential strategies, several distinguished manufacturers in an electronics industry have been making full use of the alignments at three different levels of strategic aggressiveness.

A brief explanation about the three related figures will be in order. Figure 8.6 describes a close relationship between the respective development stages of countries/companies and technologies. As easily seen, countries/companies at a high level of development stage have a wide coverage of high-tech with some dependence on medium-tech, whereas the counterparts at low development stage are forced to limit themselves mostly to low-tech with some access to medium-tech. Countries/companies at medium development stage find themselves in between the above two extremes with a wider coverage at medium-tech with some access to both high and low technologies. As shown by Interdependence Zones between L & M and M & H, the reader will see a growing interdependence between Japan, ANIEs, ASEANs and the People's Republic of China. This will facilitate some distinguished Japanese companies in an electronics industry to develop/re-develop a beautiful matrix of development stages between countries/companies in three essential strategies. Figure 8.7 illustrates this matrix. As application of Figure 8.7 to the business reality, Figure 8.8 shows how successfully these distinguished companies have been constructing/reconstructing their total picture of the corporate matrix.

A new dynamics described in the above will increasingly bring about two other new issues of corporate strategy as follows. The first issue is a more deliberate and frequent use of various supporting strategies such as tie-up, alliance, M & A, spin-out and divestment strategies. The reader has already seen significant activities of M & A and divestment taking place in Japan as well as in Western Europe. Specifically, some fully fledged MNCs including Philips have been making full use of these two extreme strategies in restructuring themselves to have a better fit with a novel and more dynamic corporate environment.

The second issue is a new dynamics of business portfolio management in the following points in particular:

(1) To use some product portfolio matrix jargons, with higher commitment to wild cat/problem child quadrant because of higher competition over longer time, business/products requirements for cash in this quadrant will become stronger over the longer term.
(2) With accelerated shift of present business/products from star to cash-cow quadrant, requirements for cash in search of an extended growth stage will become stronger over the longer term.

Figure 8.5 Aggressiveness levels of strategy

Levels / Vectors of strategy	Low	Medium	High
Internationalization	Domestic production/Sales and export	Domestic production/Sales and export + Quasi-overseas production/Sales (KD and/or JV)	Domestic production/Sales and export + Quasi-overseas production/Sales (KD and/or JV) + Overseas production/Sales and exports from the overseas manufacturing sites
High-tech	Modified existing technology strategy	Modified existing technology strategy + New technology development strategy	Modified existing technology strategy + New technology development strategy + High-tech development strategy
Diversification	Market penetration strategy	Market penetration strategy + New product/market development strategy	Market penetration strategy + New product/Market development strategy + Diversification strategy

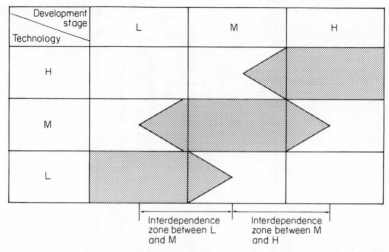

Figure 8.6   Matrix of development stages of countries/companies and technologies

(3) In order to comply with the above two points, much stronger requirements for cash generation in cash-cow quadrants will lead to much stronger requirements for a series of drastic cost reduction supported by continuous and corporate-wide efforts.

NEW DEVELOPMENTS OF CORPORATE PLANNING SYSTEM AND ORGANIZATIONAL CAPABILITY

With a growing importance of alignment between 3Ss in the 1990s, the reader will see new developments of corporate planning systems and organizational capability in terms of shift from medium to high level.

In the arena of the corporate planning system, a growing recognition is that the corporate planning process has two aspects. The first aspect is corporate planning process as information input/processing/output process. In other words, corporate planning process with an emphasis on the contents of corporate response can be identified as strategy formulation process where system is closely related to strategy with strategic planning as an output. The second aspect is corporate planning process as a systematic and organized process of involving people through participation/interaction/consensus making. In this sense, the corporate planning process is a process of generating and sharing new understanding/values leading to the development of organizational capability. Here, the corporate planning process with an emphasis on organizational capability development is closely related to structure. In view of a corporation as an organizational learning entity, corporate planning

Figure 8.7 Matrix of development stages of countries and three essential strategies

Strategy along \ Development stage of countries	I	II	III
Logistics (countries)	Less industrialized industrializing countries	Newly industrializing countries	Industrialized countries
Technology	Low technologies	Medium technologies	High technologies
Business	Old/existing products in existing industries	New products in existing industries	New businesses

	I	II	III
Countries	ASEANs (excluding Singapore and Brunei)	Asian newly industrializing economies (4 Tigers)	Japan, the US and Europe
Technologies	Labor–intensive low technologies in home appliance industry	Capital intensive medium technologies in home appliance industry	High technologies in electronics industry
Business/ Products	Preliminary products in home appliance industry + Parts/Components for countries II	Sophisticated products in home appliance industry + Parts/Components for countries III	Some sophisticated products in home appliance industry + Information equipment in consumer/electronics industry

Figure 8.8 Matrix development stages of countries and three essential strategies (cont'd). Application of matrix (Figure 8.7) to consumer and industrial electronics companies

process is an organizational learning process characterized by proactive logical learning.

The metamorphosed corporate strategy cube discussed in the previous section, together with a growing importance of converging vectors of corporate direction and people's values, will have a massive impact upon the framework and contents of corporate planning hierarchy particularly in terms of planning period/horizon. As an example, an increasing number of Japanese companies have been willing to invest a sizeable amount of time and energy in constructing a long-term vision for the year of 2001 and/or the twenty-first century. Figure 8.9 illustrates one of these new tendencies.

With a closer relation to structure than to strategy, the reader will see a shift of planning view as follows:
- From goal view to process view.
- Planning process as organizational learning process.
- Role of planning as catalyst between strategy development and organizational capability development.
- Towards a new slogan 'implementors (doers) should be planners!'

Thus, if leading companies are successful in shifting their planning views, they will effectively get rid of the following four planning syndromes which had been dominant in typical Western and Japanese companies up to the mid-1980s.

- 'One-man show' syndrome.
- 'Pie in the sky' syndrome.
- 'Paralysis by analysis' syndrome.
- 'The death in the drawer' syndrome.

Figure 8.9   Three flexibility levels of corporate planning system

Level / Range	Low	Medium	High
Long	—	—	Long-term corporate vision construct + Corporate philosophy redefined + Corporate (visual) identity
Medium	Extrapolative medium-range planning	Entrepreneurial/ strategic planning	Entrepreneurial/ strategic planning + Differential planning
Short	Operational planning/control	Operational planning/control + Strategic control	Operational planning/control + Strategic control + Shortened planning cycle

On the organizational capability front, several remarkable developments will be seen as follows.

Firstly, in accordance with heightened level of aggressiveness and flexibility of strategy and system respectively, corporate mentality will have to shift from production/supplier through marketing to strategic/entrepreneurial level.

Secondly, in the area of entrepreneurship, the reader will see more planned continuity of systematic and organized entrepreneurship even through planned discontinuity of presidency as the case of Honda Motor Company typically suggests.

Thirdly, with regard to organizational leadership, 'new leadership' will be identified as an influential power to generate organizational dynamics through the impacts upon bosses/colleagues/subordinates so that this dynamics will generate an accomplishment of strategic direction.

Fourthly, organizational learning will have to shift from the low through the medium to the high level of openness/creativity/innovativeness. Figure 8.10 illustrates these new developments.

189

Figure 8.10 Three openness levels of organizational capability

Mentality	Production/Supplier	Marketing	Strategic/Entrepreneurial
Training/Education Corporate planning Learning through doing	In-company education and training system	In-company eduction and training system + Corporate planning system as a proactive logical learning process	In-company education and training system + Corporate planning system as a proactive logical learning process + Learning through doing as realtime learning process through experience
Slogan	Do not rock the boat	Be where the action is	Success breeds failure
Preferred culture in organizational units	Production/Accounting	Marketing	Research, New venture

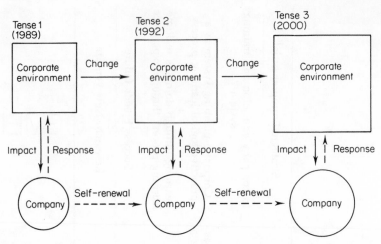

Figure 8.11   Continuous and corporate-wide/self-renewal/self-restructuring

CONCLUDING REMARKS

The new dynamics of strategic management in the global context in the 1990s has been briefly discussed considering four elements of strategic management. To sum up, strategic management in the 1990s will increasingly become a more continuous and corporate-wide willingness to realign the levels of aggressiveness of strategy, flexibility of system and openness of structure at much higher level of turbulence/dynamics of the global environment (Figure 8.11).

9

STRATEGIC INFORMATION MANAGEMENT

Helen Butcher and Michael Mainelli

BDO Binder Hamlyn

INTRODUCTION

Strategic information management is an imprecise phrase. It can mean the management of information systems in order to support a business strategy—management of information strategy. The phrase can imply the need to fully use information in order to secure competitive advantage—strategic management of information. We will use the phrase in the sense of effectively using information to develop, implement and control business strategy—management of strategic information. In doing so, we will touch on aspects of the first two interpretations.

Any interpretation of the phrase must touch on business strategy, planning, information, information technology (IT) and systems. We will refer to three functions which we presume will be present in some form in any organisation that exhibits strategic thinking:

(1) The Information Technology Unit (ITU), responsible for the delivery of information and computing services, including hardware, software and communications.
(2) The Information Services Unit (ISU), responsible for assisting management with the use of information services, including libraries, filing, external database queries, etc.
(3) The Strategic Planning Unit (SPU), responsible for the *process* of strategic plan development, which is a very large user of information services.

International Review of Strategic Management.
Edited by D. E. Hussey. © 1990 John Wiley & Sons Ltd

Each role exists, at least in a rudimentary form, in most organisations which need to react to a changing environment. Although they may be known by other names or overlap in different groups, the functions are necessary. Together, and generally led by the SPU, these three roles are responsible for strategic information management.

Strategic information can be categorised as:

- internal to the organisation;
- external about competitors;
- external about the environment.

The provision of information in any of these three categories involves a nine-step process involved in information provision, described later. The resulting information is delivered to users, typically the SPU or senior management, in order to confirm strategic assumptions, make decisions on strategic direction or measure the success of a chosen strategy and its implementation.

Strategic information, perhaps more than any other kind of organisational information, easily becomes so voluminous that it is difficult to structure effectively. For instance, a waste management firm needs to know which environmental changes are major or where the firm is weak in environmental concern. The waste management firm needs to track all types of environmental legislation, but for strategic planning purposes, only major changes or areas of weakness are important. Identifying major changes requires tracking large volumes of information before it becomes irrelevant to secure competitive advantage. The interpretation of large quantities of information, moreover information which is very sensitive to interpretation, poses special problems for an ISU with other duties of a more operational nature.

The demanding requirements of information for strategic use justify special treatment. The internal provision of information is largely done by the ITU in conjunction with other internal departments, including finance, marketing, etc. Information provided by the ISU largely comes from information sources outside the organisation. The SPU requires both internal and external information in order to manage the process of developing a strategic plan. This chapter intends to demonstrate a practical approach to coordinating the management of this strategic information.

DEFINING STRATEGIC MANAGEMENT

Purpose of Strategic Management

What counts as strategic management is a question of degree—the degree to which management takes a long-term view. The ultimate goal of strategic management is to implement a set of actions which achieve a sustainable long-term competitive advantage. Competitive advantage results from ensuring that the organisation is preferred by potential users, minimises cost and maximises revenue. For many organisations this favourable environment may be at a distant point in the future. For others the environment already exists and long-term planning is required to sustain or improve their position.

Strategic management is particularly important in:

- organisations with complex inter-relationships;
- organisations which must take long-term views on development, purchasing or investment.

Organisations characterised by complex inter-relationships typically have difficulty in focusing upon their goals and objectives in a simple, easily communicable way. Customers can be suppliers; competitors often have common goals; or various divisions may have conflicting relationships with long-term sub-contractors. Examples of complex inter-relationships can be found within organisations such as those in banking, professional services or government. Although other organisations may be characterised as exhibiting complex inter-relationships, they may perhaps be better classified as organisations needing to take a long-term view on purchasing, development and investment. Examples of such organisations include those involved in insurance, utilities, energy, defence and pharmaceuticals. However, strategic management applies to many types of successful organisation which believe in the importance of taking a long-term view of competitiveness.

Strategic management is evident when the organisation as a whole is able to provide answers to three basic questions:

- Where are we now?
- Where do we want to be in X years' time?
- How are we going to get there?

The answers to these questions should be found throughout the organisation at all levels, from an all-encompassing overview at board level to a bare bones summary on the shopfloor but supported with detail on areas of the shopfloor responsibility. Strategic management is a success when the organisation knows how it is achieving sustainable competitive advantage and everyone within the organisation knows the organisation's strengths, weaknesses and objectives—and their individual roles in making it all happen.

Forms of Strategic Management

There are five recognisable forms of strategic management:

- minimal;
- budgetary;
- annual;
- developmental;
- complete.

These five forms are often, though not necessarily, an evolutionary sequence. Companies with *minimal* strategic management often provide this through informal meetings or brainstorming sessions. Minimal strategic management relies upon individuals' ability to pursue long-term goals and visions. The incorporation of rudimentary *budgetary* procedure is frequently more profound than is commonly recognised. A formal budgetary procedure is the first sign that an organisation truly understands where it is now. The introduction of an *annual* plan can often be a major step towards complete strategic management. The annual plan is more than the sum of the budgets. The organisation recognises that subsidiary budget objectives can conflict or that additional resources are needed to achieve a sum greater than the whole of the parts in particular areas. *Developmental* strategic management comes about when the organisation, typically due to outside pressures, finds itself making long-term plans for projects that are designed to enhance its competitive position. One example of developmental strategic management might be a two-year development of a new product line. Development requires an assessment of current position, identification of the long-term positioning and strong project management to turn plans into actions. There is no single correct way to achieve *complete* strategic management in every organisation. However, some of the characteristics of complete strategic management include intensive development of integrated strategies at various levels within the organisation; the ability to take a long-term view appropriate to the organisation, possibly 3 to 10 years; documentation of the strategy; and appropriate communication throughout the organisation. The best evidence of true strategic management is when an outsider immediately feels that the purpose or mission of the organisation is clearly understood in relation to the organisation's current position and the actions it is undertaking.

Strategic Questions

Answering the three basic strategic questions (Where are we now? Where are we going? How do we get there?) raises a host of subsidiary questions such as Who are our major competitors? What are significant new developments in our environment? What major demographic changes will affect us? Where is our greatest potential for cost reduction? What are the weaknesses of our key suppliers? These quetsions exhibit four characteristics which bear upon the provision of information in the strategic management process. Strategic questions often:

- are external, i.e. directed outside the organisation;
- involve classifications which require interpretations and judgement or are difficult to classify, e.g. who are our competitors?;
- are answered with inappropriate or unreliable qualitative information;
- are fluid, i.e. the information will often generate new 'what if' questions related to the original request for information.

As we have seen, there is no totally accepted definition of strategic planning, let alone what constitutes a strategic question. However, a practical definition of a strategic question is one whose answer will provide information about actions to be taken more than one year in the future. This definition is not correct in all cases but will suffice for the purposes of this chapter.

The Basic Steps in Strategic Planning

The purpose of this chapter is to analyse the information needs of strategic planners. However, it is important to identify some basic steps of the strategic planning process and to relate them to the three basic questions identified earlier.

Question	Step
Where are we now?	Establish the need for strategy Define the environment Critically evaluate position
Where do we want to be?	Understand why we are here Determine desired position Define mission and principle
How are we going to get there?	Identify options Determine selection criteria plan Budget and implement

As mentioned earlier, strategic planning takes a variety of forms and uses a variety of methodologies and approaches. The nine steps indicated above are common to information used by most forms. Each step has a requirement for large quantities of information. The provision of timely, accurate, adequate and appropriate information at each step is discussed in succeeding chapters.

Role of Strategic Planning Units

There is no single, correct way to organise strategic planning within an organisation. For some it is a board level responsibility to develop a strategic plan. For others a dedicated planning unit provides a series of inter-linked plans. In between there is an array of approaches with varying degrees of success. In our experience, SPUs are most effective when they:

- have the highest visibility, e.g. report to the chief executive;
- facilitate, but are not responsible for, the production of a strategic plan;
- involve several layers of the organisation in the development of the strategic plans;
- are deliberately kept small and act as a support to those ultimately responsible for plan development;
- manage the incorporation of subsidiary plans and highlight areas of potential conflict or concern;
- ensure that planning drives the initiation of key development projects;
- ensure that planning drives day-to-day operations through procedures and budgets.

In short, we recommend the formation of a strong SPU, but also recommend that it be kept small and tightly focused.

DEFINING INFORMATION MANAGEMENT

Given a small specialist SPU, the question remains of how it should interact with those performing the ISU. Before turning to this, we need to consider in more detail the nature of information management and its place within organisations.

The term information management is used by both the IT and the information profession to describe the various methods of organising information. Originally coined to describe paper-based systems, it now

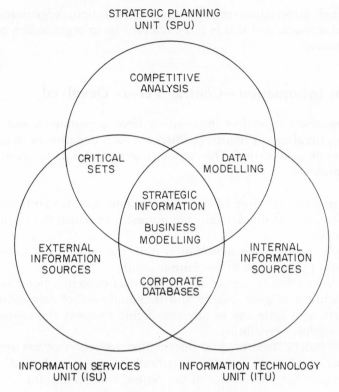

Figure 9.1. Role of strategic planning unit

encompasses computerised systems, reprographics, telecommunications and all other ways of retrieving, organising and storing information.

Organising Internal Information

Most organisations have a lot of internal information. It may take the form of mailing lists, contacts, client information, suppliers' lists and staff records. The IT industry has provided the facilities to organise this information, and most organisations expect that use of such facilities will make retrieval easier. Unfortunately, for some, computerisation of internal information has proved to be the triumph of hope over experience. The existence of IT as an aid to retrieval has been used as an excuse to amass vast quantities of information collected in the belief that it might be useful some day, rather than with organisational goals in mind. The inevitable result is that information which is relevant and useful proves difficult to locate and slow to retrieve. The collection, storage and retrieval of internal information requires careful selection, organisation and continual management if it is to be relevant to an organisation now and in the future.

Internal Information—Central Versus Devolved

Some organisations collect information from departments and store it centrally providing, in return, facilities for each department to access all the corporate information. The central collection of data frequently leads to four problems:

(1) Centralised collection of data may become too standardised and so not respond to the dynamic environment in which the organisation operates.
(2) People wish to take information from the system but are reluctant to pass information to the central point.
(3) This reluctance to service the central data collection point results in the storage of poor quality and frequently out-of-date information which is of little use to anyone. If this happens the central point quickly loses credibility.
(4) Independent departmental information collection points spring up to serve what are seen as specifically departmental needs and to overcome the deficiencies of the central collection point.

If this scenario is allowed to develop, valuable information is lost to the organisation and informal information flows may develop to the detriment of the organisation as a whole. People will only supply information to the centre if there is a clear incentive to do so. This incentive must be as immediate as possible, vague appeals to people to consider the corporate good are likely to go unheeded.

Where central collection is necessary the following guidelines should be considered:

(1) Forms should be as simple as possible, only the minimum amount of necessary information should be collected.
(2) Mechanisms should be found which ensure that data are regularly used, and through use data quality and completeness will be enhanced.
(3) Collection and input of data should be made a simple task so that it can be delegated to junior members of staff.
(4) The usefulness of the collected data should be regularly reviewed to ensure their continuing relevance.

Devolving the collection of data to the departments themselves, is not the complete answer. Though devolution may cut the cost of data collection, as only that information which is relevant and timely will be collected, and though it is likely that the information may be of better quality as departments will have an incentive to keep their own records up to date, these advantages may be considerably outweighed, by the lack of coordinated, comprehensive information available to those involved in the long-term planning of corporate strategy.

The answer lies in a careful mixture of centralised and decentralised approaches to information collection, organisation and storage. Information management will help to establish guidelines for information collection. It will also provide the disciplines to manage the structuring and storage to enable the organisation to achieve its aims.

External Information—Central Versus Devolved

It is common in large organisations to have a central library which frequently evolves into an ISU. Such a unit may perform a useful function but it can become an expensive overhead which does not fulfil the needs of the organisation. Where possible, operating departments should be provided with the means to locate a majority of their own information. In practice this situation will often happen as user discontent with the central ISU increases. Decentralisation of the information function may take the form of the provision of resources for trained researchers within the departments to perform online searches, or it may be more cost and time effective to employ an information specialist in each operating department who becomes an integral part of that department.

Re-defining the ISU's Research Role

This does not mean that the central information department should necessarily be disbanded, merely that its role should be redefined and circumscribed. It may, however, take on new tasks which may include:

- keeping departmental users up to date on new potentially useful databases, and new facilities available on systems already in use;
- teaching new users about information and systems;
- providing backup facilities for research which it is difficult to do within the operating departments;
- planning for external information sources in ITU plans.

Managing Information

The central information service should also take on the role of coordinating and managing the organisation's internal information. While some information must be provided centrally for MIS purposes, there is other potentially useful information within organisations which has been collected or created with the needs of specific departments or jobs in mind. For instance, departments often keep their own lists of contacts or experiences on a database created on proprietary software, or they may keep specialist information on legislation. This departmentally held information might be of use to other departments if its existence was more generally known. It is in these roles that a central information department can prove useful. Such roles may involve:

- organising meetings of members of each department to discuss new information initiatives and to exchange ideas about information products and services, thus preventing duplication across departments;
- ensuring that members of all departments know what information is available, e.g. information directories, and are provided with the manipulation tools and skills to use it;
- creating and maintaining standards for the internally generated information products so there are clear guidelines for the collection, retention, organisation, management and destruction of information;
- identifying commercial opportunities for internally generated information products;
- ensuring that information products and services are correctly budgeted for and that the budget is adhered to;
- ensuring that information resources and products are recognised as a corporate asset and are maintained in the best possible way;
- testing new products such as software for potential use in the organisation and manipulation of information.

Structure of an ISU

Where ISUs exist in organisations they are generally one of two types:

- staffed by professional information specialists;
- staffed by other professionals, for instance, lawyers, accountants or MBAs.

These two groups see the provision of information and their tasks as a whole, in quite different ways. Before an organisation sets up an ISU therefore it should consider the role it wishes its units to perform and appoint accordingly.

Unit Staffed by Information Specialists

Such units frequently evolve out of what was originally a library and many information specialists still regard the provision of library services as an important part of their jobs. Many such information specialists are members of the Institute of Information Scientists and possess skills in online searching and organising information for efficient retrieval as well as general research skills. A unit staffed by information specialists will be likely to provide facts only when an enquiry is made: they will rarely provide comments or opinions on their reports and their manner of working is likely to be reactive rather than proactive.

Unit Staffed by Other Professionals

Such units are generally charged with the task of providing intelligence rather than information. They draw on the skills learnt at university and in their profession to monitor the competitive environment. They are likely to be skilled in the use of IT and have some knowledge of information sources. This group can be expected to provide customised reports tailored for their organisation. These reports will contain opinion and comment. As a whole, the group will be more proactive than reactive.

Each of the above groups will approach the task of collecting, storing and distributing internal information differently. Intelligence units and indeed some ISUs send unsolicited information to users, i.e. they take a proactive approach to information provision. The recipients of these data frequently question their usefulness. It is often 'worthy' information such as industry statistics, details of raw materials and government legislation. Unfortunately, many managers do not need this kind of information and may come to believe that they cannot get the information that they really require from the information unit. In turn, ISUs labour under the misapprehension that managers *should* be reading this kind of information and that they will ultimately appreciate the value of it. The ISU often fails to understand that most senior members of organisations suffer from information overload. The ISU must understand that information is largely only recognised as valuable when it is required for a *particular* rather than a *general* purpose and can be used in a particular context to answer a specific problem. A unit charged with the job of monitoring the market or environment, or even of merely collecting information may be an expensive overhead, providing little value to the organisation.

202

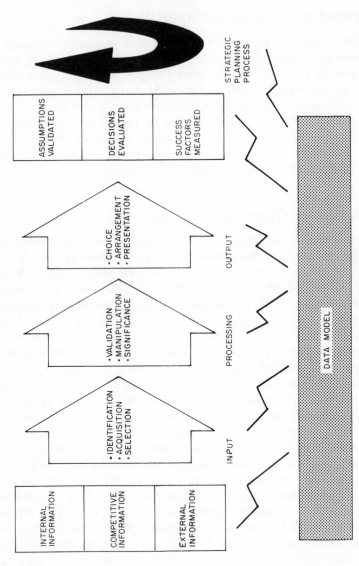

Figure 9.2. Strategic information provision

Information is only of use when it has a context, a problem which it can be used to solve. Those who are closest to the problem are those who know precisely what kind of information will be the most helpful and relevant in their search for an answer to the problem. It is therefore probably ideal to dispense with the notion of a central ISU supplying information to everyone, and for each operating or planning department to have access to its own information sources to enable it to perform a majority of its own research using the central information service as backup. The ISU should support other departments in finding their own information. It may be best for an SPU to employ its own full-time researcher who is a recognised part of the SPU team and is involved in all its work while still having available ISU specialists.

UNDERSTANDING STRATEGIC INFORMATION PROVISION

We now move from considering the organisation of the personnel involved in information provision to an analysis of the tasks they perform.

Overview of Information Provision

The practical availability of information varies considerably. A classification into five categories is useful:

- available, widely or already known;
- available but requires confirmation;
- available but requires processing;
- possibly available but requires examination;
- not practically available.

For the purposes of this chapter we will focus on the third category—available but requires processing—because this category exhibits all the tasks included in information provision. An overview of information provision can be described as a three-function model. Posing a question should result in actions by the ISU of covering:

- input;
- processing;
- output.

As mentioned in the introduction, further analysis results in nine basic steps which are relevant to most strategic questions. We now give a description of each of the nine steps from the point of view of the researcher.

Input

(1) *Identification of sources*. Asking a question or requesting information should generate an idea of possible sources, or sources of courses. A well-planned project to furnish information would endeavour to identify all possible sources at this stage.
(2) *Acquisition*. This activity involves assembling and collating information from the sources identified and selected in the previous step. This could include database retrieval, magazine searches, or market surveys.
(3) *Selection*. Acquisition can result in excessive amounts of information which may require selection or summarisation prior to processing.

Processing

(4) *Validation*. Cross-validation of items compiled from different sources is useful in ascertaining the reliability of information provided. Further selection on the basis of perceived reliability is used to determine which items of information can proceed to the next step.
(5) *Manipulation*. Information may need basic processing, e.g. statistical evaluation such as regression analysis, mean calculations, range, distribution, or sensitivity analysis.
(6) *Significance*. It is important to ensure that the information, having undergone processing, remains reasonable, reflects the situation and still remains germane to the original request for information. In addition, the researcher needs to highlight interesting discrepancies or unusual information.

Output

(7) *Choice*. A selection of the information which will be finally submitted is now made. It is important to ensure that assumptions on choice do not simply reflect preconceived ideas.
(8) *Arrangement*. The researcher now classifies the different items of information and determines the way in which they are intended to be logically presented.
(9) *Presentation*. Physical presentation of the information is determined, e.g. tables, media, graphics, etc.

INFORMATION PROVISION IN ACTUAL USE

Classifying a question as strategic or operational depends to a great degree on the use to be made of the results. If we again pose the question of who are our customers, the answer might be a list of customers with some indication of size. This answer can be used in several ways, varying from a mailshot to an attempt to correlate size with expenditure for credit control. The more strategic the use, the more the answer may need to be enhanced with additional attributes, e.g. date of becoming a customer, spending profiles, etc., and the more additional work will be required to interpret the question, e.g. what type of customer will we have over the next five years.

An example of the provision of strategic information should serve to illustrate the difference between strategic questions and operational questions. There is a continuum of degree which is affected by the form of strategic management, i.e. from minimal to complete. Our example will indicate the latitude in one basic strategic question of most SPUs—who are our customers?

Input

(1) *Identification of sources.* The ISU has a wide degree of latitude in choosing which information sources to treat as potentially relevant. An organisation in the minimal stage of strategic management would be satisfied with a list of last year's customers but the answer to the question 'who are our customers?' in other stages may include suppliers who could become customers, new entrants to the customer market, or competitors who may take partial services. Internal systems in marketing or distribution or finance should have relatively complete lists. Trade associations may provide shared information on common customers. Market surveys or government reviews can contain lists of potential customers as well as some indicative categorisations which may be suitable to the organisation.

(2) *Acquisition.* Each possible source can be tracked down and costed. After some small pre-selection with the interrogator, the information is assembled, if possible in electronic form in cases where it exists in large amounts. An organisation in a minimal stage of strategic management would use the more easily available internal sources. Organisations at other stages would broaden the search if comparative information would be used.

(3) *Selection.* The acquired information may be excessively voluminous. Customer information could include operational items such as bank account code. Customer information could also include items such

as credit references which may be useful but are difficult to interpret. Having seen what is available, the interrogator must decide on the degree of controllable detail.

Processing

(4) *Validation.* Customer information could include information on income or turnover. Validation of this kind of information may include statistical techniques ranging from sample testing of alternatives and direct selection to statistical comparisons of distribution, or more basic verification such as directly contacting the customers.

(5) *Manipulation.* The ISU can enhance the customer information by developing categorisations through means of histograms, by testing key variables in regression analyses or by cross-referencing customers by their industrial codes to see performance against industrial averages.

(6) *Significance.* The final step in processing is to ensure that the information has significance for the user. A list of 10 000 customers is unlikely to be helpful while a summary of all but the top 100 may be. The Information Service Unit can help the interrogator by suggesting, among other actions, the calculation of a ratio of customer expenditure to turnover.

Output

(7) *Choice.* Having developed the question about customers thus far, the significant information may still be voluminous or confusing.

Some areas may be incomplete or based on unreliable sources upon which it is considered inappropriate to rely. An important function of the ISU is to act as devil's advocate for the interrogator, ensuring that key questions are asked, e.g. does a prestigious but very small account qualify as significant on all lists.

(8) *Arrangement.* The ISU can help to ensure that statistical information is properly presented with minimal bias or that various areas are consistent and to similar standards of quality, e.g. customers are categorised by true presence in a market rather than total turnover across all operations.

(9) *Presentation.* An ISU, with its experience of information handling, can provide invaluable, time-saving assistance to infrequent users of information handling or presentation tools.

The above example helps to show the importance of an ISU in the collection of the vast bulk of strategic information. Strategic information poses unique problems to an ISU which has become accustomed to dealing with requests from operational departments. In addition to the long timescale associated with its use, strategic information is characterised by the following:

- *Leverage*: a little goes a long way—significant items must emerge from a large amount of background information and not be submerged in detail.
- *Ongoing requirements*: strategic information demands are continuous and increasing levels of detail are revealed.
- *Heavy and complex demands*: the above example illustrates one path through a question, 'who are our customers?' while several are possible. Interrelationships among the data are strong, requiring cross-referencing and interpretation.

Strategic information benefits from some further categorisation in order to improve our understanding of its role in strategic management. One classification method is to relate the categories of strategic information to its continued use in strategic management. We have found that the work of Henderson, Rockart and Sifonis (1984), on critical sets and the linkage between strategic business plans and information, influences our strategic development practices. Their basic categories of

- assumptions,
- decisions, and
- critical success factors.

form a critical set of items for management's strategic framework. The links of each of these with information, provide a structure for analysing strategic information provision. In this process, each item of information is categorised as being associated with assumptions to be verified, decisions to be evaluated and success factors to be measured. The strong links between the three categories become clearer when formal cross-tabulation is done. In this way, the effect of providing more information to the SPU becomes apparent.

For example, we return to the question of who are our customers. One assumption to be verified may be that they are small shopkeepers who prefer personal service over low prices; one decision to be evaluated is how to attempt to increase personal service; and one success factor to be measured is account retention. Associated information for each one involves the customer. Tracking the answer over time might show that, contrary to established opinion in the organisation, corporate growth correlates well with customer growth and so our small shopkeeper assumption should be changed to one involving larger, growing shop-keepers. Larger shopkeepers may be more interested in volume discounts than personal care. Their preference may be for maximising margins rather than personal service. With changing customers and slimmer margins, account retention, the old success factor, may show a higher percentage account loss and so the new strategy should focus on providing new success factors, for example turnover times average margin. The changed situation raises many questions—among them, what is our competition in this changed market? How can we refocus salesmen and distribution staff on margins over service? Should we be growing and changing with our customers or developing newer, smaller shopkeepers as customers who may also leave for larger discounts in the future?

With formal cross-tabulation, those responsible for strategic management are able to use the ISU to track key variables. Each variable relates to a particular portion of the strategic plan and each portion of the plan is clearly identified with an information need. The categorisation of information as aiding assumption verification, decision evaluation or success factor measurement, helps to distinguish the manner in which the information should be handled during the nine steps of information provision. In general:

- *Information for assumptions*: tends to be trend information for stable assumptions, e.g. average customer size, and discrete events for unstable assumptions, e.g. an assumption of new entrants in a market would be contradicted by news of a major acquisition of a competitor.
- *Information for decisions*: on a strategic level, the information tends to be voluminous and oriented to specific new projects or cancellations, e.g. should a new product be launched.
- *Information for success factors*: measurement tends to be exact for internally supplied information, but base statistical information may be all that is available for external information, e.g. a success factor of press coverage could be measured by column inches multiplied by impact factor of publication.

STRATEGIC INFORMATION SYSTEMS

We now turn from our analysis of the task of providing strategic information to a consideration of the systems that may be used to facilitate this task.

The use of automation as a means of acquiring, controlling and delivering information is a much-discussed subject. In actual practice, a few points do need to be drawn out about practicality. The rapidly changing competitive environment of modern business hinders the development of systematic information-handling techniques because information needs change rapidly in line with rapid business changes. Large organisations often view their total IT resources as being in a state of confusion. A simplistic categorisation of the strategic management view of IT is:

- operational IT (distribution, marketing, finance, production, etc.);
- management information systems (MIS);
- decision support systems (DSS);
- executive support systems (ESS);
- external IT (electronic data interchange, databases, etc.).

The distinctions among MIS, DSS and ESS are somewhat unclear, although much literature has been devoted to them. At the risk of oversimplification, MIS provides information necessary to run normal business operations; DSS provides assistance for task-oriented evaluation of 'what if' situations, e.g. where should we site a new development; ESS provides a highly flexible approach to direct senior executive analysis. Henderson *et al.* explain this succinctly, including the difficulty and danger of rigid classification of system types.

To a large degree the ISU has responsibility for external IT and the ITU with internal IT. The SPU's strategic plan would initiate operational IT, including IT for competitive edge. The strategic plan would also indicate the direction needed for the bulk of MIS. The SPU would work with both the ITU and ISU for development of DSS and ESS.

Strikingly, many quite large organisations have rudimentary MIS and no DSS or ESS. The effective use of external information supplied by the ISU is increased by the use of formal systems. For instance, a competitive database which listed internally known account losses to competitors would benefit greatly from comparison with external data sources searched for competitors' announcements. Controlling this external input is simplified by automation.

One reason for the lack of advanced information systems in strategic management is the difficulty in pinning the organisation down long enough to justify expenditure on automating information provision. Rapid change implies the need for flexible information structures. The critical sets of Henderson *et al.* outlined above serve as one such flexible structure by allowing information objectives to change slowly over time. What is also required is a mechanism for communicating the structure throughout the organisation.

Taking the entire IT structure into consideration, one of the most stable items is the data model. The data model, showing the entities associated with the organisation and their inter-relationships, only alters with a fundamental alteration in the business, rather than the manner in which business is conducted. For example, the data model would make clear a relationship between account manager, salesman and customer engineer and show the information which each needs to perform his tasks, e.g. account terms and conditions for the account manager, client lists and locations for the salesman and fault recording for the customer engineer. In addition, the model shows information which could be captured about tasks and about relationships between entities, e.g. engineers working for particular accounts. Completing a data model for an organisation serves to unify the operational, managerial and strategic views of corporate information and provide a mechanism for communicating throughout the organisation the relationship between information and business performance against strategic objectives.

WHAT IS THE IDEAL RELATIONSHIP BETWEEN AN INFORMATION TECHNOLOGY UNIT AND A STRATEGIC PLANNING UNIT?

In practice the ITU will be substantially larger than the SPU. The ITU will be concerned with ensuring the day-to-day functioning of a vital business component, the computer systems. The SPU will develop ideas that require evaluation; evaluation which in turn requires substantial effort on the part of the ITU in preparing information for ad hoc requests. The SPU will also develop ideas for the use of IT to promote efficiency or effectiveness. These ideas must be developed in conjunction with the ITU in order to arrive at some estimate of cost and benefit. The SPU will develop ideas that involve the application of IT in new ways. These innovative approaches to the business require the most flexible assistance.

The SPU plays a key role in promoting IT for competitive advantage. Under some definitions, all IT is for competitive advantage. A more useful definition is that IT for competitive advantage is IT which competitors do not possess or do not employ. The SPU should distinguish between various types of request and the support from ITU which they may require:

• Evaluating IT for competitive advantage: requiring innovative thought and the contribution of the best IT planners.
• Advances in operational IT which may improve the efficiency or effectiveness of the organisation: requiring the support of an IT consultancy capability.

● Ad hoc requests for IT support which may be made by the SPU at several stages in strategic planning: requiring the services of a help desk or end-user applications centre.

The ability of the ITU and ISU to communicate is essential. Communication is enhanced by agreeing the mechanisms in advance. It was brought out earlier that the SPU should promote the use of data models as a means of structuring corporate information requirements. Changes to the business data model can be discussed at an early stage to avoid later possible miscommunication. The data model is an accepted ITU tool. In turn, communication is enhanced if the ITU accepts the application of strategic planning tools to its work.

Planning methods in ITUs are often state of the art due to the long lead times for development, the dependence on large numbers of technological assumptions, and the large capital expenditure on IT. However, plans are frequently made in isolation without regard to the changing business environment. There is also a tendency for there to develop a siege mentality of implementing a plan which may have been superseded by events. This can be overcome by integrating information technology planning with strategic planning so that IT plans directly support the business. Planning for IT should be revised at least as frequently as business plans are revised. IT should be planned to deliver achievable results within the timeframe of business planning. This does not mean that IT planning cannot work to longer timeframes, merely that if the organisation's planning timescale is a few years, it is appropriate that the majority of IT plans should be delivered within that timeframe in order to realise the benefits.

Lastly, the SPU and the ITU must work together on the development of information technology applications such as ESS and DSS. The SPU should include ITU representatives in planning in order to ensure that changes in business direction are reflected in IT planning, operational IT and MIS, and that constraints of technical feasibility are taken into account in the formulation of strategic plans which depend on the implementation of information systems.

So, in summary, the ideal relationship between the ITU and SPU is characterised by:

● clear distinctions between types of information requests made by the SPU;
● coordinated planning using similar methods, e.g. relate IT plans to assumptions about business development;
● cooperative development of the business data model;
● cooperative evaluation of competitive advantage applications.

WHAT IS THE IDEAL RELATIONSHIP BETWEEN AN INFORMATION SERVICE UNIT AND A STRATEGIC PLANNING UNIT?

The ISU and the SPU are often of similar size. The ISU is concerned with corporate information in all its forms. The ISU needs to have responsibility for libraries, researchers, external databases and corporate records. The SPU relies on the ISU to varying degrees. The vast majority of background information for the SPU is provided by the ISU, such as competitor tracking, publication tracking, and large, complex statistical analyses from external databases. As with the ITU, the ISU benefits from being informed of the programme for strategic plan development.

The ISU is subject to a wide variety of requests, but may find that the overall volume of requests permits the development of routine procedures for satisfying a majority of them. In contrast, the typical SPU is a small group with complex, unplannable demands. As mentioned earlier, SPU information needs require large amounts of interpretation. The ISU must develop an iterative approach to most SPU requests, going back to the SPU frequently during the fulfilment of an information request. This iterative approach is a useful discipline for the satisfaction of requests from other departments, although it is unusual to find it in operation.

The ISU, like the SPU, is often non-operational. Frequently the two are grouped together in the same part of the organisation. Despite this, it is important to preserve their distinct roles. The role of the ISU is the provision of professional information management services. The role of the SPU is the analytical use of information in the process of aiding senior management in the formation of a strategic plan. If the ISU comes to dominate, planning in the organisation can become simply the provision of vast quantities of information to strategic planning without qualitative interpretation. If the SPU comes to dominate, the quality of information not directly related to strategic planning can diminish.

The relationship between the two benefits when the SPU:

* is clearly separated from the ISU;
* provides the ISU with information requests planned in advance of their place in the strategic planning process;
* accepts the need for iterative work on certain information requests;
* promotes the use of the ISU for factual information, clearly distinguishing assumptions from the information which supports them.

TRENDS

This chapter has emphasised the importance of promoting cooperation between the ITU, ISU and SPU, in general led by the SPU. What are the dangers of ignoring this approach? At the very least, the isolated development of strategic plans without reference to the ISU or ITU means that background information and internal information used in planning may suffer in quality and affect the quality of the business plan. Nevertheless, today's definitions of the roles in strategic information management are not static. Some basic trends can be discerned:

(1) *Development of the ISU as responsible for quality of all corporate information.* ISUs are proving their value in many organisations. The ability to respond to varying management information demands without the need to establish a permanent management function takes advantage of the centralisation of a few information specialists who have built up an understanding of the corporate data resource.

(2) *Improving external database quality.* External databases are becoming more comprehensive. Databases provided by third parties are becoming more adaptable with more applications and end user tools available on PCs. The benefits of using external information sources have never been easier to realise. What needs to be improved is the training and support that advanced database users require in order to make the most of external databases without incurring excessive cost or excessive effort.

(3) *Pervasiveness of IT.* IT has found its way into ITU planning through automated methodologies and computer aided software engineering (CASE). IT has a strong place in any ISU, particularly one which accesses external information sources. IT has also begun to find a role within the strategy planning process as an aid to developing strategy and consensus within management, as well as its traditional role within ESS and DSS. The use of IT permits advanced modelling in strategic planning work where it would have been prohibitive less than a decade ago. As an example, IT is now starting to be used in areas such as game theory which take full advantage of the quantitative frameworks previously unavailable to all but the most advanced planning units.

(4) *Integrated IT planning.* The field of IT planning has stimulated research into new areas of strategic planning, in particular, the role of a core support unit such as IT, the use of information as a competitive tool, the automation of certain areas of planning, and the importance of technological change. Further, IT planning has developed into a subset of business planning. IT plans must be based upon business

plans. As discussed earlier, the IT planning cycle should coincide
with the business planning cycle and IT should be planned to deliver
results within a timescale relevant to the organisation. This increased
integration of IT and business implies the importance of minimising
the communication gap between business and IT by using shared
tools and approaches. Look for more cross-fertilisation between ITUs
and SPUs.

(5) *Development of information and information technology for competitive
edge.* This buzzword slogan contains some important lessons. What
is clear is that the links between SPU, ISU and ITU will strengthen
due to:

(a) increasing automation of the process of strategic planning, e.g.
automated methodologies;
(b) increasing need for information in the planning process in order
to create high-quality plans;
(c) increasing automation of the results of strategic planning in MIS,
ESS and DSS;
(d) new technologies and the greater application of existing technology such as expert systems to the complexities of planning.

Because competitive edge applications based on IT often show large
returns, the ITU and SPU will be working together to develop
business planning showpieces.

CONCLUSION

We have seen how the roles of SPU, ITU and ISU interact. We examined
the provision of information to strategic planning, emphasising the high
degree of interpretation required for its use. We have also looked at some
basic ways of relating information from the ISU to the work of the SPU
and the implementation of the results by the ITU by focusing on
assumptions, decisions and success factors. Finally, we have considered
the working relationship among the three units and some trends affecting
them.

The increasingly competitive business environment forces most organisations to improve their business by improving their strategic view and
developing a more sophisticated approach to planning. Information is
the key to good strategy. Strategic information management will pull the
SPU, ITU and ISU together and push them towards developing standard
approaches and tools. One can envisage the day when strategic planning
is conducted using automated information processed by the ISU,
combined with automated approaches developed by the SPU, resulting

in automated MIS, DSS, ESS and new competitive edge systems implemented by the ITU.

REFERENCES

Henderson, J. C., Rockart, J. F., and Sifonis, J. G. (1984) *A Planning Methodology for Integrating Management Support Systems*, Center for Information Systems Research, Sloan School of Management, Massachusetts Institute of Technology.

Part 3

OTHER TOPICS

10

ADDING VALUE FROM CORPORATE HEADQUARTERS

Andrew Campbell and Michael Goold

Ashridge Strategic Management Centre

INTRODUCTION

The key issue for the chief executive of a diversified company is: do the separate businesses gain from membership of the whole? Is the whole greater than the sum of the parts? The test is whether business units perform better as part of the corporate portfolio than they would as independent companies. This is the harsh criterion that all central management groups should apply in rating their own effectiveness.

The same question also arises in comparing different companies. Often the issue is not only whether a business would be better off as part of a group than as an independent company, but also whether the business would prosper more in one group than another. In acquisition battles, such as the fight between Hanson Trust and United Biscuit for control of Imperial, the option of continued independence was ruled out early, and the outcome turned on judgements about which contender would make the better parent organisation.

For the last four years we have been studying the way that the corporate centre adds value to the business units. By looking at 16 major British companies we have defined three broad categories of management style used by the centre-Strategic Planning (such as BP and UB), Strategic Control (such as Courtaulds and ICI) and Financial Control (such as Hanson and BTR).

International Review of Strategic Management. Edited by D. E. Hussey. Published 1990 by John Wiley & Sons Ltd. This chapter was originally published in the *London Business School Journal*, Summer 1988, **12**(1), and is reprinted with permission.

We have found that the different styles cause value to be added in different ways. None of them proved to be inherently best. Each has strengths and weaknesses. Each adds value in a specific way and each can subtract value (i.e. make the business unit perform less well than it would as an independent company.) Corporate managers faced with the problem of maximising their effectiveness need to understand the strengths and weaknesses of the different styles and how to get the best from the style they have chosen.

This article summarises the results of our research, explaining the differences between the styles and the different ways in which they add value to the portfolio of business units.

WHY DIFFERENT STYLES EXIST

In our research we identified important tensions or trade-offs confronting corporate level managers. For example, the chief executive would like to help the business units by giving strong leadership from the centre, providing clear direction about which products and markets are suitable and how the units should compete. On the other hand, the chief executive would like to release the energies and entrepreneurial commitment of managers lower down by giving them wide autonomy to run their businesses as they please and to feel a sense of ownership. These two objectives are in conflict. The centre cannot simultaneously provide strong leadership and give autonomy to the business units. Hence we labelled it a tension facing corporate level managers. The chief executive needs to decide where, on the scale of leadership versus autonomy, he wants to be positioned.

THE RESEARCH

We studied 16 leading British companies to determine current practices, to identify important issues as perceived at different levels, and to relate strategic decision-making processes to the companies' results.

To that end, we conducted open-ended interviews with 5 to 20 corporate, divisional, and business managers in each company, including in almost all cases the chief executive. We also gathered internal data, usually from the head of planning, about formal aspects of the company's strategic decision-making process. Finally, we drew on published reports. The companies we studied are all publicly quoted, with headquarters in the United Kingdom. They cover a range of manufacturing and service sectors (none of the companies was in financial services or retailing). Their common characteristics are size, diversity and success.

The companies that took part in the study are British Petroleum, Imperial Chemical Industries, General Electric Company, Imperial Group, BTR, Hanson Trust, Courtaulds, STC, BOC, Cadbury Schweppes, United Biscuits, Tarmac, Plessey, Lex Service Group, Vickers, and Ferranti.

THE STYLES MATRIX

The strategic planning, strategic control, and financial control styles form part of a continuum of ways headquarters can influence business units. The continuum has two dimensions: (1) planning influence, which expresses the degree to which strategy is centralised, and (2) control influence, which shows the importance companies attach to short-term financial targets (Figure 10.1).

Companies that fall into the bottom left-hand corner can be labelled holding companies. In such organisations the centre has little influence over the subsidiaries. Our research found the successful companies moved away from the holding company style to one of the three alternatives.

The top right-hand corner of the matrix is blank because this style appears to be infeasible. Some companies in our research tried to combine a high degree of planning influence with tight short-term controls, but they have moved away from it. Either business-unit managers became demotivated by a seemingly oppressive corporate centre or headquarters failed to maintain sufficient objectivity to keep the controls tight.

We identified four other similar tensions—coordination and cooperation versus clear responsibilities and accountability; thorough analysis and planning versus entrepreneurial speed of response; long-term strategic targets versus short-term financial targets; and flexible strategies (i.e. strategies that can be changed quickly to meet competitor moves) versus tight controls.

Figure 10.1   Strategic management styles

The three different styles (Strategic Planning, Strategic Control and Financial Control) exist because it is possible to develop three different positionings against these tensions. Hence, managers in the headquarters of Hanson Trust believe in autonomy for business units, clear accountability, entrepreneurial decision making, short-term financial targets and tight controls. Alternatively, managers at the centre of BP believe in leadership from the centre, coordination and cooperation between different business units, thorough analysis and review of major decisions, long-term strategic targets and flexible strategies. Exhibit 10.1 summaries the choices underlying each of the styles and compares these to the style used by the capital markets in relation to an independent company.

In the research we also defined eight mechanisms through which the centre can add value to its business units. We recognised that the centre can only add value if it successfully influences (for the better) the strategies and actions of managers in the business units. The eight mechanisms are tools that the centre uses to influence strategy and actions. They are the organisation structure; the planning process; the use of themes, thrusts or suggestions to guide managers; the degree to which the centre managers overlap between units; the resource allocation decisions taken by the centre; the objectives set for each unit; the closeness of monitoring against objectives; and the types of incentives and sanctions applied to managers who meet or fail to meet targets.

Each style uses these mechanisms in different ways and to different degrees, depending on the choices that have been made on the tensions. For example, a company that prizes coordination and cooperation, such

Exhibit 10.1 Tensions in corporate level management

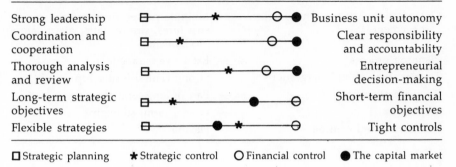

Strong leadership		Business unit autonomy
Coordination and cooperation		Clear responsibility and accountability
Thorough analysis and review		Entrepreneurial decision-making
Long-term strategic objectives		Short-term financial objectives
Flexible strategies		Tight controls

☐ Strategic planning   ✱ Strategic control   ○ Financial control   ● The capital market

as BP, has a matrix organisation structure in its oil business that forces managers to coordinate over the big decisions. A company that believes in strong leadership, such as the Lex Service Group, guides business unit managers by often repeated themes, by defining the main thrusts of the organisation, and by making frequent suggestions or instructions. The choices managers make about the tensions affect the way the company uses these mechanisms.

In the rest of the chapter, we summarise the key features of each style against the eight mechanisms and we show how the features can both add value to the subsidiaries as well as subtract value. Some of the negative consequences of a style are intrinsic and unavoidable; others are pitfalls that can be avoided. While we recognise that no style is superior for all situations, we believe that managers who understand the style they are using will be able to avoid the pitfalls and make sure that the net contribution of the centre is positive rather than negative.

STRATEGIC PLANNING

The strategic planning style is characterised by an emphasis on strategy, on long-term objectives and on a cooperative, flexible management approach. Exhibit 10.2 summarises the key features.

The complex and overlapping organisation structures of these companies ensure that a variety of views on strategy will be expressed. They also allow the centre to inject its ideas into the formulation of strategy. So they bring the judgement and experience of a cross-section of senior managers into play to help define the best ways forward. This allows a wider discussion of issues and a more comprehensive search for new strategy options than would occur in an independent company.

Exhibit 10.2 Strategic planning: key features

Organisation structure and overlap management	— Multiple perspectives, matrix structures, strong staffs, coordination mechanisms
Planning process	— Extensive, strategic
Themes, thrusts and suggestions	— Strong central leadership
Resource allocation	— Part of long-term strategy
Objectives	— Longer-term, strategic
Monitoring and controls	— Flexible

Coordinating committees and devices also allow strategies to be drawn together across a variety of businesses (or countries), to achieve benefits of synergy and integration that would not be available to separate companies. And strong staff groups at the centre allow economies of scope in the provision of central services.

The drawback of this structure is that business managers have less clear-cut individual responsibilities, less control over their own destinies. The emphasis on cooperation between businesses and across levels, and the need to coordinate strategies, means that they have less unilateral authority to take decisions for their businesses that they personally feel are right. The inevitable price of multiple viewpoints and synergy is some loss of autonomy. This, in turn, can reduce motivation, unless a sense of shared purpose compensates for the loss of individual responsibility.

The *extensive planning processes* of the Strategic Planning companies are an important means for getting different views aired. They are a test of business unit thinking, and can help to prevent businesses from falling into outdated or inappropriate strategy patterns. By challenging business managers' 'habits of mind', they perform a useful function that the independent company lacks. The questions posed by the central management in a Strategic Planning company should be much more informed, much more 'strategic' than is possible for the outside investors and bankers to whom the independent company reports. This is a prime value of the planning processes of the Strategic Planning company. They also constitute a vehicle for the exercise of central leadership in strategic decision-making, and a means by which the centre can learn more about the businesses. But extensive planning processes cannot avoid constraining business managers. As one line manager explained:

> The decision-making and planning process in our company is very professional. We are very open about discussing things. We chew over important decisions

at great length. My boss will get involved and his boss will join in the thinking. It's all very constructive and I am sure we make a better decision as a result. But somehow after all the discussion, I don't feel it's my decision any more.

The need to communicate and justify plans to the centre inhibits freedom of action, slows down the decision process, and takes some ownership from lower levels of management. The independent company can be swifter and more entrepreneurial.

Furthermore, Strategic Planning processes are often cumbersome and confusing rather than probing and insightful. At their worst, they degenerate into rigid, bureaucratic exercises. The drawbacks of bureaucracy in planning may not be intrinsic to the Strategic Planning style, but it is an occupational hazard—a potential pitfall.

By providing *strong central leadership* through themes, thrusts and suggestions, the Strategic Planning companies are able to embark on bolder, more aggressive strategies than would otherwise emerge. Central sponsorship can enlarge the ambitions of business management, ensure that resources are available to support investments, and help to overcome risk aversion. We have given examples in each Strategic Planning company of the sorts of business building strategies that result, often looking towards the building of long-term advantage in major international businesses. It is doubtful whether these strategies would have been adopted by independent companies, without a supportive and well-resourced parent in the background to underwrite the effort. It is in this context that mission statements and broad policies can be valuable, by defining what will receive priority from the centre.

The downside of strong leadership is equally clear. Close involvement by the centre in strategy development inevitably reduces both the objectivity of the centre in reviewing strategy, and the sense of personal 'ownership' at the business level. This is the strong leadership–business autonomy tension.

Moreover, strong leadership can lead to a number of pitfalls. It can be seen as autocratic or ill-informed interference that overrules business level ideas; bold strategies can become risky and over-optimistic; sound opportunities in non-core businesses may be turned down because they do not fit with the grand design. These pitfalls are frequently associated with the Strategic Planning style, although the best exponents of the style are able to avoid them. In companies such as BP, strong leadership blends into a cooperative attempt to work together for a common aim, thereby generating a sense of shared purpose and commitment that goes far to offset the disadvantages we have listed.

Resource allocation and objective-setting in the Strategic Planning companies are aimed at the long-term development of the business. The centre acts as a sort of buffer to the capital market, protecting the business units from the need to satisfy the shorter term performance criteria applied by the outside investor. This allows business managers to concentrate on building the core businesses, rather than trimming their sails with a view to meeting half-yearly earnings targets. It also means that they can make major acquisitions to support existing activities, or to build new ones, without an expectation that the pay-off to such moves will come immediately. Clear priority can be given to long-term objectives.

There are a number of businesses in the Strategic Planning companies that have benefited from this strategic, long-term resource allocation process. Without it, BOC would be a weaker force in the worldwide gases business; Lex would not have built up its electronic component distribution business; BP would not have achieved its successes in oil and gas exploration. But there are others which, it can be argued, might have reacted more quickly to adversity, or avoided risky and unpromising investments, if they *had* been exposed to the disciplines of the external capital market.

Several managers in Strategic Planning companies made us aware of the dangers of too much emphasis on strategy and the long term. 'The pressure on the long term took our eye off the short-term issues. They [corporate] and we undervalued the short-term profit impact of what we were doing', said one manager. 'Too much strategy and not enough graft', was the conclusion of another.

We have also pointed out the difficulty in defining clear, objective and measurable goals for monitoring long-term performance. This means that long-term performance measures open up the possibility of excuses. As Dick Giordano of BOC put it: 'This is probably one of the most difficult challenges. How do you have milestones that measure strategic progress without allowing excuse-making from business management?' But to point to these shortcomings is only to underline the tension that exists between giving priority to profits now or profits later, to short-term controls or long-term objectives. All Strategic Planning companies must accept some sacrifice in the clarity and enforceability of short-term objectives in order to allow for the allocation of resources to long-term aims.

Linked to this tension we noted that Strategic Planning companies are also prone to undue optimism about the future or to personal incentives that are not linked to strategies. Lacking both market disciplines and clear internal targets, the atmosphere can become too cosy. As one divisional manager put it: 'As part of the corporate entity, we have this shield and blanket around us to protect us'. This can mean that flexibility becomes tolerance, and tolerance becomes looseness. Motivation to perform is then at risk. The fact that the Strategic Planning companies have been relatively inactive in divestments, closures and portfolio rationalisations, and that some have overextended themselves through rapid growth, is all evidence of this.

Furthermore, replacing the verdict of the stock market with subjective corporate assessments of strategic progress may not be an unmitigated gain. If second guessing what will impress the centre becomes the major goal, this can be even less conducive to strategic thinking than the short-term financial pressures of the City. It is in these circumstances that corporate 'politics' flourish, with decisions taken to reinforce personal positions in the hierarchy, rather than to improve the strategies of the business.

Finally, the *flexible control system* in the Strategic Planning companies adds value. By accepting that precise, short-term targets may have to be compromised in order to stay on track to build a business, it encourages a more tenacious pursuit of long-term goals. Furthermore, it is more tolerant of innovative strategies that carry with them the risk of failure, and of strategies that evolve continuously to meet the needs of rapidly changing markets. The centre in the Strategic Planning company is more sympathetic than the capital market to the manager who is struggling to create a major new business in a highly competitive and uncertain world.

Flexible controls, however, can never provide clear and objective standards of performance. Hence it is harder for both the centre and the business manager to know whether results are 'on target'. An element of judgement enters into the assessment of performance, and increases the scope for discretion. The price of flexibility is ambiguous performance measures and a reduced sense of personal accountability.

Exhibit 10.3 summarises the key features and the added and subtracted value of the Strategic Planning style. We have divided the negative features of the style between those that are intrinsic, and those that represent pitfalls that can be avoided. With skilful management the negative features of the style can be minimised or avoided by:

- sensitive, flexible and selective planning processes;
- leadership;
- well-informed central management;
- shared purpose and commitment;
- avoiding over-optimism;
- incentives aligned with strategy;
- strenuous efforts to identify, measure and act on strategic milestones.

But the style will always give less priority to individual accountability, responsibility and incentives, and to short-term measures of performance.

Exhibit 10.3 The strategic planning style

Key features	Added value	Intrinsic subtracted value	Common but avoidable pitfalls
Complex, coordinated structure	Wider discussion of issues Synergy Central services	Less individual responsibility and authority	Can reduce motivation
Extensive, strategic planning process	More thorough search for best strategies	Less freedom of action Slower decisions	Can be cumbersome, confusing, bureaucratic
Strong central leadership	Bolder strategies Shared purpose and commitment	Less 'ownership' by business Less objectivity by centre	Can become interference Can lead to risky and overambitious strategies
Long-term criteria	Building core businesses 'Buffer' to capital market	Slower reactions to adversity Less clear targets	Can lead to over-optimism, 'lip service'
Flexible controls	More tenacious pursuit of long-term goals More innovative, responsive strategies	Subjective assessments Less accountability	Can lead to politics

Exhibit 10.4 Financial control: key features

Organisation structure and overlap management	— Clearly separate, profit centre responsibilities
Planning process	— Budgets
Themes, thrusts and suggestions	— Business autonomy stressed
Resource allocation	— Project-based; short payback criteria
Objectives	— Shorter-term, financial
Monitoring and controls	— Very tight

FINANCIAL CONTROL

At the opposite extreme to Strategic Planning lies Financial Control. Exhibit 10.4 summarises the key features of this style.

The *organisation structures* of the Financial Control companies stress *multiple, separate profit centres*, each with independent responsibilities. As far as possible, these structures replicate, for the profit centres, the circumstances of independent companies. The profit centres are set up to overlap as little as possible, and no attempt is made by the centre to coordinate between them. The profit centre manager is largely free to run his own show without interference from other parts of the company. 'We believe in the importance of the individual line manager in achieving success for his business and for the group as a whole. The management system has been devised to give maximum responsibility to the line management', said Martin Taylor of Hanson Trust. There are advantages in the simplicity and clarity of this structure. In particular it gives early general management responsibility, thereby developing the skills needed for the long-term success of the company.

But the structure is less ambitious than that of the Strategic Planning companies. It adds no value in comparison to the independent company situation; but at least it avoids the negatives which are also associated with the more complex structures of Strategic Planning companies.

The *planning process* in the Financial Control companies *concentrates on budgets*. The emphasis is on the short term, and on agreeing targets rather than on the means by which they are going to be achieved. As with Strategic Planning companies, the centre probes the plans of business managers, but the nature of the questioning is very different. For Financial Control companies the primary value arises from the pressure it creates for 'high wire' standards of profitability and growth in profits, not from probing underlying strategic logic. As Lionel Stammers of BTR put it: 'Many managers do not know what they can achieve until you ask them'. The Financial Control companies add value by asking for performance that is more demanding than that insisted on by stockholders or bankers; and they exert pressure for performance much more continuously. An independent company can produce unexciting results for long periods, in some cases for many years, before market pressure will cause a change in management. But in Financial Control companies controls are tight.

As a by-product of the budgeting process, managers may also have to think again about the validity of the strategies they are following. If they are unable to satisfy corporate requirements, they may be forced to consider changes of direction. But the centre will not typically question strategies directly, or expect to make much contribution to the definition of new and preferable strategy options. And the emphasis is on next year's results, 'the road ahead', not the long term. The focus on results not strategies leaves managers more free to make their own decisions, provided they turn in the required performance. Furthermore, the planning process can be simpler and therefore less prone to 'bureaucracy' than in Strategic Planning companies.

The major drawback of the planning process is that it cannot claim to add much value to the business manager in probing and thinking through his strategy options. Indeed the short-term results orientation may distract him from tackling long-term issues. If the stock market is felt to create an unduly short-term orientation, the Financial Control style serves to reinforce this bias. We noted, for example, that a number of the subsidiaries of Financial Control companies are losing market share. Their managers explained that they are retreating from less profitable sections of the market; and that market share is not a useful objective. As one BTR manager put it: 'We don't pride ourselves on market share. In fact, we don't like to refer to market share at all'. It is this focus on the short term that causes critics of Financial Control companies to claim that they are gradually harvesting their competitive positions. Taken to extremes the style can encourage managers to milk their businesses by cutting back too far on investment.

Although the centre may make occasional suggestions, *business autonomy* is preserved in the Financial Control companies by insisting that the final decision rests with business management, and by avoiding any broad, top–down corporate themes, missions or thrusts. This philosophy attempts to replicate the freedom of the independent company, and hence can obviously add little value when compared to it. If, however, constructive suggestions are made, but not imposed, the business manager may gain something which is denied to his fully independent counterpart. Nevertheless, it is clear that Financial Control does not attempt to add as much value in this respect as Strategic Planning;

equally, however, it runs fewer risks of subtracting value.

The *resource allocation* process in the Financial Control companies adopts *objectives and criteria similar to the capital market*. There is no attempt to buffer the businesses from requirements for short-term profit. Rather, the Financial Control style sees itself as applying capital market criteria, but in a much more thoroughgoing and efficient manner. With detailed information on each business, and the ability to discriminate between them in resource allocation, the centre can ensure that funds flow only to those businesses whose proposals meet corporate criteria, and whose track records give confidence in their ability to deliver. The system reviews each investment on its merits, rather than as part of a long-term business strategy. It adds value by insisting that proposals will only be funded if they project high returns and fast paybacks, and if business managers appear committed to achieving their forecasts and have a track record of doing so in the past. By exposing all individual investments to this test, it goes much further than the capital markets in applying tough standards. The centre, however, does not pretend to have a detailed knowledge of each business's products and markets, or to be able to criticise, shape and add value to the strategies behind the investment proposals.

The centre is more directly active in acquisitions and divestments. The search is for acquisition candidates whose assets are under-performing. Value is added to these acquisitions by increasing their profitability through the application of Financial Control disciplines. Conversely, divestments are made of businesses that do not respond to these criteria.

The clear emphasis on *short-term* profit *objectives* in resource allocation and acquisitions simplifies the management task. But it can also result in missed opportunities. We were told of a number of opportunities that had been considered and rejected because of the risk or the length of payback of the investment. Although it is not clear that the opportunities rejected would have resulted in substantial profit growth, it is probable that many more of these opportunities would have been taken up by Strategic Planning (or even Strategic Control) companies. One example is the market for standard gate arrays. Both GEC and Ferranti had the opportunity to enter the fast-growing MOS-technology segment at the early stages. Both rejected the opportunity. Ferranti chose to stay with its proven bi-polar technology and GEC, after examining options, passed up the opportunity altogether. The bold strategies they rejected were pursued by LSI Logic which now has a leading position worldwide. The short-term focus does preclude longer term, more speculative investments. The tension remains, and means that the Financial Control style will always create problems in businesses where long time scales are needed.

The main strength of the Financial Control style, however, is in the

Exhibit 10.5 The financial control style

Key feature	Added value	Intrinsic subtracted value	Common but avoidable pitfalls
Separate profit centres	Simplifies task Early general management responsibility	No coordination synergy	
Budgetary planning	Higher standards Challenges strategies that won't deliver Avoids 'potholes'	Distracts from strategic issues	Can encourage milking the business
Business autonomy	Advice, not instructions	No cooperation, no 'help' for businesses	
Short-term criteria	Clearer criteria 'Efficient' internal capital market	Missed opportunities 'Control games'	
Tight controls	Faster reaction More motivation 'Winners' psychology	Less flexibility and creativity	Can become a straitjacket

tight controls it imposes. Not only are budgets stretching; not only do investments demand short paybacks; but also the monitoring of results achieved and the feedback and follow through from the centre create strong incentives to deliver. The knowledge that there will be a speedy reaction to under- (or over-) achievement of monthly targets does create more motivation, more pressure for performance than is brought to bear on the managing director of an independent company. The simplicity of the criteria for judging performance also makes it easier for line managers to know where to focus their attention; and makes it perfectly clear who is doing a good job and succeeding, and who is not. Indeed, the knowledge that demanding standards have been set and can be seen to have been met is one of the prime motivating factors for successful managers in the Financial Control companies. A BTR division head commented that he would be willing to forgo £10 000 in salary in exchange for the psychological satisfaction of knowing he was going to be able to deliver on his budgeted objectives.

Those who do meet their objectives can be confident that they have earned the respect of the centre, and grow in self-confidence themselves. This has two benefits. It makes for a more open discussion of business issues with the centre, since the line manager can rely on his results rather than his words to impress the centre; and it creates a 'winners' psychology among business managers, which makes them feel more capable of overcoming obstacles and pushing on to further peaks of performance.

But the tight control process also has its downside. It can stifle creativity, snuff out experimentation and eliminate the entrepreneurial 'skunk works' activities. There is less flexibility to respond to opportunities. The point was made by a Hanson Trust group chairman in this way:

> Our business chief executives tend to be quite conservative in assessing the payback of potential investments. In order to preserve credibility with Hanson Trust, they will typically only promise what they are certain they can deliver. The chief executive knows he will be hung on it, and is therefore cautious rather than over-ambitious.

At its worst, tight control can mean that everything is sacrificed to meeting specified control objectives at whatever cost to the underlying health of the business. The system can become a straitjacket, not a source of added value.

Exhibit 10.5 summarises the key features and the added and subtracted value of the Financial Control style, again distinguishing between intrinsic problems and avoidable pitfalls. The negative features of this style can be minimised by:

- targets that require year-on-year *growth* in profits;
- leaving business managers in post long enough that they have to live with the consequences of the strategies they adopt.
- informed central managers who will offer constructive advice and suggestions but without imposing their views;
- willingness to question and override control objectives if it is clear that they will damage the health of the business;
- a winner's psychology to provide energy to maintain growth momentum; and
- acceptance that, in some businesses, the Financial Control style may be inappropriate.

But the style cannot avoid problems in businesses where long-term, coordinated strategies are needed, and cannot claim to provide much constructive help to business managers in the search for optimum strategies.

STRATEGIC CONTROL

Exhibit 10.6 shows the key features of the Strategic Control style, again expressed in terms that relate to our discussion of tensions. Strategic Control is a blend of the features found in Strategic Planning and Financial Control.

By *structuring themselves around individual profit centre businesses that are grouped into divisions*, Strategic Control companies claim to achieve the motivational benefits of decentralisation, while allowing important business overlaps to be managed at the business level. There is some added value from divisional coordination, but a minimum of interference with business managers.

Exhibit 10.6 Strategic control: key features

Organisation structure and overlap management	— Decentralised profit centres; some divisional coordination
Planning process	— Extensive, strategic
Themes, thrusts and suggestions	— Avoided; business autonomy stressed
Resource allocation	— Part of long-term strategy
Objectives	— Longer-term, strategic and shorter-term, financial
Monitoring and controls	— Tight

This view may justify the divisional structure. But, even if the divisional level is able to achieve synergies between businesses that would not be achieved independently, it is less clear how the corporate level adds value, structurally, to the divisions. Put simply, what would the divisions lose if they were set up as independent companies? As in Financial Control companies, the decentralised structure leaves little room for the centre to orchestrate the several businesses in the portfolio.

Strategic Control companies argue that they make a prime contribution to divisional thinking via the quality controls in the *strategic review process*. The disciplines provide a continuing challenge that sharpens the thinking in the divisions and businesses. By its probing, the centre raises minimum standards of thinking and analysis, and prevents 'habits of mind' from forming. The intention is similar to that of the Strategic Planning companies, although Strategic Control companies limit themselves to a questioning role, and do not propose their own views from the centre.

Although we have found some evidence to support these contentions, our research suggests that, in reality, the challenge to divisional thinking is not always helpful. Extensive planning processes run into the same problem of acting as a constraint that we described for the Strategic Planning companies. Moreover, bureaucracy grows quickly in Strategic Control companies because the centre is that much more distant from the businesses. One manager explained that the planning reviews in his company were a 'whole series of rakings over, all of them too shallow'. This means either that the centre may fail to be well enough informed to ask useful questions; or that any benefits may be more than offset by the time-consuming and costly processes that they involve. 'Net' added value is not always delivered by corporate planning processes. Only if these processes are sensitively designed and administered, and if the businesses in the portfolio are likely to respond to a second view, can value be added by the centre.

Strategic Control companies generally *avoid major suggestions and initiatives*, and are not active in coordinating between divisions or businesses. The emphasis on *business autonomy* is well caught by the Chairman of a Vickers division, who said:

> In giving freedom, it's a bit nerve racking at times because you feel you're not in control, not in charge. But the result is that they take more initiative and they perform better. And they feel responsible for their actions, whereas if you at the centre always ask questions, always try and monitor things very, very carefully you get a reaction that they're not really responsible for the decisions, that you're really controlling things and so if it goes wrong, it's as much your fault as it is theirs.

Strategic Control companies recognise that direction from the centre can subtract value. They stress the responsibility and independence of the business manager. However, this means that they are unlikely to add value by steering the development of strategy. Where ad hoc interventions do take place, our research would indicate that value was subtracted at least as often as it was added.

It is in *a resource allocation process that balances long- and short-term goals* that many Strategic Control companies add the most value. The centre provides access to a pool of resources, which can be made available for investment in long-term, large or risky projects. These projects might be turned down by outside investors, who have little knowledge of the business and who are often short-term or fashion driven in their attitudes, focusing more on past results than future prospects, and failing to assess technically complex or strategically innovative ideas. As Sir John Clark of Plessey argued: 'City pressures make life difficult if you're trying to balance short-term profit pressure and the requirements of the business in terms of competitive advantage.' Many of the business and divisional managements also see real value in this access to funding.

> Probably the greatest benefit of being part of ICI is that they were willing to fund us through 17 years of losses in getting the business going.
> (Chairman, ICI Pharmaceuticals.)

> We were able to take a major step forwards in investment in new production capacity that would have been beyond us as an independent company.
> (Chief executive, Howson Algraphy division, Vickers.)

The downside of the long-term investment attitude is, of course, the same as in the Strategic Planning companies: a danger of undervaluing the important of next year's profits. But the Strategic Control companies attempt to defend against this problem by balancing long-term objectives with short-term profit pressures. The ability of companies such as Courtaulds, ICI and Vickers to cut back drastically in some areas of their portfolios, while preserving growth momentum elsewhere, is evidence of their ability to make trade-offs of this sort. Indeed major corporate resource allocation decisions in the Strategic Control companies have concentrated at least as much on portfolio rationalisation and profitability improvement as on long-term investment.

In practice, however, there are numerous difficulties in achieving the right balance of objectives. Assessing more speculative, longer term investments is hard. If the centre lacks close familiarity with the business, it may be forced to rely on the credibility of the sponsoring management team, together with formal financial evaluations—much the same criteria as used by the outside investor. Where long-term projects *are* backed by the centre, the reason may be personal commitments to a business rather than clear-sighted strategic thinking. We encountered several examples of long-term and continued support for a business by the centre that cost the company far more than a hard-nosed and early closure would have done.

Reliance on corporate funds for investment can also be a source of problems, since capital scarcity can cut out investments that might have been funded by the outside market. During the years of financial crisis, Vickers was unable to finance good proposals that were coming forward, and Courtaulds was short of funds for investments even in growth areas. During this period, Courtaulds applied across-the-board cash targets to all its businesses regardless of previous success or failure. Now the company has set up its major business groups with capital structures to resemble as closely as possible the conditions of the publicly quoted parent company. It believes that the groups should be better placed to identify the consequences of their investment plans to their own balance sheets and take proper action in a more differentiated fashion to control the financing consequences of their business performance. This is a long way from viewing the value of corporate management mainly in terms of its ability to allocate resources.

Lastly, although portfolio rationalisation has improved profitability ratios for the Strategic Control companies, it is less clear that divisions of these companies would have moved any less speedily to take corrective measures had they been independently set up. Strategic Control companies may move more decisively on rationalisation and exit decisions than Strategic Planning or Holding companies, but the discipline of the outside capital markets would in some cases have been more pressing than that provided by corporate management.

The resource allocation process in the Strategic Control companies therefore attempts to combine the 'buffer' function of the Strategic Planning companies and the 'efficiency' function of the Financial Control companies. In some respects this achieves the best of both worlds; but in others it encounters the disadvantages that come from the lack of a clear commitment to either. This follows from the basic tension between short- and long-term goals. Furthermore, uninformed long-term investments, naive portfolio pruning and partisan preference for particular businesses are all potential—if avoidable—pitfalls for Strategic Control.

It is therefore only if the centre is genuinely better informed, closer to the businesses, and as objective as the outside investor that value is likely to be added.

Detailed monitoring and reporting allow the centre to pinpoint shortcomings more precisely; and incentives and *tight strategic and financial controls* create personal motivation in a much less blunt fashion

Exhibit 10.7 The Strategic Control Style

Key feature	Added value	Intrinsic subtracted value	Common but avoidable pitfalls
Decentralised profit centres: divisional coordination	Little by centre	No central coordination	
Extensive, strategic planning process	Raises minimum standards of thinking and analysis Challenges habits of mind	Constraining	Can be bureaucratic; add cost, but little value
Business autonomy			Gratuitous suggestions
Long- and short-term criteria	Acceptance of longer-term investments Balanced objectives	Ambiguous objectives	Tolerance for low performers Capital rationing Uninformed investments and divestments
Tight controls	More motivation to perform	Risk aversion Subjective balancing of objectives	'Politics' 'Lip service'

than the outside capital market, where takeovers or palace revolutions are effectively the only sanctions against non-performing management. Provided, therefore, that the control objectives are conducive to the prosperity of the business, Strategic Control adds value.

Our research suggests, however, that the definition of strategic control objectives is fraught with difficulty. First, the objectives that Strategic Control companies establish do not always embody the strategies they have agreed. Financial controls can crowd out strategic objectives, thereby damaging the long-term interests of the business. Or vague strategic goals can become an excuse for non-performance. This means that the control process becomes bogged down in arguments over trade-offs, and the intention to create tight control languishes. Second, as in Financial Control, tight controls can subtract values, through causing inflexibility and risk aversion in strategies.

There is an intrinsic conflict between encouraging long-term, creative, strategic thinking, and imposing tight, short-term controls. Two quotes from divisional managing directors in Strategic Control companies are relevant. The first illustrates the tension between strategy and control: 'The centre is pressing us to grow. But it is unwilling to accept the negative impact on profitability this may entail.' The second illustrates the uneasy balance between strategic and financial control, and the difficulty of being poised between them: 'I asked the chief executive when I was appointed whether the company was a financial conglomerate or an industrial company. After 4 years the question still seems relevant, and the answer is always: "Ask me again in 6 months' time".' This remark found echoes in almost all the Strategic Control companies.

Making the controls supportive of flexible and innovative strategies is not easy. It can even be that the stock market, whose control process is less precise and rigorous, allows more latitude for business building than strategic controls that are poorly defined and insensitively applied.

Exhibit 10.7 summarises the key features and the added and subtracted value of the Strategic Control style. The negative features of the style can be minimised by:

- flexible planning processes;
- willingness by the centre to spend the time necessary to get close to business unit strategies, to be knowledgeable about their competitive environments, and to discuss issues thoroughly;
- avoiding over-optimism;
- personal incentives aligned with strategy; and
- strenuous efforts to identify, measure and act on strategic milestones.

But the style will always encounter difficulties in setting priorities between different sorts of objectives, and in encouraging business initiatives, while at the same time providing a check on strategic thinking from the centre.

SUMMARY

The best corporate parents have an understanding of the issues, trade-offs and tension we have raised in this article. Companies like Tarmac and ICI have clearly chosen the style they want to use at the centre. They recognise the strengths and weaknesses of the style and work hard to get the most added value from the strengths and to minimise the negative consequences of the style's weak points. They are also articulate on the subject, explaining the management processes they use in terms of the benefits given to units in the portfolio.

It is common for managers in subsidiaries to complain about the interference and overhead burden of headquarters. Most corporate level managers think that this is to be expected. 'Well of course they complain about the paperwork and fight the overhead allocations', said one planning manager, 'I would do the same if I was in their shoes'.

Yet we have found companies where the units praise the centre; where managers value the review meetings and budget planning meetings and where there is an atmosphere of trust and cooperation between layers in the hierarchy. This should be an objective of all companies. By understanding the differences between styles and the strengths and the weaknesses of each style, we believe managers will be better able to create the trust and cooperation that some companies have achieved.

11

BOARD PARTICIPATION IN STRATEGY: WHEN AND HOW?

F.-F. Neubauer

*Faculty Member in Multinational Corporate Strategy and Planning IMI-Geneva**

A. Demb

Faculty Member in Organizational Systems, IMI-Geneva

THE ISSUE OF BOARDS AND STRATEGY

The dramatic restructuring of many corporations in response to the large 'tectonic' shifts in the world surrounding them has led stakeholders to demand that the board protect their interests through tighter scrutiny and a more direct involvement in the governance of the firm—particularly in the process that establishes the strategic direction of the company (Judge and Zeithaml, 1987). While this issue has received more attention recently, it is by no means new. During the last two decades, the role of boards in strategy has been an intensely debated item. Recently these discussions do not centre so much on the question of *whether* the board should get more active in strategy matters, but *how* the board can exercise its responsibilities more effectively (Smith, 1981; Pinnell, 1986).

Our analysis indicates that ample opportunities exist for boards and their directors to contribute substantively to the strategic processes of a corporation. Further, both the literature and our own research indicate that directors and boards *are* getting involved in strategy, and that corporate management—CEOs and executive directors—value that involvement.

---

* In January 1990, to join with IMEDE to form IMD, Lausanne

International Review of Strategic Management.
Edited by D. E. Hussey. © 1990 John Wiley & Sons Ltd

There are, however, several baseline conditions to achieve a meaningful involvement. First, directors must be willing to make a major investment in time and effort in order to acquire a relatively thorough knowledge of the company and its industry. This applies both to non-executive and executive directors. While executive directors may begin with a greater understanding of the corporation and its industry, in very large companies all directors experience a similar problem of limited time and attention to areas outside their personal expertise.

Second, this effort will have to be matched by a commensurate commitment and investment on the part of the company. Not only will the corporation have to provide the directors, and perhaps especially the non-executives, with complete and pertinent information, but it will also have to expose them systematically to the different parts of the organization and the people who run them. All of this requires serious attention to the scheduling of board activity and to the design of a programme that educates the directors.

To arrive at a judgement regarding the potential for meaningful board involvement, it is necessary to examine both the strategy process and the director involvement in some detail. In addition, it is essential to distinguish between the roles that can be played by executive or managing directors, and non-executive or external directors. Limitations of time and attention, as well as responsibilities for their own enterprises, importantly constrain the inputs possible from even the most diligent non-executive directors. Although executives may share a certain distancing from operational management, their familiarity with the company and its industry, as well as their managerial responsibilities for the well-being of the corporation, leave them in a different situation vis-à-vis a role in strategy. Thus, throughout this discussion we will treat the board in terms of its constituent elements: executive and non-executive directors, CEO and chairman. This will also allow us to make meaningful comments across the experience of companies with single- and two-tier board structures, e.g. in the United States, the United Kingdom and Germany.

THE STRATEGY FORMATION PROCESS

The area of strategy and strategy formation as a discipline has been subjected to considerable turmoil during the last decade. Massive criticism has been directed towards certain widespread strategic planning practices (see for instance Porter, 1987). At the same time, it has been stated over and over again that strategic thinking has never been more needed than today. In response to this criticism and the need for improved conceptual strategic thinking, several major modifications in planning theory and practice have been made. The concept of strategy and strategy formation we will use here amalgamates several approaches, particularly those outlined by Mintzberg, Quinn and Leavitt.

In particular, we are attracted to the notion that strategy can be planned, or evolve, at different levels of specificity. At one end of a continuum are those strategy formation processes which deliberately and systematically result from corporate planning processes—'intended strategies'. At the other end, is a strategy which 'emerges', en route, from the accumulation of a series or stream of important decisions (see Figure 11.1). Neither extreme in its pure form can serve large and complex corporations operating in the turbulent economic, social and technological environments of the late twentieth century.

Intended strategy   *Emergent strategy*

Figure 11.1 Continuum of planning practices

We have learned through hard experience that deliberate corporate planning processes too often generated volumes of plans which were out of date by the time they were completed, and only marginally influenced the activity that led to meaningful corporate growth and development. Similarly, we have seen that there is an important need for a shared vision, or objective, which guides the online, emergent form of 'crafted' strategy so well articulated by Mintzberg (Mintzberg and Quinn, 1988, p. 3). In this, we draw the 'pathfinding' element from the strategic management concept of Harold Leavitt (1986), and the 'metanoic organizations' of Charles Kiefer and Peter Senge (1986). Characteristic of these organizations is a central vision, well articulated and broadly communicated, which guides the behaviour of management and employees.

So, we define at least two modes of strategy formulation which may be more or less formal (intended or emergent), both of which incorporate a clear phase of defining a vision, or pathfinding. Table 11.1 outlines the relationship of our stages to the models offered by Leavitt, Mintzberg and Quinn. The table illustrates that Leavitt's three-pronged concept is broad enough to accommodate the traditional, more analytic approach to strategic planning, as well as a more modern, vision-oriented approach to charting the future course of a corporation. We will use the stages outlined in the first column to structure our examination of board involvement, grouping them in Leavitt's terms.

Most of the present discussion on the role of boards in strategy deals with involvement in the 'problem-solving' and 'implementing' stages. We will follow this sequence in our discussion (pages 245 and 251), returning to 'pathfinding' later (pages 254–255). In addition, we will

Table 11.1 Stages in the strategy formation process

Stages	Strategic Management[1]	Strategy Processes
Set path vision	Pathfinding	
Initiate process		Intended[2]
Formulate strategy	Problem solving	Emergent[2]
Evaluate strategy		
Implement strategy	Implementing	
Monitor implementation		

[1] Leavitt (1986)
[2] Mintzberg and Quinn (1988)

explore some other determinants of board involvement. Our discussion will draw on recent literature, and the interview data generated from our own research. (The IMI project on Corporate Governance and the Role of Boards will involve 14 multinational companies from nine countries in Europe, North and South America. Interviews with some 80 directors focus, among other aspects, on board decision making.)

THE INVOLVEMENT OF BOARDS IN 'PROBLEM SOLVING'

The Initiation of the Process

> A responsible and effective board should require of its management a unique and durable corporate strategy . . .

With these words, Kenneth R. Andrews, one of the most prolific and thoughtful researchers in the board area (Andrews, 1980, p. 104) suggests that boards should initiate the strategy formulation process. Blake Pinnell goes further and strongly recommends that the board insist not only on a process, but a highly quality process. He expresses fear that a main board which sets up a central planning department and then waits patiently for something to emerge, may not be happy with the outcome.

> The danger . . . is that the Board may come to view the planning activity as largely unproductive, and that this sentiment will be shared by those planning executives whose efforts come to be regarded as inadequate. To minimise this

problem, the board must somehow satisfy itself in advance that planning not only is done, but done well.

(Pinnell, 1986, p. 29)

While it is apparent that the board should trigger the planning process, it seems equally clear that the bulk of that task will fall to the CEO with the executive directors. In two-tier boards, the managing board with its corporate-wide responsibilities will play this role. In single-tier boards, the managing or executive directors carry this burden, as do the executive committees in those situations where boards are primarily comprised of outside directors. Non-executives bring an important perspective based on their experience in their own companies, but may largely play an advisory role. For example, one long-term outside director of a large British corporation whom we interviewed insistently raised an issue at a pre-board meeting of the non-executive directors, which resulted in a substantial, and clearly strategic, restructuring of the ownership profile of that company within six months.

Problem Solving: The Strategy Formulation Stage

The involvement of boards in the actual formulation of strategy seems to be rare, for practical as well as philosophical reasons. Thomas L. Whisler, an American director and professor of business policy at the University of Chicago, argues forcefully against such a direct involvement on philosophical grounds:

> We [the board members] don't set strategy. This rule is full of subtleties. To begin with, if the board were to set strategy, it would, in the process, give away its power and responsibility for questioning and evaluating strategy alternatives. It would also be separating the responsibility for setting strategy from that of implementing it—a fatal split—those responsible for implementing the strategy should be strongly influential in developing it; those who set strategy should be responsible for its implementation. Hence, those who set strategy (top management) explain it and defend it before a group of wise and experienced individuals (the board!).
>
> (Whisler, 1983)

Whisler's logic, argued primarily from an American context, is shared in the logic of the two-tier structures found in Germany, in the Netherlands and in some respects in Scandinavia. Supervisory boards generally play a review and approval role, with management boards carrying responsibility for defining and implementing strategic directions and actions.

Other practitioners, like Wommack and Pinnell, disagree and suggest that boards should indeed get involved in establishing basic objectives and a strategic philosophy, as well as goals and strategies to be used by the line as a starting point for the planning process (Wommack, 1979; Pinnell, 1986). It becomes apparent that the distinction between 'formulating strategy' and 'defining strategic directions' is fuzzy. If a supervisory board, or a unitary board approves strategic directions outlined by managing directors or management, at some point it enters into the discussion and bears responsibility for choosing or endorsing the direction. According to Andrews, it is important to understand that a board should not only evaluate a strategy, but also ratify it. By doing so it 'shares with management the risks associated with its adoption' (Andrews, 1980). We recognize, therefore, that the separation of the stages of 'strategy formulation' and 'strategy evaluation', which we discuss below, is somewhat arbitrary.

Texas Instruments, Inc. (TI), an American company with a board composed primarily of outside directors, does in fact involve the board in strategy formulation. TI's board has established a Corporate Objectives Committee composed only of outside directors.

> This committee monitors the planning system, *suggests new strategic directions*, assesses plans for meeting stated goals and evaluates outside technological and economic influences on the company's future.
>
> (Smith, 1981) (*Emphasis added*)

The involvement of the committee in strategic matters is distinctly more intensive than that of the whole board, or of the other committees. It meets for about 10 full days during the year.

Informal interaction with the CEO or managing directors is another common way for non-executive directors to participate in strategy formulation (Andrews, 1980). CEOs have indicated in our interviews that they use individual directors as 'sounding boards'; other CEOs plan time, often during a dinner preceding a board meeting, to interact with outside directors alone.

After a disturbing public crisis in one German company, the chairman of the supervisory board worked closely with the president of the management board to set detailed directions for the future handling of this aspect of the business. Similar close cooperation characterized their interaction about the domestic employment impacts of a major foreign acquisition, and about possible ways of restructuring another of their businesses.

It appears that those non-executive directors who are seriously involved in strategy formulation have made significant commitments of time and attention in order to play this role. For that reason, among others, they are also in the minority.

Problem Solving: The Evaluation Phase

There is broad agreement in the writings of both board practitioners and researchers that strategy evaluation is one of the main tasks of the board, although some writers claim that many boards fail to discharge this duty (Wommack, 1979; Grass and Zanner, 1988), or do so only in a limited fashion (Tashakori and Boulton, 1983). In order to discuss the participation of non-executive directors in strategy evaluation, we break the discussion into two parts, using Mintzberg's distinction between 'intended' and 'emergent' strategy.

Board evaluation of an 'intended' strategy

The four main reasons for a board to be fully and carefully involved in evaluating strategy can be drawn from Andrews's earlier work:

- The board needs specific evidence that management has a process for developing, considering and choosing among strategic alternatives.
- Especially if they have no personal experience in the industry, outside directors need to understand the characteristics of their company's business. Knowledge of strategy makes intelligent overview feasible.
- Understanding the overall thrust of management directions gives the board a reference point for separate decisions that come before it, and insights into those matters that should be presented to it.
- The evaluation of the corporation's strategy (and of management's adherence to it) allows the board a continued evaluation of management.

(Andrews, 1980, p. 104)

How can the involvement of board members in evaluating an 'intended' strategy be organized? Two modes seem to have developed. One school recommends that the whole board take part.

... we are responsible for assessing the long run survival of the firm ... managers come and go; internal structure changes; there are acquisitions and divestitures. The board persists, dedicated to maintaining the viability of the corporation.

(Whisler, 1983)

A second school expresses the opinion that 'most effective boards get the work done through committees that report to the full board' (Wommack, 1979). They feel that setting up a small group of directors chosen for their relevant expertise has proven an effective way to examine complex issues. In their opinion, such a committee functions best if all of its members are outside, independent directors, and thus free of the emotional commitment which competing claimants of scarce resources inevitably develop.

One North American company created a special board subcommittee to work with the chairman and CEO on a critical restructuring. The process took more than a year and involved the non-executives substantially in the process, to great advantage.

A board level committee can be involved at several points in the planning cycle. William Wommack, former Vice-Chairman of Mead Corporation, suggests that the board (with the help of a corporate objectives committee) can be involved in evaluating not only corporate objectives but also the overall strategic philosophy (Wommack, 1979). Even in cases of relatively formal involvement of a board in strategy evaluation, extensive informal discussions typically occur between the CEO and outside directors on key matters.

Texas Instruments, as we noted earlier, uses a two-pronged approach to get the board involved in strategy. In addition to the committee structure outlined above, the company holds an extensive strategic planning conference in the first quarter to discuss business opportunities for the next, say, 10 years. Early in that conference, the top executives meet with the full board to discuss their long-range goals and strategies, in an atmosphere which provides for considerable give and take.

Executive directors on unitary boards must handle a complex role in these discussions. First, they must avoid taking advocacy positions in situations where their own portfolios are under discussion. The board's concern is the overall corporate strategy. Some companies have restructured board responsibilities so that executive directors no longer carry responsibility for the operation of functions, businesses or divisions. These companies have structured performance criteria that evaluate managing directors on the basis of overall corporate performance. Second, they must respond to board members' queries and provide outside directors with sufficient information to reach an informed judgement.

In two-tier boards, evaluation of strategy naturally falls to the supervisory board whose members are all outside directors. To what extent are non-executive directors equipped to shoulder this task of evaluation? There is, of course, no simple answer to this question. It is quite obvious that certain aspects of strategy can be meaningfully assessed by almost everyone. Examples might include strategies in human resources, e.g. the introduction of a company-wide new pension plan.

In other cases, the director may have experience relevant to a specific strategic issue from personal background. Two examples can be drawn from our interview data. In both cases, the non-executive directors were invited on to the boards because of their extensive backgrounds. In one case, the director had been an executive in an industry where the company has a subsidiary business. In the other, a CEO with experience in acquisitions and mergers was asked to join the board as the company began to implement a major expansion initiative.

As a rule, strategy discussions will tend to centre around issues which require in-depth knowledge of the corporation, or its industries. Here the non-executives face tough choices, particularly if the industry is an especially complex one. They may restrict their contribution to comments based on common sense and their general business experience, or they may follow the advice of a non-executive colleague on the board who is knowledgeable on the topic. A widespread practice, it leaves the non-executive directors in a relatively uncomfortable position, particularly in the light of their legal liabilities. (In countries like the United States, this liability situation has prompted capable executives to shy away from board appointments.)

The other alternative is for the non-executives to really tool up for the task. A substantial investment of time will be necessary to familiarize themselves with the industry. This can represent a personal effort, or the company may provide specially designed briefings for them. For example, two British companies involve the board in a regular cycle of strategy reviews: one holds three-day annual meetings specifically to review corporate strategy; the other reviews each of its businesses comprehensively on a biannual basis. We found an even more direct educational approach in a large European bank, where the non-executive directors, typically non-bankers, were given special, semi-formal seminars on banking methods (e.g. on new financial instruments).

The potential for tooling-up hinges, of course, on the availability of the non-executives. Most are executives in their own right, and these efforts meet natural limits. To overcome the time constraints, other avenues have been explored. Top banking executives in Germany, who traditionally sit on the boards of many industrial companies, use special assistants (provided by their banks) to review the documentation provided to them in preparation for board meetings, as well as to review material on the industries where the corporations are active. As another means to increase the effectiveness of non-executive directors, some have raised the possibility of the corporation providing special staff for these directors as part of their board membership. While some practitioners among the non-executives favour the idea, others object. Executive directors in particular feel strongly that 'it would stress too much the "we" and "they" feeling on the board'.

In our research we encountered cases where board involvement was less than ideal. The chairman of one British company, who very much appreciates good input from the non-executive directors, soberly remarked that he doubted his board was really in a position to criticize strategic plans prepared by the executive group. This was echoed by the CEO, who believes that non-executives do not know the business well enough to get deeply involved, and stated flatly that 'his board simply does not raise questions about the future of the company'.

It is clear that meaningful involvement of non-executive directors in the strategy evaluation process will require extensive information, and a readiness on the part of the corporation to provide this information in a timely fashion (Aram and Cowen, 1986).

Board and 'emergent strategies'

How can a board participate in strategy evaluation if the corporation relies on the concept of an 'emergent strategy' to establish its future direction? In these cases, strategy evolves from a stream of important decisions which are moulded into a pattern by corporate management. This approach is far more common than the majority of textbooks make us believe; in the complex, messy and frequently contradictory world in which companies have to chart their course, clean, neat approaches to planning are not always possible. It is often necessary to use an equally messy way of proceeding when establishing the direction of a corporation. Sometimes called 'incrementalism', this approach is widely accepted as legitimate today (Quinn, 1980).

In companies where incremental or emergent strategies play a major role, meaningful involvement of the board, and particularly of the non-executive directors, is more difficult. Their role in these cases is usually restricted to the discussion and approval of major capital expenditures. If informal discussions on strategy are a major ingredient of the process for creating an 'intended strategy', it is an even more important means of exerting influence for directors in the case of 'emergent strategy'.

How difficult the role of the non-executive director becomes in this context, particularly if each investment decision is presented in isolation, was driven home to us in an interview with a North American company. The director remarked that he had to insist on the presentation of a more cohesive picture of the intentions of corporate management with respect to the future direction of the company. The company was reluctant to use elaborate formal planning systems, yet it was very difficult for him to assess individual capital expenditure proposals otherwise. His ability to contribute, or to exercise his responsibilities diligently, was dependent upon the responsiveness of the CEO to this request. Several executives, chairman and CEO, have indicated to us that as a minimum they now regularly present the board *not only* with a recommendation for action, but also with those alternatives discussed—and discarded—with the rationale.

THE BOARD'S ROLE IN 'IMPLEMENTATION'

Implementing the Strategy

Can the board be involved in implementing strategy? In a few cases, there is a fine line to be drawn between implementation and monitoring implementation. With the North American example noted above, and with two British boards, we find situations where board members have played important roles in the actual implementation of a strategic decision. In two key acquisitions, in different companies, the non-executive directors prodded the managers responsible for negotiating price offers to move quickly to set prices that were so attractive as to be virtually 'irrefusable'. In both cases, the move averted protracted and potentially difficult negotiations.

Board member intervention was possible because a close monitoring process had been set up to follow the acquisition discussions. While this might be termed 'monitoring', the process was structured with such frequent reporting to the board in each situation that board discussions actually became 'online' input to the acquisition negotiation.

Strategy implementation responsibilities more often fall to the executive management of the company. In some cases, perhaps in the majority of cases, this will include the executives who serve on the board. Certainly in the German situation, the management board executives carry implementation responsibility. In the United Kingdom, it depends upon the way the portfolios of executive directors are structured. In most companies, executive directors carry operational responsibility for the divisions or functions under their purview. For them, strategy implementation follows directly—a situation that would satisfy Whisler's preferences. In a small but growing number of companies, executive director portfolios remove them from direct operational responsibility. There, implementation is handed to the next layer of management, the heads of divisions or businesses.

Perhaps the most direct impact of the board on implementation, and particularly from non-executive directors, comes during the handling of succession. We will explore this more fully on page 255.

Monitoring Strategy Implementation

The increasing tendency to hold board members responsible for the performance of the company on one hand, and the growing volatility in the different environmental domains in which the corporation operates on the other, have moved the question of tracking a strategy and monitoring its implementation into the focal point of board attention.

While the evaluation of strategy finds ample attention in the literature, the writings on monitoring implementation are scarce (as a rare exception, see O'Connor, 1983).

The question of monitoring strategic progress revolves around the types of indicators being monitored, and who has access to them. A survey conducted a few years ago by The Conference Board on this subject came to a number of interesting conclusions. It found that the plans monitored are primarily strategic and operating plans of individual business units or divisions. Further, monitoring the implementation fell typically to the manager of the unit involved. One of the executives included in The Conference Board survey observed,

> Part of the problem is that over their histories, all corporations have developed systems for tracking short term operating and financial performance that serve their somewhat limited and short term purposes well, but that rarely serve as an effective means for tracking strategy performance . . . there are no formal means for identifying and measuring those key variables that reflect the driving forces of the business.
>
> (O'Connor, 1983, p. 2)

As a result, even in those companies that take the matter most seriously, monitoring strategy is as yet a relatively informal affair compared with the typically more structured tracking of operational plans. This result is echoed in our own research: the companies we interviewed tended to use rather short-term measurements of performance, reviewed on a quarterly basis.

Are there ways to remedy this by and large unsatisfactory situation? In answering this question, we are reminded that the tasks of strategic and operational planning are indeed different. While it is the task of operational planning to secure short-term *earnings* and *cash flows*, it is the task of strategic planning to create or maintain a solid lasting *earnings potential* (a strong strategic position) for the corporation (which, thereafter, in operational management can be coined into profits). In order to achieve these two goals, completely different actions are needed; as a consequence, their realization must be measured by different yardsticks. Trying to monitor the creation or the maintenance of a strategic position with the help of short-term performance measures—quarterly ROI or cash flow— is, as a German practitioner of planning put it 'like deciding the question whether to fill up the heating oil tank of your house on the basis of the temperature indicated on a given day on your thermometer; for decisions of that type, you better consult your calendar'.

It is certainly appropriate to try to measure the achievements of short-term performance by studying quarterly income statements. However, to judge shifts in the strategic performance of the company, other factors should be observed, e.g. market share changes, market growth rates, changes in the perception of the quality of the product or services offered by the company, as well as 'softer' indicators.

Realizing the need for better strategic indicators, more and more companies seem to be modifying their monitoring procedures. A technology firm in The Conference Board sample monitors its strategic programmes along four primary dimensions: customer satisfaction, innovation, productivity and human resources.

> In each of these areas, . . . the company has established a number of indicators of performance. In the customer satisfaction area it includes market share, product quality, delivery performance and services. Innovation indicators are concerned with the flow of new products, the percentage of revenues they contribute, and the assessment of product performance relative to competition . . .
>
> (O'Connor, 1983, p. 10)

These are questions which affect executive and non-executive directors alike. Executive directors, however, have one important advantage: because they 'live' within the corporation, they see, hear, overhear, and absorb many of the informal signals that cumulate to a judgement about the effectiveness of strategy implementation.

In our interviews, a number of non-executive directors expressed dissatisfaction with short-term measures and sought their own indicators for whether the corporation was moving towards its overall strategic position or, more importantly, whether the present strategic position was deteriorating. One alternative indicator of long-term organizational health was mentioned by both a non-executive director and the corporate secretary of a multinational oil company: the morale of the layer of executives immediately below the board. Both know the company well, as even the outside director had served 14 years on the board.

To enable a non-executive director to monitor operational as well as strategic performance, the reporting system of a company has to be organized to provide board members with two categories of information. The information flow concerning the short-term performance is usually well developed; in our interviews, some directors even complained about an overload. Despite the example of the technology company mentioned above, formal reporting of good indicators of strategic position seems to be much less developed. Comments from one German board member indicated that the CEO (head of the management board) had changed this dimension of the company culture dramatically. He developed powerful indicators to convince the two boards of the fragility of the international competitive position of the company. For example, he demonstrated a dramatic difference between total labour cost per hour of producing their product and that of an Asian producer. The role of the board of a subsidiary company may offer a way to bridge the gap between operational and strategic monitoring. In large companies, the parent board can only monitor broad strategic indicators. By nature responsible for the strategy and operations of a business on a smaller scale, the strategic indicators monitored by subsidiary boards are more likely to bring some understanding of the factors affecting the achievement of strategic goals. Good dialogue between key members of parent and subsidiary boards can bring some depth of judgement to the parent board without the overwhelming detail of operation reporting.

Valuable insights into appropriate indicators have been provided by the PIMS programme (Buzzell and Gale, 1987) and other approaches to industry and competitor analysis (Porter, 1980). It should not be impossible for management and the board to tool up for this task, although, by its very nature, it will always remain 'a difficult and sophisticated process requiring considerable thought and care' (O'Connor, 1983).

BOARD INVOLVEMENT IN 'PATHFINDING'

> I believe we need a clear understanding of the role of corporate vision or, as I prefer to denote it, a corporate dream . . . it is essential that the board of a large corporation should have a dream and the CEO a personal dream as well. Dreams do not have to be demonstrably achievable . . . they must not be precise, but they have to be ambitious, far beyond the capabilities of day-to-day operations . . . they have to attract the hearts and the minds of people who will have to accomplish them and they have a long and in some cases imprecise time horizon . . . it must inspire and stimulate and it must be deeply owned by the dreamers.
>
> (Harvey-Jones, 1988a, pp. 5–6)

Can a board, and in particular a non-executive director, get involved in developing a vision for a corporation—the grand, inspiring design of what the company wants to be 10 years hence? It is not easy to imagine how a board can get involved in the creation of such a dream. A vision is rarely a 'road to Damascus' experience; in most cases it is a design that has been shaped and reshaped over time, just as the final grandiose design of the Sydney opera house or Mao's vision of new China was not the result of a creative bolt of lightning. Both took time to evolve.

Furthermore, creative processes of this nature are difficult, if not impossible to structure ahead of time. As Harvey-Jones (1988a, p. 6) says himself:

> . . . the process of corporate dreaming is the antithesis of the [conventional] planning process. The dreams have to be the product of those at the top and

will result only from the expenditure of a great deal of time and effort. But it needs to be time and effort in sweatshirts, with cans of beer, sandwiches and flipcharts, rather than in business suits with a coffee and computer graphics.

Time and effort are not the only ingredients in a visioning endeavour; it also requires a visionary at the top, someone to lead the process, a CEO with creativity and imagination. Harvey-Jones (an imaginative corporate leader) confesses that he held his dream for many years—for ICI to be the world leading chemical service company—before he could embark on a process which allowed him to shape it. Together with the board, he realized a dream which eventually changed ICI from top to bottom.

One North American company recently split the jobs of CEO (president) and chairman. In an interview with the chairman, who had previously held both positions, we were told that the locus of strategy setting had shifted to the new president. Thus, we arrive at another powerful way for the board to influence strategy: the choice of a new CEO.

APPOINTMENT OF THE CEO

Writers, as well as the board members we interviewed, almost unanimously see the appointment of the CEO as the key task of the board. One way or another, voices like this are echoed over and over again:

> ... most executives know that the choice of the company's chief executive officer is the most important decision the board of directors and the outgoing CEO will make—the decision that determines the future course and the health of the company.
>
> (Vancil, 1987b, p. 107)

Whisler points out that this decision is 'uniquely the board's responsibility and authority' (Whisler, 1983), an opinion by no means restricted to the Anglo-Saxon world. We find agreement in countries with two-tier board systems like Germany, where the main task of supervisory boards is seen as choosing top management. Our interview data find unanimity among all the directors on this point—executive and non-executive, CEO and chairman, Canadian, British, German.

How does the choice of a CEO impact on the strategy of a company? The American philosopher Ralph Waldo Emerson once coined the phrase, that an organization is the lengthened shadow of a person, the person at the top, of course. We believe this is particularly true for corporations. There is no shortage of examples to support this point. Leaders like Lee Iacocca at Chrysler, Jan Carlzon at SAS, John Harvey-Jones at ICI, Carlo de Benedetti at Olivetti, Jack Welch at General Electric, changed their companies dramatically after being appointed.

One CEO put the relationship between the person and the strategy in sharp focus when he said:

> To me the strategy starts with the person you hire. You don't design a strategy and then hire a person because the person becomes the owner of the strategy and transferring ownership to an enterprise and then giving them the responsibility for a strategy is the way to play the game.

From this perspective, Vancil strongly encourages the board to think of succession not simply in terms of replacing the top person, but as a critical strategic process involving the selection and development of the future leadership of the firm (Vancil, 1987a). This he concludes after five years of studying CEO succession, involving interviews of 50 incumbent CEOs, prior CEOs, CEO candidates and outside directors who had participated in succession processes.

Preliminary results of our own research suggest that non-executive directors, together with the outgoing CEO, can play a particularly important role here for a number of reasons. First, non-executives have a much more detached view of the CEO than the executive directors. Second, not only are executives concerned with their vested interests and influence, but frequently the new CEO is chosen from among them. Thus, the natural politics of the situation leave them either strongly defensive, or too deeply involved.

One example taken from our research illustrates an extreme reaction to the potential personal bias of executive directors. In a large European multinational, the committee appointed to handle the succession question was exclusively composed of non-executives, plus the outgoing CEO. The committee's choice followed the suggestion of the incumbent CEO, and only later was the appointment discussed with the executive directors. Whether it is necessary to exclude so completely executive director participation is questionable; having observed colleagues at close range for many years, executive directors probably have important insights to contribute. Furthermore, unless there is a plan to 'clean house', they will make up the team of top managers who will guide the company in its new strategic directions.

How might the work of that board committee be organized? Vancil uncovered several steps in his research. First, the board and the outgoing CEO establish a scenario of the environment in which the company will have to function under the new leadership. This leads to the identification of some key criteria which the future leader should meet. Age and compatibility between the expertise of the candidates and the future strategic challenges identified in the scenario rank particularly high. Second, a group of potential candidates is selected. Then the choice of the heir apparent is made.

No matter how it is handled, the process is highly charged. When General Electric needed to replace Chairman/CEO Reginald Jones and his two vice-chairmen, there were six or seven internal candidates for the three positions, an enviable situation with some downside consequences. For very soon it became clear that those candidates not selected would probably leave the company, a fear that was later realized.

From the candidates, a special board committee selected three for positions at the top of the company, without naming a chairman/CEO. The board used the following year to know them better, by inviting their attendance at board meetings. A year elapsed before the final decision, during which time an unproductive 'horse race' developed between the three candidates. Finally, Jack Welch was named chairman and CEO.

In GE, and in other companies where the board is expected to be heavily involved in selecting not only the CEO, but other senior managers, we wonder how the boards gain sufficient familiarity with candidates to arrive at sound judgements. How does the board judge whether to look internally or externally for a candidate? Our interviewees at two companies who recently brought in CEOs from outside, indicated that the chairman—in one case of a unitary board, in the other, of the supervisory board—played a key role. These actions were based on judgements about the long-term performance of the company and reflected the sense of key members of the board that the company was performing below capacity.

In some companies where it is anticipated that the successor will be drawn from internal candidates, specific opportunities are designed for the board to meet and get to know corporate management. Occasions for interaction may be either formal or informal. Two companies make a practice of involving business and division heads in presentations to the board regarding capital investments and major new projects. Another regularly invites senior managers to lunch with the board during board meetings. During the year, the board might interact with 15–20 individuals below board level. One non-executive said that after 14 years, he felt he knew more than 50 senior managers quite well. Other non-executives, with shorter tenure on their respective boards, said they were comfortable with their knowledge of 10 to 30 individuals.

Despite the deep involvement of non-executives in this process, the dominant role of the outgoing CEO should not be underestimated. In their study of American companies, McCanna and Comte found that more than 40% of all new CEOs were selected at the initiative of their predecessors (McCanna and Comte, 1986).

OTHER DETERMINANTS OF BOARD INVOLVEMENT

In the previous sections, we have explored how the stages of the strategy process determine board involvement. In reviewing the data and opinions about the involvement of the board in strategy, we find a number of factors which importantly influence the quality of board involvement in each and every stage of the strategy process. Five can be identified which appear central.

Legal Responsibilities: Unitary versus Two-Tier

Boards and directors function within the legal frameworks of corporate law in the countries where they operate. It is not our purpose in this chapter to provide a comprehensive review of the corporate law regarding board activity. However, a few comments can highlight several important differences between countries. Commonly, corporate law speaks only in very general terms about the duties and responsibilities of the board. Terms include, for instance, responsibilities for assuring the quality and process of the management of the company (Switzerland), and for exercising diligence and prudence in decision making (United States). In the United States, and in other countries, the meaning of the law has evolved through interpretations of court decisions.

By and large, corporate law does not speak directly of the role of boards in strategy. Important exceptions are found in the legal structures for the two-tier boards in Germany, the Netherlands and, to some degree, the Scandinavian countries. While the structure and practice in these countries differ significantly, a few similarities can be noted which impact on the nature of strategy participation.

The establishment of separate 'management' and 'supervisory' boards defines spheres of activity and responsibility. Executives serve on the management board, which is chaired by a president (CEO). Non-executives and labour representatives serve in numbers specified by law on the supervisory board, headed by a chairman. Supervisory boards are usually required to meet three to five times each year, and most meet quarterly. Management boards tend to meet weekly, or fortnightly.

The ultimate approval of key strategic decisions is usually specifically reserved for the supervisory board. These may include buying or selling participation in other companies; changing production sites; setting the investment programme; approving social agreements that go beyond trade union agreements; approving investments outside the plans which exceed a certain amount (e.g. 5 million DM).

For all practical purposes, interaction between the two boards is restricted to the president of the management board and the chairman of the supervisory board, although other board members have access to supervisory board members as well. As we have noted, this can be a rich channel. This channel is augmented by the structure of labour participation on the boards, through co-determination, as information flows informally through the various work councils and other structures that support labour representation. Like executive directors in other settings, some labour representatives are employees, and thus bring the insights that go with living and working in the company. One German director commented that, in fact, an awareness of the quality of the information available to the labour representatives of the supervisory board prompted efforts by the management board of his company to ensure that the shareholder representatives on the supervisory board were equally well informed.

The logic of the two-tier structure resonates with Whisler's concern about maintaining a role for the board that permits independent evaluation of the performance of management. The structure effectively precludes supervisory board involvement in many stages of the strategy process, leaving the vision, initiation, formulation and implementation stages, de facto, in the hands of the management board.

Attitude of the CEO/Chairman

Whether operating within a two-tier or unitary structure, the attitude(s) of the CEO and/or chairman is central to the participation of the board in strategy discussions. Through the earlier part of this chapter we assumed an attitude that sought board participation. Clearly, if the CEO wished to 'run the company' without interference, within any legal framework it is possible to handle membership, information and activity so that the power, authority and responsibility for corporate strategy rests almost entirely with management.

Comments in our interviews ranged from 'you have to take a lot on trust' (non-executive director) to 'the directors are in the hands of management and they should be concerned about this' (vice-president for legal affairs). Remarked one CEO: 'The executives can feed the board any information they want'.

Significant involvement of the board, especially of the non-executive directors, requires that the chairman and CEO establish an attitude and climate which recognize the board as a resource for the company. A willingness to share power and a real tolerance for discussion and disagreement characterize those boards where directors participate actively in many stages of the process. In interviews with the directors of several companies, directors used the terms 'trust' and 'openness' to describe the nature of board relationships, among and between executive and non-executive directors. The quotations above represent cautions from directors whose companies consider the board a highly valued resource.

The Nature of the Company

Important to our discussion is an understanding that there is no single profile of board involvement in strategy that serves best. Within the legal frameworks, and given a wish to utilize the board, other structural factors will affect the potential and quality of board involvement in strategy— and these factors will result in different, effective profiles for each company. For example, the nature of the strategy process itself depends importantly on the structure of the company: is it a holding company? a conglomerate? an integrated business? The types of decisions and level of detail available to the main board differ in each case. The potential for subsidiary boards to play a substantial role, and to expand the capability of the main board to influence strategy depends upon the structure of the company.

The depth of involvement will vary also according to the state of the environment and the stage of development of the company. Economic crises, such as the stock market crash of October 1987, brought many boards into more intimate strategy consultations than previously, as corporate assets were devalued, in some cases by 30% to 40%, overnight. Internal crises, such as the recent charges of currency fraud at Volkswagen, also bring the board into closer contact with management activity. Often, in these situations, key appointments are subject to more detailed scrutiny.

Certain watershed moments may prompt closer board involvement. For example, in businesses moving into multinational or global postures for the first time, or in companies exploring structural changes to respond to imperatives of size and geographic dispersion, the board may need to move temporarily into closer participation. Certainly, the approach of a succession decision may bring the board from a posture of primarily evaluative involvement, to an active role as that decision preconditions pathfinding, and the future vision of the company.

The Types of Strategic Issues

Strategic corporate issues come in a variety of forms. As a minimum, one can distinguish strategic directions and decisions that need to be taken in at least 10 categories of activities. In outlining these categories, we draw upon a major study of decision making at the top of 30 British firms, undertaken over a 10-year period (Hickson et al., 1986). With some modification in nomenclature, they provide a fairly comprehensive typology of strategic issues (Demb and Neubauer, 1988).

(1) Technology—choices of technology, make or buy decisions.
(2) Reorganization—the structure of the company.
(3) Control/operational plans—planning, budgeting, MIS.
(4) Marketing distribution—direct, or networked.
(5) Services—the level of service provided, or purchased.
(6) Products—product lines.
(7) Personnel—all human resource issues, executive succession.
(8) Boundaries of the organization—acquisitions, mergers.
(9) Capital inputs (financial, physical, human)—sources and modes.
(10) Location—geographic spread, location of plants.

Clearly, the board—executive and non-executive directors—can and will be involved *differently* in each area. If we use the stages of strategic development to test the nature of board involvement, some examples can surface which illustrate the point (see Figure 11.2).

Board involvement can probably be most substantial in the personnel area—especially in the choice of a CEO—and also in capital and boundary decisions. For those companies considering geographic expansion, board member experience in regions or countries new to the company may be

TASKS \ STAGES	Set Path/Vision	Initiate	Formulate	Evaluate	Implement	Monitor
Technology				⊢ − − − ⊣		⊢ − − − ⊣
Reorganization			⊢ − − − ⊣			
Control/Op Plans						
Market/Distrib						
Services						
Products						
Personnel	⊢ − −	− − − − −	− − − − −	− − − − −	− − − − −	− − − ⊣
Org Boundary	⊢ − ⊣		⊢ − − − ⊣	⊢ − − − ⊣		⊢ − − − ⊣
Capital Inputs				⊢ − − − ⊣		⊢ − − − ⊣
Location						

Figure 11.2 An illustrative profile of board involvement in strategic issues

invaluable at the formulation stage. Similarly, questions of reorganization can draw usefully upon board experience.

Technology decisions represent a particularly crucial and troublesome area. Crucial because they require such large investments and may reshape entire industries; they are troublesome because even technology experts have difficulty projecting the potential impacts of new technologies on their product, manufacturing or distribution processes. It is known that a number of companies, Philips and BP among them, bring strategic technology matters to the board for consideration, and have assigned this area to one or more directors.

Examining the reality of strategic decisions brings home a point strongly voiced in our interviews: the future is unpredictable, and even good professionals err in their judgement. In response to our request to discuss a decision which later turned out to have been in error, only one of our interviewees found difficulty locating an example. For each company, there are several examples where remedial action had to be taken within six months to a year to correct an earlier judgement.

How was a poor decision made, and under what circumstances? Often, the board and management were endeavouring to break new ground: in one case, the restructuring of a subsidiary business in a form that was experimental for the company; in another, the acquisition of a similar business by a European company, in the US market. An inability to appreciate and predict the response of the new 'foreign market' to the product led to disappointing sales results. In yet a third, unfamiliarity with the technology resulted in acquisition of a company which marketed a high quality, niche product, and became the 'high cost producer' in its industry within six months. Management and the board did not have the experience or sophistication to anticipate the introduction of a new process technology that so dramatically improved the quality of competitor products, as to make them indistinguishable from the company acquired.

So we find ourselves in agreement with the non-executive director who said: 'If shareholders think the existence of the non-executives on a board will assure that the corporation does well . . . I think not'.

The Nature and Type of Resource Commitment

The bottom line in achieving appropriate, effective and substantial board involvement in the strategy process depends upon the nature and type of the resources committed. Available resources include: time, information and personal capacities.

Table 11.2 outlines the modes in which boards, and their directors, are commonly involved in strategy, and the mechanisms that have been developed to support and facilitate this involvement.

Table 11.2 Involving the board in strategy

	Modes of Board Involvement	Inputs/Mechanisms
1. Set path/vision	Hire CEO	Board committee
	Top management succession	Opportunity for interaction
	Special 'future' sessions	Time: 3–5 days
	Individual input/queries	Individual experience/ creativity
2. Initiate process	Board requires process	Culture amenable to questioning
	Set strategic goals/parameters	Informed board
	Individual/group queries	Management willing to respond
3. Formulate options	CEO/management succession	Regular interaction with top mgt
	Special director assignments	Special task forces
	Reviewing 'discarded' options	Attitude: 'partnership' vs. 'delegation/review'
4. Evaluate strategy	'Strategy review' meetings	Time: 3–5 days
	Strategy committee	Process to synthesize background material
5. Implement	CEO/succession	Good internal board communication
6. Monitor	Define broader descriptors	System to generate data on these
	Review short-term measures	Good, pointed summaries
	Compare actual/planned	Special summaries

It is clear from Table 11.2 that a significant investment of time and attention to the provision of good information is necessary to support a real board contribution to the strategy process. Whether the company situation permits substantial involvement across topics in early stages, or tends to bring board judgement to bear only at the evaluation and monitoring stages, careful background is required on both the specific decision and its context. Even if it were a matter of 'simply' evaluating an acquisition, the board must be knowledgeable about the strategic direction (or plan) the acquisition is intended to serve.

Whatever the profile of board involvement sought, the mechanisms and processes must take into account differences in the roles executive and non-executive directors can play—differences inherent in their circumstances and useful for board functioning.

The emotional attachment, commitment and sense of personal responsibility differ. By definition of their role, executive directors feel an 'ownership' for the company—its successes and failures—more keenly than non-executives. The design of performance evaluation structures for executive directors is particularly critical in providing a base from which they can take a corporate-wide perspective in their board roles. Executives who are evaluated on the basis of the performance of a function, division or subsidiary business, are put into a double-bind situation where they must protect and defend their operational responsibility while, at the same time, trying to act on behalf of the company as a whole.

To overcome this bias, and to capture the talent of the executives for the board, at least four companies in our study restructured performance evaluation methods for their executive directors, as well as their board portfolios. In one company, executive directors are only evaluated as a group, on the basis of company performance. Their collective responsibilities are designed to keep them at arm's length from operational management. Chairmen, CEOs and executive directors have described the complexity of the transition. It requires several years to create new attitudes and to break old habits. In some cases, to place individuals where they will be most effective and experience the greatest satisfaction, individuals may be counselled to step off the board, and to take the operational role. During this transition in one Dutch company, several directors volunteered to move 'off' the board, because they wanted the personal satisfaction of 'running' a piece of the business.

The knowledge base from which executives and non-executives operate also differs importantly. The majority of executive directors will have been with the company for many years. Facts, history, the culture and the people are known to them. Their personal networks, and their current day-to-day experiences given them access to a quality of information—both formal and informal—that is unavailable to non-executives.

Of course, it is their outside view that makes the non-executive directors most valuable. They represent the potential for avoiding 'tunnel vision' and for being trapped in old perspectives and habits. Non-executive contributions often improve with the length of their tenure on the board. They come to a more sophisticated and subtle understanding of the company and its industry, particularly if attention has been given to providing them with appropriate briefings and information. We found in the companies we studied that one or two senior non-executives often became reference points for other external members of the board.

Because they are often chief executives of their own companies, the time and energy a non-executive can devote to board positions is limited. The most diligent of directors spend about 25–30 days a year on board matters—often chairing subcommittees. Realistically, this also limits the number of boards on which a non-executive director can serve in an effective manner. We noted earlier the possibilities for expanding this personal capability by providing staff, either to the board, or, as in the case of some German banks, to their executives for their outside director responsibilities. Even this has its limits, if the individual is to form cogent judgements about strategic company matters.

CONCLUDING REMARKS

Our review of strategy processes and current board involvement supports the argument that there are many opportunities—formal and informal— for substantive and meaningful board input. The natural limitations of time and attention suggest that the stage of *strategy evaluation* and the moments of *CEO and top executive succession* decisions offer the broadest platform for that involvement.

The quality of involvement will depend heavily upon the attitude of the chairman/CEO, and the time and attention devoted to supporting director deliberations. The quality of the knowledge base of a director is an input to the process which rests in the hands of both the director *and* management.

Having said this, we strongly emphasize that fruitful board involvement, in our experience, has not been limited to these few situations. Board members—executive and non-executive—have played key, and even essential roles in strategy formulation in many companies we visited.

The tectonic shifts, alluded to earlier, will continue to rumble for many years to come. The adaptation that will be required of corporations to respond to market, stakeholder, and societal pressures can only accelerate. Courage, judgement and imagination will be needed. Under these circumstances, a corporation must fully utilize all the resources available to it—especially those at the top. The talent, experience, and perspective of board members, as well as their role within the governance area, must be brought to bear in shaping the future of the company. As John Harvey-Jones (1988a, p. 22) asks:

> If the board is not taking the company purposefully into the future, who is?

REFERENCES

Andrews, Kenneth R. (1980) Directors' responsibility for corporate strategy, *Harvard Business Review*, November–December, 104–108.

Aram, John J., and Cowen, Scott, S. (1986) The directors' role in planning: What information do they need?, *Journal of Long-Range Planning*, **19**(2), 117–124.

Business Graduate (1985) The role of the non-executive director, January.

Business Week (1986) A job nobody wants, 8 September.

Buzzel, Robert, and Gale, Bradley (1987) The PIMS Princip'es. The Free Press, New York and London.

Demb, Ada, and Neubauer, F.-Friedrich (1988) Perspectives on Corporate Governance, IMI Working Paper, October.

Gerum, Elmar, Steinmann, Horst, Fees, Werner (1988) Der Mitbestimmte Aufsichtsrat, Stuttgart.

Grass, Rolf-Dieter and Zanner, Harald (1988) Weder Aufsicht Noch Rat, Wirtschaftswoche, 18 March.

Harvey-Jones, Sir John (1988a) Making It Happen. Collins, London.

Harvey-Jones, Sir John (1988b) Prepared speech for the St Gallen Symposium, St Gallen.

Hickson, David J. et al. (1986) Top Decisions. Basil Blackwell, Oxford.

Judge, William Q., and Zeithaml, Care P. (1987) The Strategic Role of the Board of Directors: A Review and Model. Paper submitted to the Business Policy and Planning Division of the National Academy of Management Meeting, New Orleans.

Kiefer, Charles F., and Senge, Peter M. (1986) A Description of a Metanoic Organization. Innovation Associates, Framingham, Massachusetts.

Leavitt, Harold (1986) Corporate Pathfinders: Building Vision and Values into Organizations. Dow Jones-Irwin, Homewood, Ill.

McCanna, Walter F., and Comte, Thomas E. (1986) The CEO succession dilemma: How boards function in turnover at the top, Business Horizons, June, pp. 17–22.

Mintzberg, Henry, and Quinn, James B. (1988) The Strategy Process: Concepts, Context and Cases. Prentice-Hall, Englewood Cliffs, NJ.

O'Connor, Rochelle (1983) Trading the Strategic Plan Research. Report from The Conference Board, New York.

Pinnell, Blake (1986) The role of the board in corporate planning, Journal of Long-Range Planning, 19(5), 27–32.

Porter, Michael (1980) Competitive Strategy. Free Press, New York.

Porter, Michael (1987) The state of strategic thinking, The Economist, 23 May.

Quinn, James Brian (1980) Strategies for Change. Prentice-Hall, Englewood Cliffs, NJ.

Rosenstein, Josef (1987) Why don't US boards get more involved in strategy? Journal of Long-Range Planning, 3, 30–34.

Smith, Brian F. (1981) The Board of Directors in Strategic Planning. Touche Ross & Co., New York, 24 July.

Tashakori, Ahmet, and Boulton, William (1983) A look at the board's role in planning, Journal of Business Strategy, 3(3), Winter, 64–70.

Vancil, Richard E. (1987a) Passing the Baton: Managing the Process of CEO Succession. Harvard Business School Press, Cambridge, Mass.

Vancil, Richard E. (1987b) A look at CEO succession, Harvard Business Review, March–April, 107–117.

Whisler, Thomas L. (1983) Some do's and don't's for directors, Wall Street Journal, 21 March.

Wommack, William W. (1979) The board's most important function, Harvard Business Review, September–October, 48–62.

12

HUMAN RESOURCE MANAGEMENT, CORPORATE CULTURE AND ENTREPRENEURSHIP AS KEY ISSUES IN THE HUNGARIAN ECONOMIC REFORM

Magdolna Csath

Visiting Professor of Strategic Management
Virginia Polytechnic and State University

Home Institution: Karl Marx University of Economics
Budapest, Hungary

ECONOMIC REFORM 1968: PROBLEMS AND ACHIEVEMENT

The Hungarian economic reform in 1968 was a departure from the centralised, autocratic economic and political system which existed prior to that time. In the old system, those at the different levels of the power structure were absolutely self-confident about their ability and right to determine what was good for everybody else. They were not interested in the opinions of their subordinates, especially when those opinions concerned poor decision making at higher levels. Human resources were badly managed, and knowledge and skills were misused. This resulted in a lack of commitment by subordinates and also in lack of interest in

International Review of Strategic Management.
Edited by D. E. Hussey. © 1990 John Wiley & Sons Ltd

doing the right things. Those lacking power and responsibility were depressed with their work and held little hope for future improvement. They were not motivated to improve their performance in the absence of clear, performance-based incentive and promotion systems. Personnel departments were more concerned about the political reliability of the people in a company than about their capabilities and skills to perform. Alienation of people along with dissatisfaction has been the characteristic feeling in the workplaces, which contributed considerably to the growing incompetence in managing the economy and the companies in the changing environment of the 1960s. There appeared to be no way out of the crisis other than introducing major changes in managing the economy and the companies.

The process started in 1968 with decentralising the planning process and giving more autonomy to company managers in establishing goals and strategies. It was a revolutionary step in a country where for more than 20 years detailed instructions had been given to managers on what to produce, what resources to use, how much to pay for the resources, how much to pay to employees and where to sell the products. The changes were intended to encourage independent thinking by managers in shaping the corporate future; in matching company capabilities and actions with the opportunities and threats in the environment; in risk taking related to new product introduction; in finding new markets, and developing appropriate marketing and management methods. Unfortunately at the time when all these structural changes were introduced the acting managers were not prepared for these changes. Market orientation, concern with efficiency and effectiveness, fluctuating demand and competition were realities they were not used to. On the contrary, they were expected to implement ideas which had been imposed on them without involving them in the decision-making process. All that they were allowed and supposed to do was to fulfil the plans which were formulated far away from the companies, in the National Planning Office and in the different ministries. As managers had operated in a strongly controlled environment for a long time, it was a naive idea to expect that they would change their attitudes, thinking, managerial methods and techniques easily and quickly. That was one of the key problems of the reform which caused serious difficulties not much later: supposing that change comes easy. Apart from a few reform-minded company managers who have been involved in the reform process from the very beginning, the majority of managers in the state-owned companies learned the rhetoric of the reform but were acting in practice against the reform. They were not willing, or very often were just not able, to change their deeply rooted ways of managing. Because they had not been involved in the elaboration of the reform steps, they did not really understand what was going on and also were not sure how long the new ideas would survive. Therefore, although not openly, they resisted the intended changes by manoeuvring in the short term. Probably if the human effects of change had been better considered and analysed by reform champions in the party and the government it would have been less difficult to introduce the reform initiatives. However, the reformers themselves did not reform their own methods. Instead of imposing production and sales plans on the companies, the different reform ideas were imposed on the unprepared managers with minimum, very often 'after-the-decision' type participation. No wonder that the majority of managers were not really committed to the reform. For them, after all, it became more difficult to manage.

It needed considerable time and consistent government behaviour to develop a new generation of managers. With the help of management education, and new methods of management selection, promotion and performance evaluation, a better fit between the reform principles and management attitudes, values and methods should have been established.

It would have been also critical to the success of the reform to build a supportive environment around those managers who were willing and able to change. Instead, very often, those managers who were willing to change, and who of course made mistakes because of environmental factors or just because of their lack of knowledge or experience, got into trouble, and had to give explanations at different levels of the bureaucracy as to why they failed. On the other hand those who continued to manage as usual, although missing opportunities, were able to survive. This environment did not encourage risk taking and change, and instead reinforced the old values: *don't rock the boat*. One also has to remember that those party and government officials and company managers were also still around who definitely opposed any kind of reform. For these old-timers entrepreneurship, risk taking, profit, self-interest, etc., had been 'dirty words' for many years. They were ideologically disapproved values of capitalism. Additionally, many workers under the influence of the same ideology were averse to the harder work expected from them in a more performance-oriented environment and were natural supporters of the old-timers. Additionally, as mentioned earlier, the reform was introduced in top–down fashion without genuine participation in the preparatory process by those who were supposed to implement the reform. There was not enough enthusiasm, faith and commitment to the reform achievements against its open and hidden opposition. The opponents of the reform succeeded in stopping the process in 1972. This was very unfortunate timing because of the accumulated environmental problems caused by the energy crisis. This interruption in the reform process has caused enormous harm to the economy leaving it absolutely unprepared for the next environmental changes. After a short time of economic improvement, by the early 1970s the country had accumulated acute problems like:

- declining economic growth;
- declining work morale;
- stagnating productivity;
- increasing difficulties in providing exports to pay for imports;
- deterioration in the terms of trade;
- increasing number of enterprises producing losses or very low profits;
- accumulation of a substantial convertible currency debt.

There have been several explanations for these problems. The official explanations unfortunately have not been critical enough in analysing the real problems. Rather they have blamed the environment, the so-called 'unpredictable changes' like the oil price increase, for the poor performance of the Hungarian economy. Specialists, however, gave a different perspective of the problems. They argued that the roots of the problems had to be searched for within rather than outside the country, more specifically in the inconsistencies in the implementation of the reform principles, and especially in the problems of poor change- and human resource-management methods used by the bureaucrats in introducing the reform.

The new start in the reform came in 1978 after a six-year period of struggling for and against the reform by different power groups. Taking into consideration the increasing economic difficulties, however, there seemed to be no other option but to continue the reform. This time a limited price reform was introduced and there were also attempts to increase further company autonomy from authorities, accompanied by partial institutional reform in the government, namely the merger of three major industrial ministries into one Ministry of Industry. These were again top–down decisions including only the specialists who were working on the new rules and regulations. The general population was informed by the media, trade unions and the party. Again, almost nothing was done to get them involved, or make them excited about the future opportunities offered by the reform. Only those people who capitalised on the more relaxed environment by starting part-time or full-time private businesses welcomed the changes. Some of the more entrepreneurially oriented private businesses became attracted by the opportunities to become millionaires within a few years. A number of these opportunities have emerged because of the contradictory rules which made it easy to find 'small doors next to the regular ones'. A more common attitude was a lack of faith in the longer term future of private businesses. Research (Csath, 1986a) indicated that these attitudes were influenced by lack of confidence in the future and chances of success of private businesses in Hungary.

The need for change in these beliefs and values was not recognised as an integral and necessary part of the reform movement. Although the reform steps introduced by 1984–85 resulted again in some improvement in the economy, still several serious problems have remained unsolved like the inflexibility and slowness of government decision making, and also the inconsistencies in the reform process caused by top–down decisions and communication, and poor human resource management. These problems were analysed in several research papers (Csath, 1980a, 1980b; Kornai, 1985). Because of the slow improvement in the economic performance of the country, decision makers were urged to continue the reform. One acute problem was the over-centralised organisational structure of companies in the industry. Organisational structure, reflecting the economic structure of the country, was highly centralised, functionally designed, fitted to top–down decision making. Additionally, there were many large companies with a long history of poor performance. To try to solve these problems, a decentralisation process was started by the government in 1984. Unfortunately this process contained too many compromises. The process was directed from different ministries. Too often, those managers who had contributed to poor performance were not unseated. Often decisions made by government officials did not consider the importance of matching corporate strategies with organisational culture and management style, nor did they consider the value of a more bottom–up approach, in creating involvement and commitment from those people influenced by the changes and asked to implement changes. One solution to this problem was the alteration of corporate ownership and a partial management reform in the industry.

The 1968 reform did not affect the state ownership of the means of production. Social ownership was interpreted to mean ownership by authorities. Additionally, company management remained closely tied to and influenced by administrative hierarchies.

The enterprise management and ownership reform attempted to break these hierarchical links by handing over ownership rights (including the selection and promotion of the CEO) to the enterprise councils in approximately 60% of the industrial enterprises. These steps were followed by banking reform, the introduction of a personal income tax and a value-added tax system.

From a purely economic point of view this ongoing reform experiment seems to be the only way to narrow the gap between Hungary and the developed, industrialised countries. Unfortunately, there are several inherent problems that continue to inhibit the development of the reform. Although these problems are inter-related, they can be put into the following groups:

(1) How to build a culture, outside and inside the companies, which is supportive to the reform process.
(2) How to develop commitment among the people for the reform process.
(3) How to develop management behaviour, skills and methods necessary to shape and implement the reform process at different levels.

When analysing the reform process back to 1968 we can identify all these missing elements inherited from the time before the reform in 1968. Although there have been several arguments about the importance of solving these problems, there have never been enough deliberate, consistent, comprehensive and bold initiatives to succeed. On the basis of experience to date, it does not seem probable that the reform will succeed and neither can the economic performance of the country improve significantly unless these problems are seriously addressed in the near future.

WHAT ARE THE PROBLEMS INHERITED FROM THE YEARS BEFORE THE REFORM IN 1968?

To understand the current difficulties in Hungary, it is necessary to review the basic problems inherited from before 1968, but which continue to influence the implementation of reform today.

For more than 20 years, managers in the companies have been implementers of decisions made by central authorities. Most of these managers lacked education and managerial skills. In the best cases they had some technical background. Those having higher education were mostly engineers. Although they had little say in decisions about either the present or the future, they had power to control people inside the corporations. The companies were very centralised to provide a convenient way of controlling them by the central authorities. This kind of organisational structure increased the power of the top management over the members of the companies. The basic focus of management for a long time had been production. People having skills and knowledge in areas like marketing, finance and human resource management were not needed. As a matter of fact those who had got some knowledge of these topics were better off not voicing these 'suspicious' ideas. Colleges had not offered these disciplines for a long time. I remember well when I was in college in the mid-1960s, marketing had just been introduced into the curriculum. Finance courses were limited to the state budget and the operations of the Central Bank. There were no business schools at all, nor any kind of management education in the country. Ideology did not tolerate private enterprise, or any kind of motivation but the ideological ones. Entrepreneurship was equated with 'cheating' or even a criminal activity. Risk taking had no meaning in a society where everything was certain, planned 5–10 years ahead. People were not expected to think about necessary adaptations to changes in the world. As a matter of fact the world was not really all that important. Political leaders suggested to the people that they need not bother with what was going on in any part of the world except the other COMECON countries.

The list of characteristics of the system could be even longer, however these basic ideas already indicate a very serious problem. In spite of the fact that the great majority of people did not agree with many of these basic ideas, they have left their mark on society. Then came the economic reform of 1968, with the aspiration to improve a sick economy as soon as possible.

What were those very basic problems which were supposed to be solved by the reform?

Managerial Problems

(1) To change managerial attitudes, behaviour and relations of authorities and companies.
(2) To find ways to furnish managers with the necessary knowledge and skills to make them capable of coping with the new environment.
(3) To find ways to unseat those managers who were not able to change and develop.
(4) To establish selection, promotion and evaluation methods compatible with the reform principles and objectives.
(5) To offer proper, up-to-date managerial training opportunities.
(6) To encourage entrepreneurship and risk taking as accepted values of the society.
(7) To supply company managers with role models from the higher leadership.
(8) To decentralise 'top-heavy' companies and get rid of managers who have retired on the job.

(9) To reinforce and encourage positive attitudes, change-orientation, risk taking and the use of new managerial methods; not to discourage managers still hesitant to change by blaming the more risk-taking, entrepreneurial-type managers for making mistakes.
(10) To develop the educational system to be able to produce competent managers.
(11) To build a strong and growing lobby of reform supporters by involving more and more managers and potential managers in the reform process: to learn from them and also to commit them.

Human Resource Management Problems Within Companies

Some of these problems are reflections of those mentioned in relation to management problems at lower levels within the companies. These problems were supposed to be solved by those managers who themselves—because of the above-mentioned problems—were not capable or willing to deal with these human resource management problems, for example:

(1) Lack of interest or faith in management.
(2) Being used to hearing how important people are experiencing different treatment in several areas of private and company life.
(3) Lack of involvement in any kind of important company decisions.
(4) Lack of clear hiring, promotion, evaluation practices.
(5) 'Contra-selection' in management positions: incompetent leaders at the different levels, including supervisors, being selected on the basis of political reliability or personal relations rather than knowledge and competence.
(6) Lack of future perspectives for people solely on the basis of better performance, more skills and knowledge.
(7) Very few differences in salaries, wages and bonuses, no interest in working better or harder.
(8) Overemployment, low productivity and low morale.
(9) Morale problems because of poor management, shortage of materials, bad communication, poor organisation of work.
(10) Poor usage of knowledge, talents and energies.

Problems Related to Values Inside and Outside Companies

(1) Deeply rooted ideological values against entrepreneurship, profit orientation, risk taking, future orientation, criticism or desire for

changing, or improving performance.

(2) Practice of promoting leaders to their levels of incompetence.

(3) 'You better buy into the company's cultural values or get out' atmosphere.

(4) Lack of confidence among members of organisations.

(5) Top–down decision-making practices.

(6) 'Driving with rearview-mirror' attitudes.

(7) Ideological chaos around 'role-models'; too many changes in role-models without giving clear, honest explanations why.

(8) 'Keeping mistakes secret' practices, 'collective responsibility' of leaders for bad decisions.

(9) Opportunities to criticise problems and initiate courses of change only for those who made the mistakes.

(10) Practice of blaming the environment for even those mistakes made by leaders or for those opportunities missed because of poor management and slow decision making.

(11) No appreciation for quality work or for quality knowledge ('cheap knowledge').

(12) Lack of support for innovative, creative attitudes.

(13) Oversized bureaucracy, inflexibility, slow decision-making practices in government and companies.

(14) 'Satisficing philosophies' used in decision making instead of proactive, future-oriented ones.

It would be easy to continue any of these three lists, but they are already long enough to demonstrate the nature and seriousness of the problems with which the reform was supposed to deal. It is evident that the problems mentioned here are strongly inter-related, and therefore tend to strengthen one another. It does not require too much imagination to understand how much burden it was on the reform to cope with this complexity of managerial, human resource and cultural problems. Therefore, it was impossible to expect that the reform would be able to cope with all these system elements from the very beginning. Solutions to some elements of the problems have necessarily been postponed. The 1968 reform concentrated on introducing economic reforms. Using strategic management terms, those elaborating the reform principles were concentrating on the strategy formulation process rather than on the implementation process. The reformers might have all the other elements in mind. Unfortunately the reform was stopped before a practical solution to these problems could have been found to support the implementation process.

ANY PROGRESS SINCE THEN?

Taking into consideration the many adjustements made to the reform since 1968, it is evident that there has been a tremendous effort to solve the problems mentioned earlier.

Below is a list of achievements which have contributed to solving the problems mentioned so far:

(1) Greater autonomy is being given to company managers.
(2) Several business schools have opened since 1968, and new management subjects have been introduced to university curricula.
(3) New value systems are being encouraged by government including profit orientation, the importance of entrepreneurship, risk taking, honest differentiation in salaries, wages and bonuses on the basis of performance, and the priority given to quality, knowledge and innovation.
(4) Encouragement is being given to private businesses.
(5) Personal management practices in the area of selection and promotion of managers are improving.
(6) More open criticism of problems is encouraged.
(7) A more honest evaluation of the economic environment around the country is encouraged and practised.
(8) There are several new achievements in the economic arena: price reform, banking reform, some institutional reform in the government and in the industry structure, and a partial financial reform.

To sum up the achievements, the most salient move since 1968 worth mentioning has been the partial restoration of the market. From the companies' point of view this means more independence in

- setting prices,
- establishing profit incentives within companies,
- setting wages,
- making investments, and
- using the after-tax profit as they want.

Additionally, a bankruptcy law was introduced in 1988 with the idea of preventing unprofitable state-owned companies from surviving on costly government subsidies.

The ongoing economic reform has been accompanied by another significant phenomenon: the partial restoration of private property. People have been encouraged to start private businesses of different kinds to help solve the problem of market deficiencies and shortages.

The alteration in ownership has produced an interesting symbiosis of organisational and institutional forms of private businesses including small teams working on private projects within state-owned firms, small-scale private businesses managed on a part-time basis, and a growing number of full-time private businesses among them the most successful formations, the so-called 'small cooperatives'.

Private businesses operate throughout the economy, but they hold an especially strong position in the service and the retail trade sectors.

In spite of all these promising results, several problems have remained to be solved:

(1) Management problems still dominate the economy, at all levels. There is an increasing need for well-trained, competent, future-oriented, strategist-type managers, who are eager to change and to take initiatives in a proactive manner.
(2) Value systems and corporate culture need to be actively shaped to support entrepreneurship, knowledge, achievement, performance, innovativeness and creativeness.
(3) Because there are shortages of almost all resources except human capital, it is time to acknowledge that people are the most valuable assets of many enterprises by installing modern, future-oriented human resource management methods in companies.
(4) It is necessary to combine top–down decisions with bottom–up initiatives and ideas in order to create a more participative type of management at all levels of the economy.

The seriousness of these problems is reflected in the worsening economic situation which can be characterised by:

- Structural problems in the economy, especially within the industry.
- Decreasing competitiveness and market share in the world market.
- A slow rate of improvement in productivity.
- Quality problems with products and services.
- Lack of innovation, and very slow commercialisation of original ideas, slow adaptation to the changing global environment.
- Stagnant economic growth.
- Further deterioration in terms of trade.
- Further accumulation of substantial convertible currency debt.
- A short-run orientation, usage of fire-fighting methods which causes companies to be victims rather than masters of change.
- Survival of dinosaur companies at the expense of the well-managed companies with the ability to be competitive in world markets.

WHAT IS STILL WRONG? SOME PRACTICAL CASES

I should like to present some practical cases based on my experiences as a consultant to several companies and also as a professor of strategic management. These cases will illustrate those company management problems I have summarised so far.

Case 1: An Electronics Company

The company management realised that the old ways of doing business needed some adjustments. Therefore, consultants were invited to analyse the situation and to suggest some ideas for a new strategic management system. The consultants worked together with management, with specialists from different areas, and with young graduates recently hired by the company. Several approaches and methods were applied to identify the opportunities and threats to the company's environment, and the strengths and weaknesses of the company itself. Questionnaires, interviews, Delphi techniques and Nominal Group Method were used to evaluate the corporate culture, the human resource management and the top management methods. Working together with specialists from within the company, a competitive analysis of products and market was done and various industry scenarios were elaborated. After working together for almost one year the following characteristics were identified by the consultants:

(1) Strong technical and production orientation; lack of a keen interest in future changes in the markets; not too much understanding about the company's standing compared to leading companies in the world; no desire to be a market leader in any segment of the world market; almost absolute monopoly situation in the home market and desire to keep it; 'imitative' and 'buy in' type of innovation—with tendency to introduce new technologies much later than the leaders—through licences in spite of the fact that there were a number of excellent engineers capable of doing first class original work. The company maintained an oversized production capacity and overemployment although there was much talk about increasing productivity. The economic performance of the company has been excellent compared to the industry average. One reason for this was the monopoly situation, it enjoyed. Another reason was a good relationship with government authorities.

(2) *Management.* The decision-making process is centralised. The top management team is absolutely confident about its competence and does not consider it necessary to listen to ideas from below.

Communication is poor, employees and even lower level managers are not aware of what is going on in the 'board room'. They are not invited to contribute their ideas to the future-shaping decisions made by the top management. They are not familiar with the mission and objectives of the company and very often have no idea why a new product has been introduced, a market has been given up or what the company's financial situation looks like. Due to the production and technical orientation of the top people, the managers of sales and finance are not seriously involved in the decision-making process either. The sales manager's responsibility is to sell what is produced and the finance director's job is to make sure that there will be enough money for the planned investments and wage increases in a given year. On one occasion the CEO declared to the consultants that he was not going to participate in a session on analysing the external and internal environment because he felt confident that he would not hear anything new. After reading the consultants' reports he expressed his disappointment with the criticism found there. Additionally, he maintained that the consultants were incompetent, not having the proper technical and technological background to understand the situation of such a company. Also he tried to convince the members of the management team that the consultants had been strongly influenced by people who had never been satisfied with anything and had been eager to frustrate management any time they could. After long discussions and arguments the work was terminated.

Case 2: A Company with a Famous Past, a Declining Present and a Future Full of Question Marks

One of my graduate students had been working for an earlier world-famous company for a long time. She was very familiar with the history of the company, and the strategies the management has pursued since the time of the foundation. She had worked in several different positions, and had gained an understanding of the problems. I encouraged her to write a dissertation on the history of the management and strategy making in the company. She did a fine job. The dissertation was a detailed, candid analysis of the history, and of the series of decisions which gradually had caused the company's situation, image and performance to deteriorate.

She conducted a number of interviews with people inside and outside the company and analysed a great quantity of data. While working on the dissertation she tried to interview the top manager but he was never available.

Her conclusions were not very flattering to management. She showed that the decline of the company was due to poor management, lack of strategy, lack of interest in getting back the 'old glory' of the company. The company's CEO was an 'old-timer', without proper management skills and knowledge. To secure his position, he had chosen deputies and middle managers with attitudes similar to his own. They were satisfied with an average performance, and were content to get ideas and initiatives from the branch ministry they belonged to. They had a typically reactive kind of behaviour: waiting and wondering what changes had happened in the environment and then trying to move ahead as safely as possible. There was no human resource planning in the company, including a lack of career and succession planning for management. They had been living from one day to the next for a long time, and had no desire to take risk or to be creative. In this environment employees had not been encouraged to be innovative. As a matter of fact, those who had creative ideas had left the company to find jobs with better managed companies.

The student's dissertation was very well accepted at the university. She defended the dissertation and received an excellent grade. Some months later she visited me at the university and told me the end of the story. She had got into trouble very soon after graduation. Although she had not been directly fired (she was a valuable employee and there was no real reason to fire her), by the time we met she had left the company voluntarily. Management had effectively 'poisoned the air' around her to the extent that she knew there was no future for her in the company.

Case 3: A Powerful CEO Without Vision

This company is one of the largest in the country. The manager came from a political background and had good tactical skills and also strong connections with the central authorities. Unfortunately the company was in a declining industry nearing crisis. What was necessary was a vision of how to avoid the coming crisis. Instead of thinking about necessary changes, the CEO visited the different authorities asking for money, to supplement the poor internal cash flow. He argued that the problems came from external sources and that there were no options for the company to cope with the environmental changes. His pleas were successful and the company has been heavily subsidised for a long time.

Employees, in the meantime, were not familiar with the situation. They had been led to believe that they had been producing good quality products, which were being sold for good prices all over the world.

The company was overcentralised, with all major decisions being made by the CEO himself. He was convinced that this was the best managerial style. When anyone talked with him about the necessity of strategic change he argued that there was no need for radical change. A gradual upgrading of technologies and products with the help of government money would solve the problems. The government indeed has been pouring money into the company with no sign of improvement. The company practically went bankrupt before the government authorities started to think seriously about the future of the company.

Case 4: A Manufacturing Company with a Great Past and a Gradually Deteriorating Current Performance

This company has been famous for well-known quality products all over the world for some time. Some new products came from inventions of excellent people working for the company. The employees were proud of being a part of the company's success. In recent years, however, the company has experienced serious problems: losing market share, and suffering declining performance in terms of quality, productivity, profits and innovation of products and technologies. Analysis revealed that the company had:

- a long history of government intervention in product and market decisions; and
- become dependent on financial support of the government.

In addition to these environmental factors, some of the managers had been selected on the basis of political reliability and willingness to cooperate with the supervisory authorities. The company was near bankruptcy, but because of government support, it was not apparent how great the problem was. Employee motivation was low. They did not realise the difficulties faced by their organisation because wages and bonuses had increased from year to year. The performance of the company as a whole and that of the individuals was disconnected from the money earned by the company because of the subsidies. In the meantime management had not improved either. Good people were frustrated and left the company. It became more and more difficult to sell the products. In spite of this not much has happened with the product line. Minor technological improvements have been introduced, but the real problem has not been solved. From among several inter-related reasons some have been definitely striking: the company lacks adequate management talent. In close relation to this the corporate culture is gradually worsening. In addition, the human resource management of the company is inadequate. At the 'twenty-fourth hour' a new, dynamic manager was appointed and asked to turn the company around. Short-term solutions were proposed for the financial problems and strategic changes were made to address long-term problems. The manager was determined to solve the problems by making decisions that had been postponed for a long time: like drastic changes in the product portfolio, in management, in organisation and knowledge structure of the company. He hired young specialists and involved them in the formulation of a new long-term strategy. He has been eager to establish a strategic human resource planning system, too. With the help of consultants and people committed to change from inside he started a project that had never been done before: to understand who the employees were, and to discover their basic skills, knowledge and ideas about the company. He was also determined to build up a selection, motivation, training and control system in harmony with the strategy. He wanted to decentralise the company by delegating responsibility to the lower levels. Unfortunately these moves were seen as too radical when compared with previous CEOs. The company's situation was in such a poor state that it was not possible to turn it around in a short time. More time would have been necessary. People, including several powerful managers and the majority of the employees, who preferred the security of government support, turned against the new CEO. The internal climate deteriorated to the point that even newly hired people were blocked and paralysed.

The CEO, although working hard to change the situation, could not do much against the established, change-resistant culture of the company. If he could have fired some members of the management team maybe it would have been easier to cope with the situation. But it was difficult to identify those who were the most responsible for the troubles because of continuous government intervention, and the high turnover rate in management. It was also impossible to fire employees because of ideological problems. It was said that employees should not suffer because of mistakes made by management or by supervising government authorities. It has been a 'catch-22 situation'. The new manager came in too late, and the company had gone too far on the wrong track. There were no friendly solutions available any more. Only one solution remained: bankruptcy followed by a radical downsizing, decentralisation and restructuring of the company.

These cases have been chosen deliberately from among the poorly managed companies. Naturally there are many companies with very capable managers. Unfortunately poorly performing companies present a greater problem than one might imagine. The reason for this is the practice of the government of taxing away the profits of the well-run companies and pouring money into the poorly run companies to keep them alive. Among these poorly managed companies one can easily identify the problems mentioned before: the managerial, human resource and cultural problems. As these latter companies represent the majority of companies, they have contributed mightily to the accumulated economic woes of the country.

The other aspect of the same problem is equally important. Let us imagine for a moment being a capable manager and working for a company that performs well. The fact that improvement in performance results in losing the majority of the additional profit to support the subsidies paid to poorly managed companies presents a moral problem. Sooner or later people will tend to withhold their work efforts because of this practice. They are likely to control their achievements in order to avoid surpassing an average performance. This attitude has a profound negative effect on the economic performance of the country. Putting everything together, these reasons explain rather clearly why it has been so difficult to improve the performance of the economy in spite of the attempts of reform since 1968.

At this point it is worth summarising who are the managers of public companies in Hungary.

COMPANY MANAGEMENT AND ENTREPRENEURSHIP IN HUNGARY

Let me start with two fundamental questions:

- How are managers selected and promoted?
- Who evaluates, and on what basis, their performance?

Until 1984–85 managers were selected and promoted by the branch ministries. Even the deputies were selected by the branch ministries without asking about the opinion of the CEO. (In Hungary they are called directors, or chief-directors, depending on the size of the company.) At that time top managers used to say that they had the spies of the ministry around who were checking whether they were following the directions and 'expectations' of the authorities properly.

The list of characteristics used in the selection process basically had three major items: political reliability, personal traits and professional background. It has never been absolutely clear how these three require- ments had been weighted in the selection process. It is also worth mentioning that personal traits like change orientation, problem sensi- tivity, criticism, risk taking, independent thinking, originality very often were not welcomed by those involved in the selection process, because managers having these characteristics would have been too difficult to cope with and also not reliable enough to implement decisions made by the ministries, and to fulfil objectives and targets set by the ministries.

The evaluation system used by the branch ministries was complicated, having sometimes more than 20 measures, including some very vague ones, which made the performance evaluation process very subjective. I remember several cases when the managers of the companies were decorated and rewarded one year and in the next year the company almost went bankrupt. One reason for this phenomenon was past orientation and short-term orientation of the whole evaluation system.

Consequently, the managers of the state-owned companies, with a few exceptions, were much more concerned about pleasing the authorities than elaborating competitive strategies for shaping the future of the companies. Evidently this situation did not encourage entrepreneurship in the state-owned companies at all. However, this system was not changed for a long time after the reform was started in 1968, causing serious managerial problems in the companies including:

- lack of strategic thinking;
- lack of corporate culture supportive to innovation and entrepreneurship;
- lack of risk-taking attitudes; and consequently
- lack of change orientation.

It is important to emphasise here that since the beginning of the reform there have been more and more arguments and political declarations about the importance of these managerial characteristics. In practice the national planning system, the economic regulators, the exceptions made by government authorities to help companies to escape from the influences of the economic regulation and also the direct interventions of government authorities into the companies' life, discouraged managers from developing these personal traits.

The motivation and interests of managers changed radically in 1984–85 with the introduction of new forms of ownership. However, there is still a long way to go before these managerial characteristics will dominate the public sector. In particular there is another important change which must happen before company managers will be truly convinced about the importance of these managerial capabilities. This is government attitudes towards companies. The ways in which government authorities operate and manage have to be changed, too. As an old Hungarian proverb says: 'you should not preach water and drink wine'. More specifically it is also necessary to develop similar kinds of behaviour and attitudes, including more future orientation, strategic thinking, innovation and entrepreneurship supportive behaviour, etc., in the government offices dealing with companies. Otherwise it is difficult to expect that managers themselves are going to change their ways of managing the public companies. This explains the importance of human factors in implementing the economic reform ideas which would need more change acceptance, risk taking and entrepreneurship from all actors on the economic and political stage. This seems to be attainable only through mutual understanding, trust and commitment, which on the other hand cry out for more involvement, better communication, further delegation of decisions to the business level. But who are those managers at the top having the responsibility for putting the reform ideas into practice? A brief summary of earlier research (Csath, 1986) tries to give some answers to this question.

The research focused on analysing 100 companies using the following characteristics:

- Age of top managers.
- Professional background of top managers.
- Corporate structure.
- Strategic planning practices.
- Major changes, innovations in the last five to ten years.
- Government involvement.

Let me summarise the research findings very briefly.

Age of Managers

There were three easily identifiable groups as far as age was concerned. In the majority of companies managers' ages were between 55 and 60. These people became managers in the time of central planning, when managers were implementers of central decisions. In most cases these people have not received proper managerial education. Risk taking did not mean anything for them when everything seemed to be certain and planned five years ahead. They were not expected to think about changes or new ideas. They were supposed to implement decisions made outside, or more precisely above, the companies. They had a hard time understanding the new directions of the reforms and especially how to apply them in their managerial practice.

In the second group managers represented the so-called 'reform generation', at ages between 45 and 55. They had direct experiences with the economic reform, having tried to get by during the 'ups and downs' of the reform process. Some of them seemed to be disappointed, even cynical, because of the contradictions and inconsistencies in the ways the reform has been implemented. The majority of these managers have been keen supporters of the reform, and have tried hard to use new managerial approaches although they, too, lack formal managerial training. However, what they experienced in practice was very often in opposition to the theories. One good example which illustrates this problem is the profit orientation principle of the reform. As was mentioned earlier, what happened in real life was against this principle. Companies that were not able to produce profit, still got money from the government to increase wages of workers, and buy equipment. They were subsidised at the expense of the profit-making companies. So it did not prove to be a good strategy to be really good or innovative. Therefore, these managers lost enthusiasm and just tried to survive, aiming neither to be too bad, nor too good.

Unfortunately the government continued punishing good companies, taking their profits with heavy taxes and putting billions of forints (Hungarian monetary unit) into the badly managed companies for such a long time that it was easy to destroy entrepreneurship and creativity just because it was not worth the effort.

In addition, the extremely short-term orientation of the economic regulators, and other government incentives and measures, made it stupid to be risk taking and future oriented.

In the third group there were managers under age 45. The majority of these acquired managerial knowledge and skills, partly in the educational system, partly their own. These young managers represented a minority group in the sample. However, their number seems to be increasing recently. These managers were more interested in adopting modern managerial techniques. Very often, in spite of the problems mentioned earlier, they were just enthusiastic about proving their abilities to manage the company strategically and to get lasting results in a short-term oriented economic environment created by the regulations, rules, measures and government interventions.

Professional Background

The majority of managers, especially in the first and second group, had an engineering kind of education. There were more managers in the second group who earned a second diploma later, which was some kind of management diploma. There were more managers in the third group with an economic type of educational background, or again with a double diploma in engineering and economics. The situation is understandable: it is more important to have people with technical education at the top if the most important problem to decide on is production.

Corporate Structure

Corporate structures were very highly centralised, more or less copies of the earlier system of managing the companies by the branch ministries. This system supported the centralised control of all operations throughout the companies by top people who were also heavily involved in short-term problem solving. Therefore, they were overburdened which resulted in slow decision making without (or with insignificant) participation from lower level management. The most typical structure was a functional structure with very powerful functional managers, especially manufacturing managers (assistant directors). This situation created inefficient decisions about markets and product lines and was not able to create clear views about the profitability of different products and divisions. Also it hindered creativity, entrepreneurship, adaptation to change and innovation throughout the company.

However, in some instances we found some initiatives for, and also minor results in, developing new organisational structures. The most typical of them was a kind of project-oriented structure and different versions of divisional structures. Also, especially in the third group of companies, there was an interest in, and even experimentation with, strategic business units.

Strategic Planning Practices

In the majority of the companies we did not find any other type of planning than the traditional five-year planning practice. This planning method can be characterised by:

- fixed time-horizon;
- past orientation;
- periodical planning;
- lack of interest in opportunities and threats in the future environment;
- inflexibility;
- unsophisticated methodologies;
- enormous amount of numerical and verbal details; and
- concentration on continuing trends, improving over the past performances rather than searching for ways to change in order to find a better match between the companies' capabilities and the future environment.

However, some managers seriously considered introducing strategic planning instead of the traditional planning method. But they found it really difficult to overcome the constraint imposed on them by the short-term oriented economic regulations.

On the basis of these findings it is easy to understand that we could not identify too many radical changes—departures from the past introduced in the examined companies in the last five to ten years. There were some minor changes in the product lines, and frequently some improvement in quality or service. Also we found a few new markets these companies had entered recently.

Government interventions were quite frequent and often also direct. Additionally, because of the permanently and often hastily changing economic regulations, companies found themselves to be strongly controlled, that is kept within boundaries. Some of them used the following illustration when I asked them about possibilities to be entrepreneurs in this environment: 'it is difficult to dance if your legs are tied together'.

I tried to approach the problem of lack of entrepreneurship from two different perspectives:

(1) From the perspective of managers and managerial capabilities.
(2) From the perspective of the environment created by the economic regulators and government measures.

My point here is that without strategic thinking and long-term orientation it is impossible to be an entrepreneur in a rapidly changing world. Although this is true in every country, there are additional factors to be taken into consideration in countries with a long history of central planning, like Hungary. The factors discussed so far are:

• government methods for controlling the economy;
• the way managers are selected, promoted and motivated.

ENTREPRENEURSHIP IN PRIVATE BUSINESSES

Entrepreneurship is a great economic and social force driving businesses toward creative, innovative performance, growth and competitiveness. To flourish entrepreneurship needs a proper environment, which if not supportive must at least not be hostile. After examining the several problems of economic reform in Hungary, one can easily suggest that one important way of improving performance throughout the economy would be the creation of an environment which is not against entrepreneurship at any level and in any segment of society. However, so far we have identified too many problems outside and inside the companies which have made it very difficult, and often even simply senseless, to be an entrepreneur in a public company. But how different is it to be an entrepreneur in private businesses?

Private businesses do not represent a large portion of the industry. They are, however, more prevalent in agriculture and service industries. According to a study by the International Monetary Fund (1987), in 1986 approximately 30% of the country's production was carried out in the private sector. Private businesses seem to operate very successfully in spite of the heavy taxes they have to pay. One evident reason is that they are operating in the so-called shortage segments of the economy.

Also, competition still has not developed to be very tough for them because of the shortage situation. However, there must be additional reasons why they keep prospering. I was curious to find reasons for this. Therefore, I joined the research project started originally by New York University, Center for Entrepreneur Studies in 1987. The research was truly international, including more than 20 countries, with the objective of comparing motivations of entrepreneurs in different political, social and cultural environments. I modified the questionnaire, originally prepared by NYU, in order to adjust it to the characteristics of local conditions.

First I tried to find a good representation of entrepreneurs from different sectors of the economy, different parts of the country and also different sizes of businesses.

I sent out the questionnaire to 600 private businesses and I got back 25% of the questionnaires. The people who filled out the questionnaires mainly represented the age group between 35 and 44. More than half came from a professional, intellectual family background. The majority held a college degree, some of them a Ph.D. Original training of more than 50% was some type of technical one.

They operated in the following manufacturing and service areas:

- *Manufacturing*
    - machine-building industry,
    - construction,
    - electronics,
    - computer manufacturing (PCs),
    - technical design,
    - cosmetics manufacturing,
    - plastic manufacturing,
    - food processing.
- *Service*
    - software development,
    - beauty salons and shops,

- laundries,
- restaurants and bars,
- car, shoe, home appliances, etc., repair,
- film processing,
- retail trade,
- consultancy,
- training,
- gardening,
- house cleaning, etc.

The most questions were asked about the motivations of starting one's own business. Here are the most common reasons for starting a private business:

- Desire to use my training and skills better.
- To be challenged by problems of starting a new business.
- Sense of adventure.
- Desire to develop an own idea for product.
- To be able to work with people I chose.
- To achieve personal sense of accomplishment.
- To work in an unstructured position.
- To control my own time.
- To take advantage of an opportunity I created.
- To be my own boss.
- To broaden experience.
- Not to work for an unreasonable boss.
- To be in a position of day-to-day learning.
- The desire for financial independence.

The least important motivational factors were the following:

- To follow the example of a person I admire.
- To continue family traditions.
- To achieve higher position in society.
- To have good physical working conditions.
- The desire to be wealthy.
- To have more influence in the community.
- A step towards achievement of political ambitions.

If we look at the list of the strongest motives then we can easily identify common elements here which are the entrepreneur personality traits, like:

- future and change orientation;
- curiosity;
- desire for personal growth and challenges;
- innovativeness, creativeness;
- risk taking;
- result orientations;
- desire to create and capitalise on opportunities.

If we examine the outside, environmental reasons of starting a private business the most commonly mentioned ones are the following:

- I didn't like my previous job.
- I didn't see any opportunity for being promoted.
- I could not use my knowledge and skills properly.
- I did not find my boss competent.

Here we have an interesting match. These people, the majority of whom had a higher education, were not able to find satisfying and challenging jobs in the state-owned companies they left behind when starting a private business. This problem goes far beyond the facts I was interested in analysing in the context of private businesses. This is a clear indication of the major problem in the state-owned companies which we discussed earlier in detail, namely poor human resource management, which results in lack of motivation, lack of innovation and entrepreneurship and ultimately lack of performance by individuals and by companies.

I was also interested in the training needs of these private entrepreneurs, because if these people, who were brave and innovative enough to start a private business operating in a much more uncertain environment, felt they needed extra knowledge and skills to be more successful, it seems evident that the same kind of knowledge might be needed also for the managers of the state-owned companies.

On the whole the knowledge areas these entrepreneurs felt uncomfortable with were the following:

- Marketing, pricing, trade, foreign trade.
- Communication, human resource management, human relations, relation building, lobbying.
- The latest technologies, materials.
- Management methods, economics.
- Computer application.
- Languages.
- Laws and regulations.

The last item on the list can easily be explained by the answers given to the following question: What major obstacles did you face in setting up you own business? The most frequently given answers were the following:

- Lots of rules and regulations that were often confusing and difficult to understand.
- Too many people and departments had to be consulted for approval.
- Too many papers, questionnaires and forms to be filled in.
- Too many permissions to get.
- Extensive and complicated negotiations with officials and offices.

This list gives a good picture of the difficulties these people had to cope with before starting their own businesses.

The overwhelming need for managerial knowledge and skills indicates the same problem we discussed in the context of the state-owned companies, which is the technical background. However, if the private entrepreneurs found this a weak point which they had to strengthen in order to be able to manage their businesses better, then it is clearly a much more serious issue for managers managing large companies with several thousand employees and operating in at least four different markets:

- In the home market.
- In the COMECON market.
- In the market of the developed countries.
- In the market of the developing countries.

The findings of the two researches seem to support each other very well, and also lead to the same conclusions: there are several important steps to be taken in order to let entrepreneurship flourish in Hungary. These steps should be initiated partly by government authorities and partly by company managers, but of course in an inter-related manner, relying on good communication, clear views and open discussions. But what are those problems that have to be seriously addressed?

CONCLUSION: PROBLEM WHICH NEEDS TO BE SERIOUSLY ADDRESSED IN ORDER TO IMPROVE ECONOMIC PERFORMANCE

To solve the basic problems of the Hungarian economy and businesses several changes seem to be urgent and necessary. These changes need to focus on more decentralisation, more involvement of lower levels in decision making, more reliance on knowledgeable and skilled people, and more motivation and encouragement for achievement and creativity. On the other hand, laziness, resistance to change, backward thinking, and irresponsible or incompetent decision making must be discouraged. Taken all together we get back to the original hypothesis: what is most needed is a fundamental change in values and culture together with a significant improvement in human resource management at all levels. The economy seriously needs innovation, entrepreneurship and renewal in all areas. Ideas and innovation can come only from committed, involved people. There are many talented, creative people in different jobs whose opinions have never been asked and listened to. Only when this waste of talent and knowledge is ended will there be a chance to turn the economy around. At the same time it is necessary to change the management style from a reactive to a proactive, problem-solving mode. As far as management selection and promotion is concerned, it is important to establish a clear, understandable and acceptable system which opens up opportunities for a larger population of qualified candidates for management positions. It is also critical to develop clear-cut motivation and reward systems which emphasise strategic activities and create a proper atmosphere for innovation and strong performance.

To enhance future effectiveness, it is equally significant to build future-oriented training and retraining systems inside and outside the companies. These systems should involve cost-effective methods such as distance learning, and open learning. The way to get people excited about learning is to favour knowledge and skills over previously established norms and values.

Although a complex array of dimensions of societal culture has a strong effect on these human resource issues, the following seem to be among the most critical ones:

(1) Establishing clear responsibility for decisions at all levels including the government decision-making authorities.
(2) Tolerating and encouraging open criticism and arguments about possible courses of actions, especially those of strategic importance for organisations, and for the country, too.
(3) Strongly encouraging people to come up with original, creative ideas, no matter how radical they seem to be compared with the usual ways of doing things.

The strengthening of these values would help to implant more dynamism into the society. This would consequently support implementing the changes necessary to improve the performance of the economy.

Unfortunately the latest steps in the economic reform process do not seem to be aligned with these arguments. On the contrary, the newly introduced personal taxation system does not seem to encourage creativeness, or inject a bigger dose of performance orientation into the economy. The reason for this is the way the tax reform was introduced. It puts an extra burden on those people having second or third jobs in dynamic areas of the economy, while not offering the opportunity to be better paid for better performance in the first job. Professionals and specialists not working in management positions are going to suffer the most. They are underpaid for the first job, which is usually a job in the public sector. To establish a proper living standard, they work in additional jobs either in the public or in the private sector. If they are not able to keep a reasonable part of their extra earnings, they will not be motivated to keep these jobs. Unfortunately the majority of these activities, including consulting, software design, and support services, are of key importance to meet market demands. The taxation system does not seem to be able to control the so-called 'hidden activities', which never appear on any document and are therefore exempt from taxation. This situation can easily have an additional negative impact on the societal culture, causing value confusion and embarrassment. It may also result in lower motivation for better performance, in creativity, by working against those new values which are of crucial importance for improving economic performance. It is also probable that the high taxes on the legal private businesses will not encourage present businesses to increase their production and service activities. Nor will people be attracted to enter this sector, which is the most dynamic sector of the economy at present. It would be much more consistent with the principles of the reform to encourage private businesses to contribute further to the revitalisation of market forces.

FINAL COMMENTS AND SUGGESTIONS

The coming years are not going to be easy for Hungary. Accumulated problems from the past must be solved or the economic performance of the economy will continue to deteriorate and consequently social tension will increase. In this chapter I have tried to highlight those problem areas which have not been analysed and explored to date in the context of the economic reform. I am aware of the fact that I might have overemphasised the elements of human resource management, corporate culture and entrepreneurship relative to other important preconditions for improving the economic efficiency of the country. The reason for this is that I believe that the values and attitudes of society are far more important than physical assets in the achievement of economic success in the long run and particularly right now in Hungary.

The most important changes, which cannot be delayed any longer, are the following:

(1) To stop subsidising poorly performing companies at the expense of the good companies.
(2) To stop subsidising poorly performing managers by moving them around the industry and allowing them to make additional mistakes after they have proved their managerial incompetence several times.
(3) To create a real market situation by:
    (a) decentralising overly concentrated and centralised enterprises;
    (b) establishing new businesses, especially medium sized and small ones;
    (c) encouraging the start of new private businesses;
    (d) loosening the restrictions of the private businesses including the introduction of a more favourable taxation system;
    (e) finding ways to unseat those managers of any level who are no longer able to change;
    (f) establishing selection, promotion and evaluation methods compatible with the reform objectives and principles;
    (g) strengthening competition in the home market, with any possible and available method, including foreign (import) competition;
    (h) encouraging international cooperation;
    (i) easing the entry of foreign firms into the Hungarian market to create genuine competition.
(4) To develop a general climate which supports highly performing individuals, appreciates knowledge, tolerates differences, and is receptive to and positive about new ideas, change, and entrepreneurial-type behaviour.
(5) To develop further the higher education system in order to produce competent managers.
(6) To create more personal encouragement and freedom for personal achievements.
(7) To delegate much more responsibility and decision-making opportunities to lower levels, including radical downsizing of government authorities, and a radical decrease of government involvement in businesses.

The problems that have to be solved within companies, but in harmony with dealing with the above-mentioned problems are the following:

(1) Decentralization in company decision making: creating more involvement, building up more flexible organisations.

(2) Strong motivation for performance.
(3) Building up innovation and creativeness supporting corporate cultures.
(4) Appreciation of quality, knowledge and discipline.
(5) Establishing clear, future oriented and honest human resource management practices.
(6) More emphasis to be put on continuous training of management and employees.
(7) Introduction of rigorous productivity and quality standards.
(8) Building up strategies for shaping the future instead of 'fire fighting'.

These two levels, government and management have to work together in order to get results. The government has created a major part of the home environment for the companies, therefore it has to be a pioneer in introducing the necessary and real changes. To develop and encourage more entrepreneurship and innovation in the economy, there is an urgent need for more flexibility, less bureaucracy, more involvement and open discussion about problems and possible solutions. And the best, maybe the only, opportunity for solving the problems is to capitalise on human knowledge, initiatives, aspirations, innovativeness and entrepreneurship.

Unless these changes are introduced in a determined and practical way, the future of the country as an industrialised nation might be put in jeopardy, especially with regard to the coming of a United Europe in 1992.

REFERENCES

Csath, M. (1980a) Problems of the recent economic controlling system (Based on interviews). *Karl Marx University Review*.

Csath, M. (1980b) *Problems of Structural Adaptation in the Hungarian Industry*, Vols I–II. Academic research papers.

Csath, M. (1986a) *Motivations of Private Entrepreneurs in Hungary*. Research paper presented at the Conference on International Management Development, University of Lancaster.

Csath, M. (1986b) *Corporate Management and Strategic Planning in the Hungarian Industry*. Research paper. Budapest.

International Monetary Fund Study (1987) *Washington Post*, 6 April.

Kornai, J. (1985) *Contradictions and Dilemmas*. Corvina, Budapest.

13

STRATEGIC PLANNING IN THE PUBLIC SECTOR

Kate Ascher

Port Authority of New York and New Jersey

Blair Nare

New York State Division of the Budget

Expectations of corporate strategic planning, though lowered by painful experience over the past decade, were in the early days of the discipline quite high. In the case of public sector strategic planning, however, even initial hopes for success were fairly low. Public sector planners had to contend with assumptions that their organizations were too politically constrained and their goals too vague to 'do' strategic planning.

The commonly held distinction between public and private sector organizations in this regard was expressed by Barry and Maryann Keating in the February 1981 issue of *Long Range Planning* as follows:

> The use of profit as an indicator greatly simplifies the measurement of output and measurement of efficiency in profit-seeking firms. Because of vague goals and the difficulty of formulating targets and indicators, a non-profit agency often does not measure output in any way and the management is severely impeded. Furthermore, an organization with no targets or indicators is unable to measure progress in any way toward the ultimate objectives of the organization. . .

As if vindicating those early criticisms, strategic planning in the public sector has indeed foundered frequently since its inception, both on the shoals described above as well as on those encountered by private sector

International Review of Strategic Management.
Edited by D. E. Hussey. © 1990 John Wiley & Sons Ltd

strategists. Nonetheless, through trial and error, the activity has survived (and in some cases prospered), despite the fact that the forms it has taken in order to do so might not be recognizable to its early practitioners. This chapter will examine developments in public sector strategic planning over the past 20 years, as experienced by a variety of American, British and Canadian organizations. Compare those developments to trends in corporate practice, analyse key points of similarity and difference, and offer an outlook for the 1990s based on the experience of the 1970s and 1980s.

BACKGROUND: THE RISE AND FALL OF PRIVATE SECTOR STRATEGIC PLANNING

There has been no lack of commentary on the failure of private sector strategic planning to live up to its early billing. Most of this disillusionment was the result of what Michael Porter (1987) recently described as:

> . . . a growing recognition that the processes for strategic planning were not promoting strategic thinking. Instead of clarifying and communicating strategy, the outcome of laborious strategic-planning exercises was thick binders which had little, if any, impact on action. Form dominated substance. Meaningless long-term projections obscured strategic insight. Strategic planners had captured the process, filling out plans which were reviewed by yet other planners. Line managers tolerated planning, but increasingly dismissed it as an irrelevant ritual.
>
> (*The Economist*, 5/23/87)

As a result of these experiences, some companies dropped strategic planning not only from their organization charts but from their calendars; others moved toward an emphasis on strategic 'thinking' or 'management' with a new focus on the role of line management. Figure 13.1, adapted from a paper by Ian Wilson of SRI, summarizes these trends and indicates the approximate time lag with which they later occurred in the public sector.

THE ORIGINS OF PUBLIC SECTOR STRATEGIC PLANNING

General Electric (USA) and the other private sector strategic planning pioneers were motivated by their organizations' need to respond quickly to rapid and unexpected change in their competitive environments. Similar external pressures drove the public sector's initial interest in

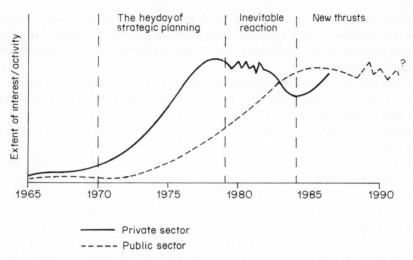

Figure 13.1 The evolution of strategic planning. Source: SRI International, Ascher & Nare

strategic planning: an ever more fragmented and unruly political process in legislatures and elsewhere; strident demands from the public for new services such as environmental protection and new controls such as local consent for capital projects; and the increasing ability of new technologies to outrun both legislative and regulatory oversight. Finally, taxpayer revolts and other shifts in the political winds worldwide were resulting in greater competition for shrinking resources just at service demand was expanding.

In response to these external pressures, larger and more complex organizations emerged in government as well as in industry, making effective management of resources more difficult. It was inevitable under the circumstances that government would also begin casting about for techniques that would help it define—or redefine—its mission, develop rational resource allocations and improve its organizational performance.

It is important to note, before beginning to discuss specific examples of strategic planning in the public sector, that the term 'public sector' itself includes a wide variety of organizational types. We have included, among other examples, traditional government departments (on the national, state/provincial and local level), state corporations and quasi-governmental agencies such as independent public authorities. Despite the fact that these types of organizations may operate in very different political, legal and market environments, their special public responsibilities and the fact that the lines between them are becoming increasingly blurred by privatization and other forms of innovation argue for their inclusion. Also, while national-level initiatives were the focus of most earlier analysis, experience and politics have pushed planning into more decentralized forms and many recent innovations have taken place at the local government level.

Perhaps the earliest high-visibility effort by the US government to 'focus on output categories like goals, objectives and end products instead of inputs like personnel, equipment and maintenance' (Wildavsky, 1974) was the Planning, Programming and Budgeting Systems (PPBS), espoused by President Lyndon Johnson in 1965. PPBS was intended to establish priorities among various government objectives and then determine appropriate levels of investment among them. It was widely attempted, not only in the United States but in other countries and multinational agencies. Nevertheless, Aaron Wildavsky (1974) was able to state in the second edition of *The Politics of the Budgetary Process* that 'PPBS has failed everywhere and at all times'. Studies of PPBS efforts cited in his book contain conclusions with an eerily prescient ring: 'Detailed PPBS processes have been developed in a number of agencies; [however] the materials produced through these processes have not been used extensively by decisionmakers...''... This systems approach simply adds another layer to the existing excess of reports and paperwork.'

Earlier and smaller scale efforts such as zero-based budgeting and the State Department's Comprehensive Country Programming Systems met with similar complaints. Probably as a result of these experiences, no federal strategic planning mandate replaced the ill-fated PPBS initiative and subsequent US public sector experiments with the process did not get under way much before the early 1980s. Many of these first efforts were the result of state and local 'futures' activities, beginning with the Hawaii Commission on the Year 2000, created in 1970. Between 1970 and 1982, according to the Council of State Government, 39 futures programs were undertaken by 29 states. The majortiy of these were time-limited exercises; however, their conclusions and recommendations often included provisions for ongoing planning activities once the 'task force' mandate expired. This was the case, for example, with the Port Authority of New York and New Jersey's Committee on the Future, which will be discussed in some detail below.

Meanwhile, beginning in 1970–71 with GE's new planning system and accelerating through the early 1970s, the private sector was also experimenting with new approaches to the process of goal definition and resource allocation. These approaches constituted the new discipline of 'strategic planning'. Although a wide variety of strategic planning concepts were advanced by consulting firms and corporate planning staffs during this period, common characteristics of these early activities included a relatively long planning horizon (usually five years), a budget-driven planning cycle, and a focus on preparation of relatively formal annual documents and management presentations.

Early public sector efforts in the United Kingdom followed the private sector lead more closely than had US initiatives, both in order to take advantage of its growing experience base and because the United Kingdom's initial focus was on nationalized industries rather than traditional government agencies. The first corporate plan of the British Steel Corporation, for example, was completed in 1971 and later became the model (the 'Benson Brochures') recommended by the government for all nationalized industries. The Benson Brochures specified a three-tier system of planning, involving production of an annual operating plan, a strategic plan (ten years or more) and a development plan (five years). These documents, as well as quarterly progress reports, were then to be submitted to the sponsor department and the Treasury.

In 1978, a government White Paper acknowledged that a variety of obstacles to the successful implementation of corporate planning in nationalized industries existed, among them the problem of diverse, if not competing, objectives (i.e. efficiency versus maintenance of employment). Managers in the industries in question also pointed out, in evaluating their own efforts, that government interference had affected and distorted those objectives even once such conflicts were resolved (Harris and Davies). As a result, between 1973 and 1981 a number of adaptations were made to the process to clarify the relationship between the industries and the British government, similar to the changes by then underway in the private sector.

A broader strategic planning initiative than that of the United Kingdom was undertaken by the new Liberal Government of Canada in 1980–84, after an experience with PPBS similar to that of the United States. Each government agency was required to prepare a Strategic Plan for review by the Planning and Priorities Committee of the Prime Minister's Cabinet. That requirement was subsequently dropped by the Mulroney Government, although Canadian agencies continue to perform the function in a variety of different ways as they deem appropriate. The Province of Ontario's Ministry of Transportation, for example, still follows the process initiated by that agency in 1977: an 'environmental scan' in the fall of the year, followed by regional managers' presentations on Strategic Business Units (SBUs) such as highway, regulatory and municipal transit programs, and development of program priorities over the five-year period, under each of which are established the necessary implementation strategies. The federal government's Environment Canada, on the other hand, performs much the same process (moving from a planning framework to program objectives for each of 20 'result areas' corresponding, again, to SBUs) but on what they describe as an 'ad hoc' rather than a calendar basis.

The United Kingdom's experience with strategic planning in nationalized industry also has at least one Canadian counterpart in Air Canada. This airline faced both the shock of deregulation (until the late 1970s, Air Canada's market share of air passenger travel was guaranteed by law) and the equally profound organizational changes due to privatization. Over its six-year strategic planning history, it has therefore had to behave much more like a private sector organization than the agencies described above. After several management changes, strategic planning at Air Canada has been decentralized into the major SBUs (domestic passenger, international passenger, domestic cargo and international cargo). It has moved from a five-year to a three-year planning horizon with the majority of staff time spent on the first year to deal with the fast-moving competitive environment of the nation industry. Its strategic emphasis has been on improving productivity and changing its stakeholder focus from the elected official to the shareholder. Results so far have been impressive, with net profits doubling in the year of the company's initial stock sale. Air Canada's experience has particular relevance in light of the privatization movement underway in many countries—in itself a major shift in strategic direction.

Without the incentive of a federal government mandate, US public sector agencies did not begin serious experimentation with strategic planning until the early 1980s. The first efforts tended, as in Canada, to be undertaken by those organizations with capital-intensive, long-range investment programs such as transportation and other infrastructure-related agencies (the Port Authority of New York and New Jersey, the Pennsylvania Department of Transportation), whose planning processes were the most disrupted by the rapid changes in their political and competitive environments.

These early efforts at strategic planning in the US public sector generally involved attempts to apply the original (early 1970s) concepts and practices of private sector firms as closely as possible to public sector entities. For example, the Transportation Research Board's 'checklist' for strategic planners in transportation agencies included the following seven elements: examination of mission, environmental scanning, market analysis, strengths and limitations analysis, shareholder analysis, analysis of threats and opportunities, and critical issues and strategies. Similarly, the strategic planning process initiated by New Jersey Transit (a public transportation agency operating bus and rail passenger services throughout New Jersey) in 1985 involved segmenting its geographic routes into markets and evaluating the attractiveness of each. The special nature of public sector strategic planning was acknowledged, however, by assuming that the agency's mission required the maintenance of some unattractive routes where no alternatives were available to the public (Mark Howard, Transportation Research Record 1156).

Case Study: Strategic Planning for New York's Port

As noted above, one of the earliest stategic planning efforts in the United States was undertaken by the Port Authority of New York and New Jersey. The ten-year experience of that agency merits detailed discussion, as it illustrates many of the positives and negatives encountered along the public sector learning curve.

The Port Authority of New York and New Jersey, formed in 1921 by a compact between the two states, was the first public authority in the United States. While it served as a model for dozens of agencies created during and after the Depression, its structure and operations today are by no means typical of other such authorities. As a bi-state agency, it is directly answerable to the governors of two states on both policy and administrative matters. It is involved in a wide range of businesses, employs 9000 people and has an annual operating budget of US$1.2 billion. In addition to its original role in port commerce, the agency today operates an interstate rail system, bus terminals, bridges, tunnels and the metropolitan region's three airports. It is also involved heavily in the promotion of world trade—including the operation of the World Trade Center office complex, an educational arm—the World Trade Institute, and an export trading company.

Most Port Authority business has historically been tied to either transportation or trade activities. Both sectors felt the impact of major changes in the local and national economies during the 1970s. A leveling off of traffic on the Authority's trans-Hudson crossings signified an end to years of increasing toll revenues. Simultaneously, the globalization of the world economy led to concerns about the competitiveness of high-cost regions such as New York. Since the late 1960s manufacturing firms had been leaving New York City in droves, headed either for less costly premises in the region's suburbs or for other parts of the nation.

To compound economic uncertainties, the year 1977 witnessed the arrival of a new Executive Director at the agency. In contrast to the inwardly focused approach which had characterized the 29-year reign of Austin Tobin, Peter Goldmark's outlook was inquisitive and expansive. With one eye on a tightly wound bureaucratic machine and another on a rapidly changing economic climate, he concluded that his new organization was poorly suited to deal with the coming decade. As one commentator noted, 'Peter felt that the agency didn't known where it was going, and set out to find some answers'.

As a centerpiece of his initiative, Goldmark established what became known as 'The Committee on the Future'. Consisting of five separate task forces—four outwardly oriented and one focusing on institutional capacity—the Committee's brief was to identify areas where the agency had a competitive advantage it could bring to bear on development in the region. Within a year the exercise was completed, with recommendations that would eventually lead to a variety of new business opportunities—from industrial parks to waterfront development—for the agency.

The Committee on the Future also led to organizational changes, and one was a decision to institutionalize the spirit and discipline of strategic planning within the Port Authority. In 1979, an Office of Strategic Planning was set up to develop and implement a strategic planning process. The establishment of this office was a clear sign that corporate planning was to be seen as a separate function—distinct from planning efforts that occurred within line departments, which had historically run the area's ports, airports and interstate subway with a high degree of autonomy. A staff of three was assigned to the office, which itself was placed within the larger Planning and Development Department. This placement of the function was itself probably a tactical mistake; line department planners had traditionally viewed Planning and Development staff as rivals, with whom they often quarreled over responsibility for planning or new projects.

While the Executive Director was instrumental in the creation of this office, he played little or no role in the development of the new strategic planning process. Staff of the newly formed office were given a brief to implement 'strategic planning' but no guidance as to how to do so. As a result, these three individuals—none of whom had any background in the new field of strategic planning—spent months learning about techniques used elsewhere and trying to draw parallels with the agency's own situation.

Their educational process began in Boston, with visits to consulting firms at the forefront of the new discipline—among them McKinsey and the Boston Consulting Group. They also called on practitioners of the new techniques, including private sector firms such as General Electric and public sector bodies in Canada, and participated in a variety of conferences on strategic planning. It was at one of these conferences that staff encountered representatives of New York Telephone, an organization similar to the Port Authority in terms of both its industry environment and the size of its capital program. New York Telephone's strategic planning process—already in place—would become the model for the Port Authority's new approach.

What ultimately emerged from this fieldwork was a rather generic strategic planning process, more a modification of the existing ten-year long-range planning and financial forecasting process than an entirely new approach. A three-year time frame was set to ensure planning beyond the budget year. The process itself, as shown in Figure 13.2, involved seven stages—from assessing the environment and defining goals to identifying critical issues and implementing strategies. Both line and staff departments were asked to prepare plans, all of which were reviewed by the Office of Strategic Planning staff before being presented to the Executive Director. The Office's staff also played a role in identifying ways to measure the success of particular strategies, and in hosting meetings between top management and individual line managers.

According to one participant in the process, strategic planning was introduced to the agency 'Like a Trojan Horse'. It was portrayed as a friendly, non-threatening process—one which would provide a formal showcase for displaying 'what they'd always done'. Inside, however, were real questions about the assumptions behind various activities and the strategic directions being followed. Participants were offered an introduction to the concept through 'classes' sponsored by the Office of Strategic Planning. Immediately thereafter, they were asked to fill out the fairly extensive forms which would serve as the basis for questioning by senior management.

Despite attempts to portray the new process as an extension of existing department planning efforts, managers in both line and staff departments resisted its application to their areas. Many argued that results in their businesses were not readily measurable. Most saw the substantial volume of paperwork associated with the process as an unnecessary diversion from 'real work'. Particularly strong resistance came from the Controller's Department, which rejected efforts to link strategic planning in any meaningful way to the annual budget process.

The result was a strategic planning exercise that had very little effect on either major business decisions in their line departments, or on

---

1. Assess the external environment

2. Define the mission, objectives and goals

3. Prepare a 'situational analysis' for each business area

4. Determine critical issues

5. Develop alternative strategies for dealing with the critical issues

6. Decide on the optimal strategy

7. Implement and track strategies

Figure 13.2.   The Port Authority's planning process

specific resource allocation decisions. Seeing little real payoff for the time and effort invested, the Executive Director soon lost interest in the process. Senior line managers, in turn, quickly perceived that strategic planning was not being used as a vehicle for making critical decisions—and therefore took it even less seriously. While Office of Strategic Planning staff did work successfully with individual managers in some cases—for example, in helping the Port Department develop a new strategic plan—formal strategic planning was largely discredited, and in 1983 was abandoned.

The seeds of change, however, were planted in 1984, when the Authority established a new Management and Budget Department. The new department's first director, unlike her predecessors in the Controller's Department, was strongly committed to the idea of linking the budgetary process and the strategic planning process, and began working toward that end with Office of Strategic Planning staff. Their work bore fruit a year later, with the appointment of a new Executive Director. Stephen Berger saw 'business planning', as the joint effort was called by Budget and the Office of Strategic Planning, as an opportunity to put his own stamp on the Authority's decision making. He used the process as a means for reviewing departmental plans for the next several years—and went one better by insisting that departmental capital programs, which previously had been developed separately from either strategic plans or operating budgets, be justified in light of departmental business strategies. Out of this process came a 'Five-Year Business and Capital Plan' that spelled out overall strategies, operating requirements, capital projects and new business initiatives in each of the Authority's major business area.

Strategic planning had clearly attained a new level of corporate commitment—but it was still viewed by most line managers as a set of reporting requirements imposed from above, rather than as an inherent part of their own management responsibilities. During the next two years, Berger gave high priority to getting his line department directors to 'internalize' the process—to view it as theirs, rather than something belonging to any staff department. The task was no doubt made easier by the directors' perception that Berger took business planning seriously, and expected them to do the same—but it was also helped by the readiness of planners in the staff units, who recognized that the directors' commitment to the process was essential and that their role was more supportive than directive in nature.

By the end of 1986, the process of establishing strategic planning as part of the department directors' management responsibility had succeeded to the point that the Office of Strategic Planning was simply abolished. The Port Authority now has a strategic planning process that is fully integrated with budgeting and capital planning, that involves the Executive Director in regularly scheduled discussions of major strategic issues with his top line managers and that operates without any central strategic planning staff.

Resolving the process questions posed by strategic planning, of course, does not guarantee success in helping an organization plan or implement desired change. Here also the Port Authority's experience is instructive. An example of successful change occurred when the agency, in response to a political mandate to initiate a new commuter ferry service between New Jersey and New York, was able to privatize the service instead of assuming direct operating responsibility. This initiative, the agency's first significant experience with privatization, was a major departure from tradition. It both saved the Port Authority substantial sums of money and allowed the development of the service to proceed at a much faster rate than originally anticipated.

On the other hand, efforts to increase the organization's planning and resource investments in air cargo activities, a step explicitly called for in the agency's strategic plan, have been slowed considerably by internal conflicts stemming from a continued focus on passenger travel as the primary, if not exclusive, mission of the aviation department. These conflicts have prevented air cargo, a growing and lucrative business in a highly competitive environment, from receiving an appropriate level of management attention and development. Similarly, the agency has not yet been able to develop an effective strategic response to the market share decline faced by its marine cargo business (in fact, sharply increased competition in the port business has sparked in recent years a 'boomlet' in strategic planning by US port authorities).

Thus, even once process questions are resolved, implementation and evaluation problems remain. Having agreed on a desired strategic direction, how does management convince a skeptical operations staff to make the required personnel and procedural changes? How do management and operations then reach a shared definition of 'success' or 'failure' by which they can evaluate the initiative once implemented? At the end of the day, the Port Authority's struggles with these questions, and the process issues described above, differ very little from those encountered by private sector management.

IS STRATEGIC PLANNING POSSIBLE?

As the experience of the Port Authority shows, the essential value of strategic planning—forcing an organization to develop processes for thinking about and responding to real change—proved too important for public agencies to discard. The case also suggests that the problems in implementing strategic planning in the public sector have been more similar to the problems the private sector experienced than different from them. In both sectors, it took planners some time to learn that centralized strategic planning processes and separate strategic planning staffs proved themselves too divorced from the real decision-making processes of the organization to be effective; that implementation of strategic plans was significantly more difficult than their design; that complex methodologies tended to obscure rather than illuminate key issues facing the organization; and that line managers were unwilling to cede responsibility for the mission and objectives of their organization to 'professional planners'.

The fact that public and private sectors have encountered similar problems in implementing strategic planning leads us to question the notion that it is structural factors peculiar to the public sector which prevent the application of strategic planning techniques. Factors such as legislative mandates to stay in business, political influences on decision making, lack of clarity about mission, and unionization have traditionally been thought of as major obstacles to effective strategic planning. Yet, as the case of the Port Authority shows, such structural factors never entered into the internal battles over strategic planning. And while it is true that these factors affect decision making in public agencies, similar environmental constraints operate in the private sector. Tobacco companies and car companies are good examples of firms facing environmental constraints—specifically politics and labor—critical to business decisions.

Far from undermining planning efforts in the public sector, the presence of certain complex structural factors is precisely what creates the need for careful and deliberate strategic planning. One could argue that strategic planning, defined as techniques geared to detecting and reacting to changes in the environment, is even more critical to planning in the public sector—where political winds shift frequently and radically—than it is to the somewhat more stable world of private business. The same logic would suggest that long-range planning, with its longer time horizons and internal focus, is a more useful tool in the private sector than it is in the public sector.

That is not to say that the approaches to strategic planning developed for private industry during the 1970s are all directly transferable to the public sector. Some are clearly more applicable than others, and part of the difficulties public agencies have experienced can be traced to their failure to distinguish between these approaches. The following brief review of some of the major approaches to strategic planning illustrates this point.

Portfolio Approaches

Portfolio approaches to strategic planning offer a way to evaluate an organization's business(es). Among the most popular of these was that put forward by the Boston Consulting Group in the late 1960s and early 1970s, involving a matrix by which market share was plotted against overall market growth. An evaluation of these two factors allowed corporate managers to distinguish businesses which require significant investment and generate significant cash from those which do not. The key principle was that a company should maintain a portfolio of businesses which would generate sufficient cash to meet investment needs.

Portfolio models such as this one may be of limited value in some public agency settings. For example, agencies operating in only one business or service sector may not need to choose between competing businesses in making resource allocation decisions. Further, most portfolio models are based around strategic dimensions that are financial in nature (i.e. market share and market growth). In many areas of the public sector, non-financial dimensions such as availability or quality of service are more important than financial targets.

But portfolio models have indeed proved useful in certain types of public agencies. Deregulation in the shipping and aviation sectors has meant that both port and airport operators must now compete for business that was once taken for granted; similar changes have occurred in the telecommunications field. Market share and market growth are now serious considerations behind investment decisions in all three of these industries. And for agencies with multiple businesses like the Port Authority, portfolio analysis is a particularly useful tool in facilitating medium and longer range financial planning.

Competitive Analysis

Competitive analysis, as an approach to strategic planning, can be traced back to Michael Porter (1980) and his seminal book, *Competitive Strategy*. Porter suggested that organizations must focus on a variety of factors affecting the industry in which they operate before they can devise an appropriate strategy. Among the aspects he identified were entry and exist barriers, the availability of substitute products, the relative power of buyers and suppliers, and the nature of competition within the industry.

Like portfolio models, competitive analysis is more useful in certain areas of the public sector than in others. Defining the relevant industry, the first step in such analysis may be difficult if not impossible in many areas of governmental activity. Social services, health care and emergency services are just a few of the tougher cases. In these areas, the concept of competition may not be particularly relevant and the notion of an industry rather abstract. There are of course other areas, such as power generation, telecommunications and transportation, where industry structure analysis can be a more powerful tool.

Competitive analysis is likely to become more relevant to public sector agencies as privatization and deregulation initiatives continue. Organizations like Air Canada, British Telecom and the US Post Office now operate in increasingly competitive environments; the same is true in the health care field, where a variety of new health care providers have entered the market in the United States and in Britain. Greater competition in these and other sectors will require more comprehensive industry analysis.

SWOT Analysis

A third approach to strategic planning is often referred to as SWOT analysis, an acronym referring to the strengths, weaknesses, opportunities and threats associated with any business. This form of analysis, which emphasizes both internal and external factors in devising an appropriate strategy, operates at the level of the strategic business unit. By analyzing the way particular business units fit into their environment, SWOT analysis provides the foundation upon which a corporate strategy can be built.

SWOT analysis is more easily translatable to a public sector context than either portfolio or competitive analysis models, and the earliest public sector forays into strategic planning were based squarely on this approach. The major difficulty associated with SWOT analysis is the definition of an appropriate strategic business unit. While this is relatively easy for single-purpose authorities or agencies, it is more difficult where a variety of programs and initiatives operate from under one roof.

The beauty of SWOT analysis is that it forces planners to evaluate the peculiar constraints and limitations placed upon public sector bodies alongside other environmental factors in devising strategies and goals. It also places particular emphasis on management values and social obligations—both of which are of particular relevance to decision making in the public sector.

Stakeholder Analysis

A fourth approach to strategic planning, and another which is particularly relevant to the public sector, is known as stakeholder analysis. It requires identification of those individuals or groups who have a stake in the success of the organization—from customers and suppliers to employees and shareholders—and suggests that corporate strategies must take into account all of these varied interests. To do this, organizations must identify the needs and demands of these groups and develop strategies which strike an appropriate balance where competing needs exist.

Like SWOT analysis, stakeholder approaches are easily translatable to the public sector and can be applied to almost any public agency. Here stakeholders might include taxpayers, politicians, the local community and special interest groups, in addition to employees and service recipients. That successful public policy requires the cooperation of so many groups illustrates the importance—rather than the futility—of careful strategic planning.

These approaches—portfolio, competitor, SWOT and stakeholder analysis—are by no means the only techniques in use today, and approaches like strategic issue analysis also have applications in a public sector setting. Nevertheless, a discussion of these four approaches is sufficient to illustrate several important points. The first is that certain approaches to strategic planning are of greater relevance in a public sector context than others. SWOT and stakeholder analysis have been shown to be particularly applicable, as they are able to address and incorporate into the analysis constraints peculiar to the public sector. While neither approach dictates substantive answers as to what types of strategies are likely to be successful, they are important in identifying environmental factors that might otherwise be overlooked.

A second point concerns the utility of the more business-oriented approaches. Techniques such as portfolio and competitive analysis clearly have value for certain types of public bodies. Agencies with multiple businesses, such as the Port Authority of New York and New Jersey or its counterpart in Boston, Massport, are one natural audience; those facing competitive pressures for the first time, such as Air Canada, are another. By and large, agencies with clearly definable outputs that cater to specific markets are in the best position to take advantage of these techniques.

PROGRESS TO DATE

The problems that the public sector has experienced in implementing strategic planning have stemmed from a variety of sources. In some cases, public sector managers failed to distinguish between different planning approaches and selected inappropriate models as the basis of their new planning process. In others, they selected appropriate approaches but failed to tailor them to the needs of the organization. Quite often, managers overlooked the fact that these techniques are merely tools for decision making, rather than formulas which would provide them with answers.

Public sector agencies at the forefront of the strategic planning wave in the early 1980s made many of the same mistakes that private industry had made in the mid- and late 1970s. Viewing strategic planning as something separate from line department business, they set up quasi-independent corporate planning units which imposed laborious, paper-intensive processes upon organizations. Even in bureaucracies familiar with process, line managers tended to react negatively to what they saw as a threat to their decision-making autonomy. As the case of the Port Authority shows, without strong support from the top, both the process and the concepts that lay behind it were easily discredited.

The lessons of these early years were learned by an unfortunate few, and more recent entrants to the world of strategic planned have benefited from their mistakes. Public sector agencies now engaged in strategic planning exercises have a more realistic view of the limitations of such initiatives and more are experimenting with new forms of strategic planning. Most of these forms parallel similar private sector trends: decentralization, integration with line functions, task forces instead of planning staffs. Increasingly, they are undertaken jointly with private or non-profit sector partners. In short, they have moved toward more flexible, less process-driven systems controlled not by specialists but by executives. Strategic planning has, in other words, given way to strategic management.

The evidence of better and more strategic management in the public sector is everywhere. The development of innovative financing techniques, the complexity of local government deals with private developers, increased use of the private and voluntary sectors for service delivery, and more careful staging of large capital projects are all evidence of a more 'businesslike' approach on the part of public sector managers. They also reveal an external orientation all but absent from public sector planning in the 1960s and 1970s.

These systems have also moved beyond their initial universe to include human service agencies, local (as well as state and federal) governments and the private and non-profit sectors. For example, the New York State Comprehensive Mental Health Plan Act of 1986 required the development of a five-year state plan for mental health services to include a statement of goals, priorities for resource allocation, facility utilization forecast and proposals for service improvement. This plan is being developed through a system of regional and state-wide advisory committees representing the mental health system's major 'stakeholders', a feature typical of the human service-oriented planning processes.

The City of Albany, New York, in 1984 designated a public–private Strategic Planning Committee to scan the city's external environment, identify trends, assess strengths and weaknesses and design a development strategy. Similarly, the State of Pennsylvania recently concluded a strategic planning process with private sector participation (see Figure 13.3 for an excerpt of the final report's goals and objectives), while the California Engineering Foundation, a non-governmental group, performed a comparable exercise on behalf of that state during 1985–87.

These developments, as noted above, all point to a burst of experimentation and innovation on the part of public sector planners comparable

GOAL: TO IMPROVE THE COMPETITIVE POSITION AND COMPARATIVE ADVANTAGE OF PENNSYLVANIA (PA.) COMPANIES IN NATIONAL AND INTERNATIONAL MARKETS.

OBJECTIVE: TO CREATE 50,000 NET NEW JOBS PER YEAR IN PENNSYLVANIA

State Government	Other Government	Business and Labor	Education
• Recruitment of new companies to Pa. and retention of existing firms	• Local—improve regulations and taxes which currently restrict business.	• Cooperation to accelerate transition to high growth activities, to increase competitive advantages and to reduce the costs of production, providing new and better jobs and increasing firm competitiveness.	• Revise curriculum to foster skills which enhance employability.
• Provide necessary services to help business expand its employment, provide greater emphasis on performance objectives and adopt a quality orientation process for Commonwealth employees.	• Federal—use the strategy as a guide to effectively target area and industry public investments.		• Deliver custom-trained workers.
	• Maximize integration of state priorities in key federal programs.	• Start-up or growth of development departments by banks, utilities and others.	• Strengthen current programs in continuing education.
• Public financing assistance for infrastructure projects directly linked to industry expansion of employment.	• State Congressional Delegation—assist in securing federal selection/funding for Pa.	• Serve on task force.	• Upgrade the economic development content of curricula to support other public/private efforts.
• Identify growth opportunity "targets" for Pa.	• Obtain Congressional Delegation support for military facilities in Pa.	• Special commitments to support attraction of military facilities.	• Serve on task force.
• Push for the establishment or expansion of military facilities in Pa.			• Research on potential sites and function for military facilities in Pa.

Excerpt from comprehensive strategic plan.

Figure 13.3 State of Pennsylvania's economic development strategy

to Ian Wilson's 'new thrusts' and reflecting those planners' desire, like Michael Porter's, to see strategic planning 'transformed into the vital management discipline it needs to be'.

A LOOK TOWARDS THE FUTURE

Strategic management is likely to become more prominent in the public sector as we move into the 1990s, due to a number of factors. The decline of central government funding for a variety of programs is forecast to continue in Britain and in the United States. This will force state and local government sectors to find alternative sources of revenue and to manage existing resources more strategically. It will also provide increased local control over expenditure decisions.

Another factor likely to affect public agencies is deregulation. The past ten years have witnessed a number of deregulation initiatives in the United States, Canada and Britain. In many cases, deregulation has led to major changes in industry, which in turn has forced public sector agencies to rethink their long-range plans. Air Canada's experience in adjusting to a new competitive environment is a good example of this. Similar moves toward deregulation in Europe would suggest that public sector agencies there—ranging from airport operators to telecommunications companies to postal services—will need to adjust their own planning efforts to a new economic climate.

The globalization of the world economy is a third factor which suggests the need for more strategic thinking on the part of the public sector. Cities and towns—and in some cases countries—now compete against one another for the jobs and ancillary benefits associated with large multinationals' operations. Recent competition for Japanese manufacturing plants in Europe, for example, has pitted region against region—first in Britain and now elsewhere on the Continent. Simultaneously, improvements in telecommunications offer companies greater freedom to relocate in low-cost areas. As a result, many older cities and urban areas are being forced to fight hard to retain their existing industrial base—and to attract new investment.

The popularity of privatization initiatives is a fourth and final factor supporting continued strategic planning in the public sector. Privatization in the United States has offered a range of government agencies a way to do more with less—from private delivery of public services to joint public/private partnerships. In Britain, the notion of privatization extends to the sale of state holdings in a range of large industries—from British Telecom and British Gas to British Petroleum. These firms are now held accountable to their investors, hence increasing the importance of strategic and financial considerations in their planning efforts.

What is fascinating about these four factors—decreased central funding, deregulation, globalization of the world's economy, and privatization of public services—is that they are themselves the result of more businesslike approaches taken by public agencies—primarily central governments—throughout the world. Thus while the processes associated with strategic planning may have been discredited over the past decade, the ideas behind them have indeed borne fruit. Public sector managers throughout the Western world are now learning what their private sector counterparts already know: that to succeed in a rapidly changing competitive environment, organizations will need to plan, think, and, above all, manage more strategically than ever before.

REFERENCES

Bishop-Edkins, Christine, and Nethercut, Cynthia (1986) Initiating the strategic planning process at NJ transit, *Transportation Research Record*, **1156**, 81–87.

Harris, D. J., and Davies, B. C. L. Corporate planning as a control system in United Kingdom nationalized industries. *Long Range Planning*, **14**, 15–22.

Keating, Barry P., and Maryann, O. (1981) Goal setting and efficiency in social service agencies, *Long Range Planning*, **14**, 40–48.

Porter, Michael E. (1980) *Competitive Strategy: Techniques for Analyzing Industries and Competitors*. Free Press, New York.

Porter, Michael E. (1987) The state of strategic thinking, *The Economist*, 23 May, 17–20.

Wildavsky, Aaron (1974) *The Politics of the Budgetary Process*. Little, Brown and Company, Boston.

Wilson, Ian (1988) The state of strategic planning: What went wrong? What goes right. *Business Intelligence Program Publication D88–1254*, SRI International, Menlo Park.

14

A PERSONAL
READING LIST

D. E. Hussey

Managing Director, Harbridge Consulting Group Ltd

There are now many books available on strategic management, so many that it is a mammoth task for any one to attempt a full bibliography. The last full bibliography of European publications with which I was associated was published in one of my earlier books and covered the period until 1979. This was difficult enough, but of insignificance compared with the work needed to update that bibliography to 1989, and to include the enormous stream of material from the United States and other non-European sources. In any case the bibliography was limited to English language material.

A detailed bibliography would double the length of this book (at least), and would probably be of limited value to most readers. Instead I thought that it might be useful for me to provide a personal reading list, which gives guidance not only on books that may help the professional, but also others that they might like to suggest to colleagues with less knowledge of the subject.

By definition, a reading list does not try to embrace all books, nor would I claim to have read everything that has been published. A personal recommendation is also biased to the ideas and preferences of its originator, and when the originator also writes on the topic there may be additional biases. I have not listed *every* book I have written or edited although the list includes several of my own books. Clearly there are many excellent books by numerous authors which for one reason or another, usually ignorance, cannot find their way into my list. It is hoped that whatever its shortcomings, this list will be helpful as a supplement to the references that appear in most chapters. All the books are recommended, but my personal rating system_(stars) may be useful to anyone who needs to choose only a few books from the list.

International Review of Strategic Management.
Edited by D. E. Hussey. © 1990 John Wiley & Sons Ltd

GENERAL BOOKS

**G. Steiner (1979)	*Strategic Planning: What Every Manager Must Know*. Macmillan, 383pp. A step-by-step guide to strategic planning of the 'how to' type (but contrasting various approaches). Includes chapters on personal planning and planning for non-profit organisations. Primarily aimed at the manager.
***D. E. Hussey (1985)	*Introducing Corporate Planning* (3rd Edition). Pergamon, 256pp. Well-established introduction written for managers, new planners, and students takes the reader through all the basic issues he needs to consider to establish a planning process or to contribute to an existing process. A standard book for some business school courses.
***D. E. Hussey (1982)	*Corporate Planning: Theory and Practice* (2nd Edition). Pergamon, 399pp. Comprehensive and readable coverage of most aspects of the subject, with planning principles and procedures treated in depth, peripheral techniques put in context, summarised, and referenced to further sources. Good practical examples, combining an academic study of the subject with personal experience as a practitioner. Won the John Player Management Author of the Year Award.
***P. McNamee (1988)	*Strategic Planning and Marketing*. Heinemann/CIMA, 477pp. This is an official text for the British professional accounting examinations, wrriten by a faculty member at the University of Ulster. A good, broad-based text.
*D. E. Hussey (1985)	*Corporate Planning*. BIM/ICA, 91pp. A very basic, short introductory book. Useful if you want someone else to get a quick feel of the subject. Not recommended for those who have a good background in strategic management.

THE EARLY CLASSICS

These books will be of value to anyone wanting to pursue the subject in greater depth. The busy manager, wanting to expand his practical knowledge in a short time might be better advised to choose some more recent books.

*H. I. Ansoff (1965)	*Corporate Strategy.* McGraw-Hill, 241pp. One of the classics of planning literature and of value to the serious student of the subject, although difficult to read and dated in planning philosophy. This book was the basis of many of the analytical contributions to planning.
*H. I. Ansoff (Ed.) (1969)	*Business Strategy.* Penguin, 388pp. This book of readings reproduces a number of worthwhile articles on planning. Worth reading if only for Lindblom's article. 'The science of muddling through'.
**R. N. Anthony (1965)	*Planning and Control Systems.* Harvard, 180pp. One of the classics, designed to provide a framework for analysis. Includes useful comparative studies of various writers' concepts of *management* and *planning.* Mainly a book for the specialist, academic and student.
**E. K. Warren (1966)	*Long Range Planning: The Executive Viewpoint.* Prentice Hall, 108pp. Another classic, providing a research-based view of planning processes. More of a lightship than a pilot boat, in that it points to dangers without always giving a course. Very readable. Useful for planner, manager and student (essential for any serious student of planning).

COMPETITOR ANALYSIS

***M. E. Porter (1980)	*Competitive Strategy: Techniques for Analysing Industries and Competitors.* Free Press, 396pp. This book takes the concepts of industry structure analysis to a deep degree of analysis.

**M. E. Porter (1985) *Competitive Advantage.* Free Press, 557pp. Builds on his first book, and introduces the concept of value chains.

*W. Sammon *et al.* (Ed.) (1984) *Business Competitor Intelligence.* John Wiley, 357pp. A useful coverage of the subject including chapters on organising the competitor intelligence function.

*L. M. Fuld (1987) *Competitor Intelligence.* John Wiley. This is an audio cassette 'book', containing interviews and 'sound' plays. Gives useful insight into sources and uses of competitor information. Less helpful on approaches to analysis.

**B. S. James (1984) *Business Wargames.* Penguin. Relates corporate competitive strategies to military strategy. Many examples.

ANALYTICAL CONCEPTS

***K. Ohmae (1982) *The Mind of the Strategist.* Penguin, 283pp. A very good book on strategy—Japanese examples—and includes many simple but effective approaches to analysis. It is unfair to see this as a 'techniques' book: its philosophy is more about human creativity than analysis.

***C. V. Hofer and D. Schendel (1978) *Strategy Formulation: Analytical Concepts.* West, 219pp. An excellent brief guide to portfolio analysis and other techniques.

**P. McNamee (1985) *Techniques of Strategic Management.* Pergamon, 319pp. Good on portfolio analysis and experience curves. Provides PC programs to use the techniques in the book.

*D. Abell (1980) *Defining the Business.* Prentice Hall, 257pp. This deals with one analytical concept, a form of three-dimensional strategic segmentation (customer functions, customer groups, alternative technologies). A useful approach in comparing competitor positioning.

*J. Chandler and P. Cockle (1982) *Techniques of Scenario Planning.* McGraw-Hill, 170pp. Demonstrates the Reed International approach to scenario planning.

| **R. D. Buzzell and
B. T. Gale (1987) | *The PIMS Principles.* Free Press, 322pp. Strategic principles derived from the PIMS database of 3000 SBUs, many of which have provided strategic information for 15 years. |

GLOBAL COMPETITION

| *M. E. Porter (Ed.)
(1986) | *Competition in Global Industries.* Harvard, 581pp. A collection of papers on globalisation, many of which give useful insight into the issue. |
| *J. Stopford and
L. Turner (1985) | *Britain and the Multinationals.* John Wiley, 282pp. An assessment of how UK multinationals have changed in recent years, and the impact of global competition on the MNCs. |

HUMAN RESOURCE AND BEHAVIOURAL ISSUES

**J. Bramham (1975)	*Practical Manpower Planning.* Institute of Personnel Management, 200pp. A very good basic book on planning the 'people' aspects of the business, providing guidance on concepts and techniques. Does not deal with the behavioural problems of organisational development and change. Of value to planning and personnel specialists, and managers.
*R. L. Desatnick and M. Bennet (1977)	*Human Resource Management in the Multinational Company.* Gower, 411pp. Although not specifically a planning book, this is essential reading for any one wishing to design a manpower planning system for a multinational company. It deals with many of the problems for which organisations must plan, and many of the environmental issues. For planners, personnel specialists and managers.
***J. R. Galbraith (1976) and D. A. Nathanson	*Strategy Implementation. The Role of Structure and Process.* West, 155pp. An excellent book, surveying the main research, linking strategy and structure and providing a number of useful ideas and concepts.

D. E. Hussey and M. J. Langham (1965)   *Corporate Planning: The Human Factor.* Pergamon, 298pp. A good overall coverage of corporate planning with specific emphasis on behavioural issues. Brings together the analytical and behavioural streams of thought, and fills a gap in the literature. As useful to personnel and OD practitioners as it is to planners and managers.

M. Gould and A. Campbell (1987)   *Strategies and Styles.* Blackwell, 374pp. This book identifies different styles of strategic management, and the influence of those styles on operations.

*J. B. Quinn (1980)   *Strategies for Change: Logical Incrementalism.* Irwin, 222pp. An interesting study of how major strategic decisions are made. The sample is very small (nine companies) and the book is longer than its content justifies.

***D. E. Hussey (1988)   *Management Training and Corporate Strategy.* Pergamon, 201pp. A research-based book which demonstrates how management training should be planned to help achieve corporate aims. Of value to those concerned in implementation issues of planning.

T. J. Peters and R. H. Waterman (1982)   *In Search of Excellence.* Harper and Row, 360pp. A runaway best seller, too long for its content, but very useful in drawing attention to the importance of behavioural issues in business success.

*R. H. Waterman (1987)   *The Renewal Factor.* Bantam, 338pp. An attempt to show how modern business should cope with change.

**G. Donaldson and J. Lorsch   *Decision Making at the Top.* Basic Books, 208pp. Sub-titled 'The shaping of strategic direction', this research-based book shows how chief executives set corporate strategy.

**P. Martin and J. Nicholls (1987)   *Creating a Commited Workforce.* IPM, 212pp. This is important reading for those concerned with implementation of strategy. It is about achieving major change throughout an organisation.

OTHER TOPICS

**B. Taylor (Ed.) (1988)   *Strategic Planning, the Chief Executive and the Board.* Pergamon, 115pp. A collection of useful articles which first appeared in *Long Range Planning*. Includes case studies on ICI, 3Ms, SAS, NFC and Philips.

***D. E. Hussey (Ed.) (1983)   *The Truth about Corporate Planning.* Pergamon, 586pp. A collection of research based articles on various aspects of planning. Includes considerable research on the success and failure of planning systems.

*T. Hill (1985)   *Manufacturing Strategy.* Macmillan, 230pp. One of the few books published which deals with the strategic issues of manufacturing.

**W. Skinner (1978)   *Manufacturing in the Corporate Strategy.* John Wiley, 327pp. This is the pioneer book of this subject, and still very valid.

*E. Tozer (1988)   *Planning for Effective Business Information Systems.* Pergamon, 265pp. One of the few books on IS strategy planning.

MAILING ADDRESSES
OF CONTRIBUTORS

Dr K. Asher   *New York Port Authority, New York, NY, USA*

Ms H. Butcher   *BDO Binder Hamlyn, 8 St Bride Street, London EC4A 4DA*

Mr A. Campbell   *Ashridge Strategic Management Centre, 1 Kingsway, London WC2B 6XF*

Dr M. Csath   *Virginia Polytechnic Institute and State University Department of Management, Blacksburg, Virginia 24061, USA*

Ms A. Demb   *IMI, 4 Chemin de Conches, CH 1231 Conches-Geneva, Switzerland*

Mr M. Goold   *Ashridge Strategic Management Centre, 1 Kingsway, London WC2B 6XF*

Dr J. P. Henry   *SRI International, 333 Ravenswood Avenue, Menlo Park, CA 94025, USA*

Mr D. E. Hussey   *Managing Director, Harbridge Consulting Group Ltd, Harbridge House, 3 Hanover Square, London W1R 9RD*

Ms M. McHugh   *University of Ulster, Shore Road, Newtownabbey, Co Antrim, Northern Ireland Bt37 OQB*

Mr P. McNamee   *University of Ulster, Shore Road, Newtownabbey, Co Antrim, Northern Ireland Bt37 OQB*

Mr M. Mainelli   *BDO Binder Hamlyn, 8 St Bride Street, London EC4A 4DA*

Professor Gen-Ichi Nakamura *604 Sun Rise, Meguro Building 3-4-6, Shimomeguro Meguro-ku, Tokyo 153, Japan*

Ms B. Nare *Director of Fiscal Policy Analysis, New York State Division of the Budget, New York, NY, USA*

Dr F.-F. Neubauer *IMI, 4 Chemin de Conches, CH 1231 Conches-Geneva, Switzerland*

Dr A. J. Pendlebury *Coopers & Lybrand Associates Europe, Plumtree Court, London EC4A 4HT*

Professor M. Porter *Harvard Business School, Cambridge, MA 02163, USA*

Mr E. Tozer *67 Andover Road, Winchester, Hampshire SO22 6AU*

Dr T. S. Wurster *Vice President, The Boston Consulting Group Inc, 333 South Grand Avenue, Los Angeles, CA 900712, USA*

INDEX

327